Praise for *The Kuhreihen Melody*

"The riveting quality of this startling collection of essays strips it of even a whiff of sentimentality. Selgin understands that nostalgia means 'the return of pain'; that it is in longing that we discover the existential grief of being human. Desire weaves its way through this book like a river."
—Dustin Beall Smith, author of *Key Grip*

"Titled after a 17th century Swiss cattle herding song that, when heard, produced an intense nostalgia or ache to return home, *The Kuhreihen Melody* is a collection of fifteen truly brilliant essays that explore the longing to return to a home or a place that never really was. Reminiscent of W.G. Sebald and other masters of describing the acute "nothing," the unrecoverable and impermanent, Peter Selgin patiently—and always entertainingly—uncovers nostalgia's complex, contradictory relationship to time. Selgin's recall of his own past is as eidetic as Proust's, and whether he is writing of his childhood, his history of swimming with Oliver Sacks, his romance with New York City, a history of vests or the pleasure of stripes, Selgin, also an artist, is irresistible, colorfully philosophical and frequently profound."
—Melissa Pritchard, author of *Palmerino* and *A Solemn Pleasure*

"Such strong, vivid, haunting stories. Whether set in wintry 1970's Brooklyn or sultry New Orleans or the jungles of Mexico or in the streets of a vanished hometown, Selgin's tales convey the texture of the human condition in ways that make each a singular, indelible experience."
—Peter Nichols, author of *The Rocks*

"Listen: Peter Selgin has come unstuck in time, time being the fourth dimension of being. But way beyond that the essays found in *The Kuhreihen Melody* suggest a whole new saturated string theory of remembering. Into rivers that we cannot step into twice, Selgin choreographs a bevy of these sublime plasmatic memoirs, a squad of synchronized swimmers, syncopated and panting, doing a solid time step with a murmuring heart in the deep end of congested confluences, pooling estuaries of emotion. Buoyant and effervescent, rip-tided and torpedoed, the melodies herein are as persistent (and resistant) as forever and so beautiful, beautiful enough to launch 1,000 clocks."
—Michael Martone, author of *The Moon Over Wapakoneta* and *Brooding*

I

"'Be at life's mercy,' young, wannabe-actor Peter Selgin is told by a New York casting agent in "The Bones of Love," one of fifteen 'nostalgic essays' in this wonderful collection that is, by turns, harrowing and delightful, heartbreaking and comical, gritty and erudite. As deceitful as those words may have been, the advice is sage. And Peter took it—is haunted by it, in fact— remaining vulnerable despite his scars to life's pleasures and pains, triumphs and tragedies as he struggled to fathom the man he was, is, and wants to be. It is tautological to point out that doing so he must indulge in nostalgia, a word that has in serious literary circles been spelled with four letters for quite some time. Peter, however, redeems nostalgia through an alchemical mix of wide-ranging curiosity, nimble intelligence, candidness, and felicity, turning it into the gold of these vital, magical essays."
—Mark Drew, Editor, *The Gettysburg Review*

"In *The Kuhreihen Melody,* Peter Selgin invites us to observe, through the simultaneously comforting and painful lens of nostalgia, a variety of experiences ranging from the ordinary to the extraordinary: the history of muffins, the dreaded childhood haircut, the joy of stripes, the pleasure of swimming, seeing *Rebel Without a Cause* for the first time, living in New York, the unexpected gift that comes from befriending the worst neighbor, friendship, art, and fatherhood. Warm and sincere, these essays read as though you have spent an afternoon with a dear friend who tells amazing stories and leaves you hungry for more."
—Stephanie G'Schwind, Editor, *Colorado Review*

Praise for *The Inventors*

"[A] book destined to become a modern classic... A remarkable model of the art of the memoir, this book will satisfy all readers. Highly recommended."
—Derek Sanderson, *Library Journal*

Praise for *Confessions of a Left-Handed Man*

"Peter Selgin is a born writer, capable of taking any subject and exploring it from a new angle, with wit, grace, and erudition."
—Oliver Sacks

THE KUHREIHEN MELODY

The Kuhreihen Melody

nostalgic essays by PETER SELGIN

SERVING HOUSE BOOKS

The Kuhreihen Melody: Nostalgic Essays by Peter Selgin

Copyright © Peter Selgin

All rights reserved.

No part of this book may be used or reproduced in any manner whatsoever without the prior written permission of the copyright holder except for brief quotations in critical articles or reviews.

Library of Congress Control Number: 2019942835

ISBN: 978-1-947175-16-7

Cover design by the author

Serving House Books logo by Barry Lereng Wilmont

Published by Serving House Books
Copenhagen, Denmark and Florham Park, NJ
www.servinghousebooks.com

Member of The Independent Book Publishers Association

First Serving House Books Edition 2019

for Pinuccia, my mother

also by Peter Selgin:

Fiction:
Drowning Lessons (story collection), University of Georgia Press, 2008
Life Goes to the Movies, Dzanc Books, 2009

Nonfiction:
Confessions of a Left-Handed Man (essays), University of Iowa Press, 2012
The Inventors (memoir), Hawthorne Press, 2016

Writing Craft:
By Cunning and Craft, Writer's Digest Books, 2006
179 Ways to Save a Novel, Writer's Digest Books, 2010
Your First Page, Serving House Books, 2017
　　　　Broadview Press, 2019 (classroom edition)

Children's Books:
S.S. Gigantic Across the Atlantic, Simon & Schuster, 1999
L'uomo che viveva da solo ("The Man Who Lived Alone"), Falzea Editore, 2011

Plays:
Night Blooming Serious
A God in the House

❖ Contents

The Kuhreihen Melody	1
Black Bubbles	35
The Muffin Man	47
Eagle Electric	57
The Opening Credits to *Rebel Without a Cause*	81
Some Field Notes on Setting	111
The Bones of Love	119
Barber	137
Noise	143
In Praise of Stripes	157
My New York: a Romance in Eight Parts	163
How the Vest Was Won	187
Swimming to The End	191
Swimming with Oliver	195
The Strange Case of Arthur Silz	219

❖ The Kuhreihen Melody

"I have returned there / where I had never been."
—Giorgio Caproni, *The Last Homecoming*

SOMETIMES, WHILE DRIFTING OFF TO SLEEP, I play a game with myself. I imagine myself in Bethel, Connecticut, my hometown, circa 1964, when I was six or seven. I imagine myself walking down Greenwood Avenue, the town's Main Street, slipping into its shops and stores as they were then. The object of the game is simple: to piece together, out of the Tinkertoys, Lincoln Logs, and Lego bricks of memory, the place where I grew up, down to the smallest trivial details. Store by store, night after night, I reassemble my past.

It doesn't matter where I start. The Bethel Food Market, at the north end of town, will do. I begin at the meat counter, behind which Tony stands in his bloody butcher's smock, his hair not yet gone gray. The mounds of ground beef remind me of spaghetti. From there I inspect the aisles, admiring whimsical cereals in tidy boxes, cans of soup lined up like toy soldiers in their red-and-white uniforms, cardboard

I

cartons of ice cream in freezer cases, racks of spices and baby food, plums, pears, tomatoes and grapefruits arrayed like cannon balls. Past the checkout counters I glide like a ghost, neither seen nor heard by the lady with the big hair and cat-eye glasses manning the bulky silver cash register, chewing Juicy Fruit, her false nails snapping the keys, unaware that she is now grown old, her children married with children of their own, she herself condemned to an assisted-living facility somewhere in the low-tax Carolinas.

From Tony's I head down the hill to Noe's, the clothing store at the corner of Greenwood and Rector, where Mom used to buy my brother and me dungarees. As soon as I enter, while the doorbells are still jingling, a rich, chemical scent of un-broken-in denim leaps up my nostrils. There stands Mr. Noe, in shirtsleeves behind the counter, his tape measure draped like a surplice over his shoulders. Mixed with the smells of cotton and clothes is that of old wood, along with a faint odor of dust and something like vinegar—the smell of old days.

From Noe's I may make my way down to the five-and-dime store, or to Mulhaney's, where we used to pinch Matchbox toys, or I may drop in on Old Man Nelson at the hardware store named for him.

Of course they don't see, let alone remember, me, these ghoulish actors in my lucid dream, or sense my longing to hug them all, like Emily in the last scene in *Our Town*, when she visits her past from beyond the grave.

For the past three years I've been a visiting professor. Last year I was in Georgia, this year in upstate New York. Next year: Florida. Call me a "nomacademic." As I write this, my belongings, the few that I need, fill a half-dozen cardboard boxes on the ground floor of the house that came with this latest job. Though for the past year I've referred to it as my home, for a visiting professor "home" is a concept, nothing more. My house isn't my house, my students aren't my students, and my colleagues aren't really my colleagues. These things are no more mine than a river one swims across once. Meanwhile my sixteen-month-old daughter, Audrey, is in Carbondale, Illinois, where her mother has gone for her graduate degree. It's been over six weeks since I last saw either of them, and longer since I've seen anyone else in my immediate family.

The last time I saw my mother was this past January when, for the first time in over a year, I returned to Connecticut. Soon after my father died, my mother sold the house in Bethel and bought a condominium in nearby Danbury, at a place called Kenosia Estates, named for the lake that was once home to Kenosia Amusement Park. The park, which opened at the turn of the century and was accessible by a five-cent trolley ride, featured gazebos, a merry-go-round, a horse track, a roller coaster, and sail and rowboats for hire. A passenger steamer plied its crystal waters. A grand Victorian hotel overlooked its shores. At the height of its popularity, seven hundred people a day—men in striped blazers and straw boaters, women twirling parasols in knickerbockers—took the twenty-minute trip from town. Though the amusement park no longer exists (its grounds are now occupied by Mom's condo complex), the lake is still there. Soon after my mother moved, against the advice of her new neighbors, I tried to swim across it. I got a dozen yards before the weeds stopped me. For days afterward my skin itched. I've disliked the place ever since, though I'd never say so to my mother, who is vehemently house proud. She never tires of saying to me, every time I visit, "I like my house." (It's *not* a house, I'm tempted to say; it's a *condominium*.)

In Bethel we lived in a house, a Cape Cod, halfway up a hill at the far end of a driveway lined with weeping willow trees, their trunks as gray and wide as rhinoceroces. I dream of that house, too, of those weeping willows lining its driveway, and of the hill behind it, of the woods where my twin brother and I got lost when we were five years old, sending half the neighborhood out into the woods to search for us, strangers armed with flashlights, whistles, and lanterns (dusk had fallen), and all the while we crouched behind the rotting hulk of what was once a guest cottage a few dozen yards from the back yard of our home.

In my dreams I run a finger along the pickets of the white fence enclosing one side of the yard, at one end of which a mulberry tree grows. The fence's chalky paint leaves the tip of my finger white, the color of the bird droppings that coat some of the mulberries and that reminded me of cake frosting (an analogy I resisted testing). In a nearby meadow everything from strawberries to rhubarb grew. There was a slate stone patio outside of our grandmother's room. A forsythia bush erupted there, its yellow petals blazing in her window.

All kinds of things like this I remember. I remember the draw fan at the top of the staircase, above the linen closet, and the sound it made thrumming through muggy summer nights. My inventor papa had rigged up a crude timer switch with a pulley wheel for the dial. I used to imagine that a mythical creature, half vulture, half vampire, made its home in the draw fan's louvers (which opened impressively when the fan turned on). Though the switch was off limits to me, I'd still sneak out there in my pajamas in the middle of the night and give the pulley a hefty twist so the fan would run all night long, billowing the blue ocean-liner curtains near my bed. Most nights, my mother would waken and sabotage my mission. I'd hear her open the door to the linen closet (where the switch was), and then the fan would stop, leaving me lying there, helpless, hostage to the rasps and chirps of cicadas and crickets. It wasn't just coolness that I was after, but the noise of the fan, its rumbling steady rhythm like the turbines of a passenger steamship. Its thrumming assured me that—no matter how hot and humid and long—I'd survive the night, somehow.

But what I most like to remember is riding around in my mother's black Mercury, in the backseat with its scratchy houndstooth upholstery and bulky transmission hump. I remember shopping trips to Danbury, to Genung's, to McRorey's, to the Bargain World . . . all those shops fronting Main Street. At the lollipop rack at Woolworth's I'd search for my favorite flavor—root beer—this after gulping down two frankfurters smeared with emerald relish from a stainless-steel lidded bowl while seated on a swiveling chair at the counter. Another store, too, stands out in my memory. I can't remember its name or what was sold there, only it stretching on and on and on into infinity, obligingly, since like all good childhood things I never wanted it to end, but then it did, though with a free carousel ride that made the end almost worth it. Then back to Mom's Mercury, which by then would be either as cold as freezer or as hot as an oven, depending on the season, and could could generate as much seasickness as the *Queen Mary* in a 70-knot squall.

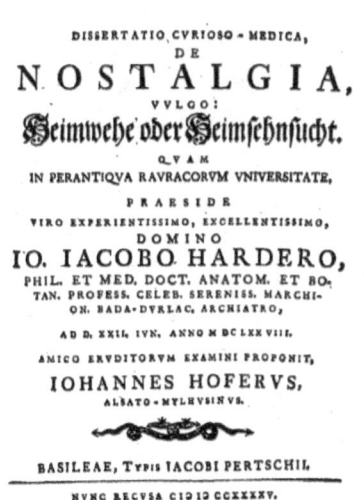

When I relive such memories, I don't know whether to feel glad or sad, grateful or sorry, cursed or blessed with what seems like total recall. There are days when I miss *everything*, when the innocence, simplicity, continuity and security that I felt as a child seem as irrecoverable as childhood itself. The disease has a name: *nostalgia*, from the Greek *nastas* ("return home") and *algia* ("pain or ache; longing"). In most cases the longing isn't so much for a real home as for one that never really existed or that exists only in memory. The term "nostalgia" was originally coined by Johannes Hofer, a Swiss medical doctor, in his 1688 dissertation describing the sometimes paralyzing sadness that overwhelmed Swiss university students, domestic workers and soldiers fighting abroad. This undifferentiated longing afflicted its victims' imaginations, incapacitated their bodies, and exhausted their "vital spirits." Physical symptoms included everything from loss of appetite to a propensity for suicide. According to Dr. Hofer's thesis, the "nostalgic" suffered from his longing as if from a persecution complex, driven to the very urges that caused his suffering much as a paranoid is driven toward his dark visions. By a crude irony, victims displayed a remarkable ability to recall sounds, sights, smells and other sensations with acute and even uncanny accuracy, down to the smallest mundane details—things that most people, experiencing them in real time, would scarcely notice—the better to torture themselves.

In experiments conducted with Swiss soldiers, Hofer found that certain memories were especially likely to trigger nostalgic responses. These included memories of certain tastes and sounds—like the taste of fresh milk or the melodies of certain folk songs. One rustic cantilena in particular was said to trigger nostalgic longings, a tune played on a horn by Alpine herdsmen as they drove their cattle to and from pasture. Known as the "Ranz des Vaches" or the "Kuhreihen melody," when heard by Swiss mercenaries in the service of the king of France it supposedly produced such an intense longing for home that those who heard it were moved to illness, desertion, and suicide. So strong was the link between this melody and what the French called *mal du Suisse* that Swiss soldiers were threatened with severe punishment for singing or even whistling or humming it.

Long before Hofer first described the symptoms the concept of *heimweh* (homesickness) had already been embraced. In a letter to the Council of Lucerne in 1569, at least one death—that of a man named Sunneberg—was attributed to the phenomenon. As for the cure for homesickness or *mal du pays*, doctors prescribed everything from purging to opium, leeches, and "warm hypnotic emulsions." During the war of Polish Succession (1733– 1738), a Russian army officer, disgusted by the number of nostalgia cases cropping up among his soldiers, discovered yet another cure whose dispensation was as cruel as its efficacy was assured: he buried one "nostalgic" alive and promised to do likewise to others who complained of the ailment, markedly decreasing its prevalence. A fitting cure, since nostalgia similarly suffocates its victims under a mountain of memories.

But the most obvious cure for nostalgia was to send the victim home or, short of that, to merely suggest the possibility, as Lieutenant Robert Hamilton, commander of light infantry in the British army's 82nd regiment, learned:

> [The soldier] had now been in hospital three months, and was quite emaciated, and like one in the last stage of consumption ... He asked me, with earnestness, if I would let him go home. I pointed out to him how unfit he was from his weakness to undertake such a journey ... but promised him, assuredly, without farther hesitation, that as soon as he was able he should have six weeks to go home. He revived at the very thought of it ... His appetite soon mended; and I saw in less than a week, evident signs of recovery.

My mother is in her eighties but looks younger. She is healthy and spry and has no trouble getting around by foot or by car. Left to her own devices, however, she prefers to sit in the dark playing solitaire with the TV on. As Judge Judy chews out her latest shameless litigants, my mother slaps one card after another down on her glass-topped coffee table, all the while puffing like a locomotive. *Snap, puff. Snap, puff.* She claims it is something to do with her heart, some vague undiagnosed condition that makes her breathe that way, though I know it's just one of her plethora of pathological habits, like overcooking vegetables and making certain that every cabinet and drawer in her home is filled to brimming and common household objects are impossible to find.

Unlike the house in Bethel, this has never been my house. There's a guest room, and though I'm one of the few people who sleeps there, it is decidedly not *my* room. The handful of my belongings that are still here, old notebooks and such, feel as foreign to me as everything else. Even my dead papa's slapdash oil paintings, which I love so and which line every wall, look strange here, and might as well adorn the walls of a barricaded embassy in Jakarta. Not a trace of "home" survives.

Meanwhile my mother plays solitaire. *Snap, puff; snap, puff.* . . .

When I can't stand it anymore, I suggest a drive and a walk. It's January; the roads are treacherous with ice and snow. Still I insist. *Judge Judy* is over, I say, and we've perused all of the photo albums. My mother gives an extra-loud puff. Why do I want to drag her, an old woman, out into that mess? But I stick to my guns.

"Come on, Mom," I say. "It'll do us both good."

And so we head downtown, to Main Street in Danbury, to where Mom used to park her black Mercury, only now it's my beige Honda Civic. In the old days parking was a problem. No longer, thanks to the Danbury Fair Mall, which as soon as it opened on the former grounds of the state fair for which it was named transformed Main Street into a ghost town. I remember the fair, sandwiched between the interstate and Route 7 across from the local airport, a shoddy enterprise, with its crowded thoroughfares of dust and mud. There was a Dutch village, complete with windmill, and a frontier town where shootouts were staged. Under the Big Top farmers showed off tomatoes, pumpkins, and poultry. There were Clydesdale horses, men on stilts, polka bands, a lake with ducks and a paddlewheel steamer. But what I recall most were the Saturday evening stock-car races. From my house you heard the roar of engines and smelled rubber burning. For two dollars each, we'd jam into the stands, myself and my brother and Lenny Polis and Victor Virgilio and other kids from the neighborhood. We'd buy boxes of French fries and slather them with ketchup—to eat, sure, but also to hurl down from high bleachers onto unsuspecting heads.

I park my Honda in front of the old movie theater, the Palace, where as a boy I watched the Beatles in *Help!* and *Those Magnificent Men in Their Flying Machines*—quite possibly the only movie my inventor father ever enjoyed with me. The bulky marquee is still there, dented where a truck driver misjudged his clearance, as are the framed cases where movie stills and posters once hung, though no movie has played there in decades. Through a crack in the plywood covering the main entrance I peer inside, hoping to glimpse rows of plush folding seats and a grand if peeling proscenium, but see only darkness.

"*Ma cosa stai cercando?*" "What are you looking for?" my Italian mother says, impatient in coat and gloves. Unlike her son she doesn't suffer from nostalgia.

"Do you remember the last movie we saw here?"

She can't. Neither can I, though for some reason *If It's Tuesday This Must Be Belgium* comes to mind.

From the Palace Theater we make our way north up Main Street, with me poking my head into every storefront, looking for the store that never ends, the one with the carousel. Though most of the buildings still stand, the businesses that used to occupy them have fled, drawn to or chased off by the mall, replaced by Asian and Hispanic grocery stores, thrift shops, and stores selling insurance, phone cards, postage stamps and louche women's fashions. A few are empty shells. It's as if one of those neutron bombs hit the place, the kind that decimates populations but leaves structures intact.

"Hey, look!" I say and point to the pavement. "Woolworth's!" The name's still there, brass letters in pink terrazzo squares. "Wasn't there a policeman's kiosk out here, in front of this store? Or was that farther down?"

My mother shakes her head. She can't imagine what I'm up to.

"Help me remember," I say.

"*Ma perché?*"

"Why not? Don't *you* want to remember?"

Mom gives me a strange look that I ignore, asking her instead to name some of those old stores for me, the ones she always took us to: this eighty-two-year-old Italian woman who this morning couldn't remember the word for "pancake," whose command of English is at best subadequate and whose vocabulary has started to erode in earnest. I press her a bit, but then, seeing the aggravated look on her face and remembering the strokes that killed my father, I lay off.

We walk past the former post office, down a side street, past a bar named Tuxedo Junction—formerly the Top Hat Lounge, but in any case a dive, its neon beer signs blushing in dark windows. Across the way, lining the parapet of a recently constructed building, a dozen black birds stand like statues. At first I assume they *are* statues, until one by one they spread their raven wings, putting me in mind of one of Hitchcock's more unsettling movies. Like crows they are, but bigger, reminiscent of those half-bat, half-owl monsters that crowd out the artist's dreams in Goya's *The Sleep of Reason Produces Monsters*. A man in a hooded sweat suit who speaks no English joins us, wondering too about the birds. Nor are the two dozing bums we come upon on the sidewalk much help.

"*Dio,*" says my mother tripping over one, and for a moment I feel like Beatrice leading Dante down through the crusty layers of Hell.

We're on our way to a diner. The Holiday. Or the Windmill. Two Brothers. The Peter Pan: these are all names of diners I recall, though what they have in common, apart from a vague fairy-tale resonance, I've no idea. I've long been a fan of diners, especially the stainless-steel kind shaped like Pullman cars, with their buck-toothed frappe machines, arrayed ketchup bottles and glutinous pies hardening under glass domes. What I love most about them is that anywhere in America, in the Northeast anyway, you could walk into one and know what you're in for, that for instance, arranged along a phalanx of stools, I'd find rugged men in green and blue work uniforms, while across the counter a waitress grips a Pyrex carafe while wearing a pencil tucked behind her ear. The food's nothing to write home about. Still, it beats McDonald's, and anyway you don't go to diners for gourmet meals; you go for a sense of continuity, to feel at home. I do, anyway.

Once, at the very diner to which my mother and I are presently headed, I encountered love of the sweetest sort—yes, nostalgic love. It came in the form of a waitress whose name reminded me of rain. I saw the name first, on the plastic name tag she wore on her bosom, though I had no idea, would never have known, that this was the very same April with whom I'd ridden the school bus in second grade, bus number 9, driven by overweight Miss Hatt ("Miss Hatt is fat she's a dirty rat!"). On the backseat of that bus all through second grade George and I belted out Beatles' songs— "Ticket to Ride," "You're Gonna Lose that Girl"—songs from *Help!* that we first heard when the movie of the same name played at the Palace Theater. We were a hit, George and I, with our twin voices and bold harmonies. April, our biggest fan, always sat nearby. She had a crush on me. Or was it the other way around? I can't recall. But having served me my coffee and a corn muffin, she said, "You don't remember me, do you?" I looked at the nametag again, then up at her. "No," I said. "I'm sorry." Then she told me. This must have been ten years ago; I would have been in my mid forties. The last time we'd seen each other, April and I had been seven years old (after second grade she transferred to St. Mary's). Forty years stood between us. How could she have remembered, let alone recognized, me? As I kept looking at her, the memory of April's face superimposed itself on the present reality until the two images merged. She hadn't changed. Her hair was still dark and long; she had the same full face, and, though her lips were stingy, her generous smile more than made up for them. I'm not sure what we talked about after that. I guess she asked me what I'd been up to, and I guess I told her. At the time I was still married, still living in New York City, surviving as an artist. I'm sure I painted a far more romantic and successful picture of my life than I might have, my feeble attempts at modesty notwithstanding. And there was April, a waitress at the Holiday (or the Peter Pan, or the Windmill, or Two Brothers) with a pencil behind her ear. She'd been married, she said, and having recently come through a rough divorce was struggling to make ends meet, hence the waitressing job. I didn't ask for details. It seemed to me that the moment didn't call for them, that it was like a song, and, like a song, should be short and sweet. I finished my coffee and muffin and — having debated whether to do so — left a dollar on the table. With a peck on her cheek and having said, "Take care of yourself," I left the diner and April and ran out through the rain to my car. Did I happen to mention that it was raining?

And now we've arrived at the same diner, my mother and I, or what used to be the same diner, but isn't anymore. The stainless-steel sides have been plastered over with rugged stucco, while the Pullman-style roof is covered with terra-cotta tiles. Christmas lights are strung along the eaves. A big wooden sign hovers over it: *La Playa*. From two dozen feet away we can hear the music drifting out into the street, along with an odor of fried food. We look at each other, my mother and I. Italians are naturally suspicious of their Latin cousins, especially concerning food and drink. My mother and I are no exception. It's a case of familiarity breeding — not contempt, exactly, but something closer to competition, where authenticity comes into question, along with a dose of chauvinistic pride. Never mind: we're hungry, and here's a place to eat. We no sooner step inside than a wall of greasy air and loud music confronts us bully-like, pushing us away, and back outdoors we go.

"*Per l'amor di dio*," my mother says.

It is now four thirty. Behind the Catholic church's black witch's hat of a steeple the sun hangs exhausted and orange. We haven't eaten since breakfast, though I'm not hungry — or I am, but my appetite is strictly for nostalgia. We're on a back street, walking behind a row of stores, behind Genung's — or what used to be Genung's. I recognize it by the configuration of its back doors, and am even able to imagine, based on an autochthonous memory, how their handles will feel against my hand when touched, as well as the odor of perfume and soft fabrics, subtle as my grandmother's kiss, that would greet us the moment we entered the place — a soft, luxurious fragrance. There was a time when for me Genung's stood as magnificently for luxury as the Taj Mahal, when I could no more imagine the universe without Genung's than I could imagine the night sky minus the Big Dipper. With its glass display cases of glimmering watches and jewelry, its endless racks of dresses, its twirling displays of lipsticks and perfumes and women's hosiery extending over three levels (reached via escalators whose iron treads would suck me in by my untied sneaker laces and slice me to ribbons with their thin iron teeth if I failed to leap off at just the right instant), Genung's was for this son of an avowed atheist a combination holy shrine and a museum to rival the Smithsonian. It didn't matter that the objects on display had little to do with me; they were mine: their shapes, their colors, their folds, their textures, the glimmers of jewels and metal, the swirling patterns in a blouse or a skirt, they belonged to me, to my greedy, ravenous senses. I'm reminded of the last time I saw Audrey, my daughter. We were in Carbondale, where we visited a big department store not unlike Genung's. I forget what her mother was shopping for. While she shopped we had the run of the place. Audrey was especially taken with the male mannequins: sleek, faceless aliens modeling dress shirts and designer blue jeans. Every time she saw one she'd run up and hug—him? it?—around the knees. That store was more edifying to her by far than the science museum we'd gone to the day before and that cost us seventeen dollars' admission, and where, within twenty minutes, Audrey fell asleep in her stroller.

As for what was once Genung's, the place (I discover when I try the door, the handles of which do indeed conform to memory) is locked. Where not plastered with FOR LEASE signs, the once seductive display windows are painted with some opaque substance to prevent prying eyes like mine from peering inside and seeing—what? An opium den? A bookie joint? A covert surveillance installation? The source of the next bubonic plague?

As children we assume with a conviction bordering on righteousness the permanence of all things. Whatever it touches, childhood consecrates. How can Genung's no longer be? Yet like the Temple of Artemis it is no longer. The Big Dipper has quit the sky.

Lately I have less and less patience for reading. Novels no longer hold any interest for me. Reading them for me is like eating cotton candy.

Newspapers I rarely touch; magazines are even worse. As for nonfiction in general, I've no more interest these days in reading up on, say, the Berlin Olympics of 1936 than in immersing myself in the Codex Theodosianus. The only books that interest me are those with nothing as their subject. Such books exist. Pessoa's *Book of Disquiet* is one; so are what Georg Lichtenburg called his "Waste Books" *("Sudelbücher")*; so is *Efraim's Book,* by Alfred Andersch; so, essentially, are the "novels" of Sebald. To this list one might add Burton's *Anatomy of Melancholy* and Miller's *Tropic of Cancer,* though the first is practically unreadable, and time has turned Henry Miller into the great misogynistic windbag of modern letters.

Among my favorite books about nothing is one titled *Tsurezuregusa* (translated as *Essays in Idleness* or *The Harvest of Leisure).* Written in the fourteenth century by the Japanese monk Yoshida Kenko, it consists of 238 essays of various length arranged in no particular order except insofar as the arrangement pleased its author. It is one of the earliest examples of the genre known as *zuihitsu,* meaning "follow the brush," a metaphor for a stream-of-consciousness technique that not only allowed but encouraged authors to flit randomly from topic to topic at their whim, guided only by the flow of their thoughts. If Kenko's free-flowing book has a subject, it is the awareness of impermanence, or "mono no aware," the melancholy born of the passing of all things:

> The world is as unstable as the pools and shadows of Asuka River. Times change and things disappear; joy and sorrow come and go; a place that once thrived turns into an uninhabited moor; a house may remain unaltered, but its occupants will have changed. The peach and the damson trees in the garden say nothing—with whom is one to reminisce about the past? I feel this sense of impermanence even more sharply when I see the remains of a house, which long ago, before I knew it, must have been imposing.

Dr. Hofer was wrong. Nostalgia isn't a disease; it's a symptom of a greater malaise, an unwillingness to accept, let alone embrace, the future. Nostalgia isn't merely an "expression of local longing"; it is a new and disturbing relationship to time, or a longing to return to an old relationship. The healthy man, on the other hand, lives in the present with an eye to the future. In pop-psychology terms, he sees the glass as half-full; time will fill the other half (and empty it, and fill it again, and so on). Whatever has been will be again—in one form or another. This notion of a continuous cycle of birth and death—the concept of "eternal return" or "eternal recurrence"—has its roots in Jainism and Buddhism and other Indian creeds, and is often symbolized by a wheel. In ancient Egypt the dung beetle provided a parallel, if less appetizing, metaphor: out of shit comes life, and vice versa. As Kenko writes: "[T]he old leaves fall due to pressure from underneath of new leaves." Nietzsche, who called modern man "a depraved creature racked with homesickness for the wild," references the doctrine of eternal recurrence, which he most likely encountered in Heinrich Heine, who offers this description:

> Now, however long a time may pass, according to the eternal laws governing the combinations of this eternal play of repetition, all configurations which have previously existed on this earth must yet meet, attract, repulse, kiss, and corrupt each other again.

For the nostalgic, the cycle is broken; the hourglass is cracked. He yearns for its repair, for a slowing—if not a reversal—of the sands. He has no faith whatever in the future's ability to replenish what has been sacrificed to time. If it spins at all, the wheel of life spins toward decay, destruction, desolation, and doom.

Along Main Street—we're back on the front sidewalk again—all the shops I recall are gone. Feinson's Men's Clothing, Sturdevant's Photo Shop, the New Englander Motel, Buster Brown Shoes ... What isn't gone appears reduced, the streets narrowed and shortened, inhabited by ghouls. We pass the hulk of the savings and loan where my grandmother kept her money. In that yawning cool echo chamber, on an octagonal table surfaced with thick glass, she'd fill out a deposit slip (I doubt she ever made withdrawals) and then I'd stand in line behind her in her brown polka-dotted dress as she waited for *her* teller. She always went to the same teller: a short, plump woman with a beehive of red hair, Thelma Dudley—who could forget that name? To reward me for my patience, Miss Dudley would reach deep into her teller's drawer and hand me a lollipop—root beer, if I had my druthers. Then Nonnie and I would cross the street to the New Englander, where, in a restaurant under the main floor called the Mad Hatter, decorated with flocked red velvet fleur-de-lis wallpaper and an *Alice in Wonderland* mural, she would order us each the Salisbury steak, smothered with mushrooms and gravy, from a waiter in an ocher Eton jacket, and made sure that I tucked my *salvietta* into my shirt collar, chewed with my mouth closed, and sipped, not gulped, my water: commands I

Mad Hatter sign outside Hotel Green

happily obeyed given the momentous elegance of the occasion. Now that restaurant and the New Englander both are gone, as is the bank. Only their buildings remain, the latter still with its imposingly impenetrable bronze doors protecting nothing but a hollow granite bunker. As for the New Englander, it is now a senior citizen complex called Ives Manor, after the maverick composer Charles Edward Ives, born in Danbury, whose house was moved at great expense from its original Main Street location and now sits on a barren parcel abutting the town playground, its clapboards rotting, its roof beginning to sag. The museum society that owns it has struggled to raise money to repair it, no mean feat in this economy and given that very few people today even know who Charles Ives was, or would care much for him or his music if they did. So his house sits there, empty and forlorn, not yet a ruin, but rapidly becoming one.

A few doors past the bank we find an open restaurant. A baize curtain on a brass rod divides the plate-glass window. The restaurant's name fails to register with me. There are three tables within, each covered by an oilcloth imprinted with a hodgepodge of Italian tableaux, the Rialto Bridge on my end, the Trevi Fountain at my mother's. The place reeks of oregano-heavy tomato sauce. We are the only patrons. Over cups of obviously canned soup my mother conducts her own nostalgic inventory, remembering Tripoli, where she was born, and where she rode everywhere on the back of her brother's Lambretta, how every kind of fruit grew in her backyard: figs, olives, lemons, dates. It was a sunny landscape unsullied by war, insurrection, hunger, death, disease, or despots. She had a pet monkey named Guerlina (Trans: Little War).

She tells me not for the first time how her mother was close friends with Italo Balbo, the pilot; how Italian guns shot him down. "They say was accident, but Mussolini, he kill him. And now dey have dat *maledetto* Gaddafi. I hope dey kill him, too." She slurps her soup. In the past she has spoken well of Colonel Gaddafi; she even once remarked to me how handsome he was. She must be in a bad mood. Outside the snow is melting; water drips from the awning. Though the sun is nearly gone, I'm eager to get back to our walk, feeling as if I've walked into my own dream, as if already I'm remembering this moment with my mother in this sad excuse for a restaurant, a moment lived ages ago, in another life, as if my mother is already gone and I am dreaming of her alive and well and here sipping lukewarm barley soup with me, now. I used to have such dreams about my father years after he died, of us together riding up Mount Beacon on the creaky wooden funicular that once led to a pavilion overlooking the Hudson River, where people danced, though the pavilion had long since vanished, burned down. Now the funicular too is gone. In my dreams I saw the breeze through the open car stirring my father's gray hair, its few remaining strands. That's how lucid those dreams were. It's the same here with my mother right now, though the dream is real. Still, I have to resist reaching across the oilcloth-covered table, over the Rialto Bridge and the Fontana di Trevi, and taking her hand in mine like a suitor. Though other sons might, I have never done such a thing, perhaps because even at eighty-two my mother is still so much more beautiful than average mothers, let alone grandmothers.

Instead I change the subject. "What about that other store we used to go to, the one that went on forever?" I'm referring to that other department store, the one with the endless narrow configuration that wound its way to a carousel at its terminus. My mother's gaze drops; while blowing into her by now lukewarm soup, she refuses to make eye contact with me. She's upset, I can tell.

"I no like this," she tells me.

"What—the soup? It's canned."

"No the soup, what you doing. Dis game! Remember dis, remember dat! What is wrong wid you, Peter?"

"Weren't you just doing the same thing?"

"Is no the same! I am an old lady!"

She's right, of course; it's not the same thing. She's also right that something is wrong with me; there's no denying it. The disease called nostalgia has me in its grip.

"I tink you depressed," my mother decides.

I nod into my soup and own that it may just be so. She suggests that while in town I visit her doctor.

"Maybe he help you," she says.

So I make an appointment with Dr. Jerome. If memory serves, he always wore a bow tie. His office is on Sandpit Road, in Germantown. What the heck; maybe he'll prescribe me some interesting pills. I go by way of Bethel. It's not on the way; in fact it's in the other direction. But there's a breakfast place there, a diner, as a matter of fact, one that, if it still exists, has very good corn muffins, and right now I need a good corn muffin no less than I need to see a doctor.

But what I really need, what I'm really after, is to see my hometown, something I've resisted until now. All those places in my waking dreams? I want to see what time has done to them. I can't resist.

And so along shady back roads whose names (Long Ridge Road, Reservoir Street, Saxon Drive...) I recall along with the name of those I knew who once lived on them, I drive to Bethel. In his boxy little ranch house on Saxon Drive, with Billy Norse I first listened to the Beatle's *White Album*. I was thunderstruck by "Why Don't We Do it in the Road?" (a good question, I must have thought then, to which the world offered too many equally good answers).

I drive on. Soon I'm passing Pete Smith's house, or rather the house where he and his numerous brothers and sisters grew up, a disheveled Victorian with a wraparound porch and abundant gables. He was the first in my class to marry and, at the ripe old age of twenty-three, father a child, beating me by thirty-four years. The same year he had his kid, I wrote my first (bad, unpublished) novel. I recall him saying to me apropos our progeny, "Until you've have a kid, Pete, you'll never know the meaning of creativity." The remark rankled. It still does.

I drive on, past the tire shop and the liquor store and other cultural landmarks, Bethel style. Soon I'm crossing the railroad tracks by the old station, passing in front of the building that once housed The Vaghi Woodworking Company, now boarded up and with a For Lease Sign

on it, like so many other buildings around here. In addition to being Bethel's finest mill worker, Dante Vaghi was the town's flying saucer authority, and had been since the night in 1950 when he sighted his first UFO in the night skies over Bethel. On that night Dante saw what he would later describe as a luminous, wing-shaped object hovering in the sky, a quarter-mile or so above the earth. The UFO appeared to hover directly over the neighborhood known as Dodgingtown (275° azimuth; elevation 1.5°). As it hovered, a group of patchy clouds swept over it, enhancing the impression of luminosity. Having hovered there that way for a minute or two, the luminous, wing-shaped object dispersed, leaving no doubt in Dante's mind that he had borne witness to an utterly novel event. Following that night, Dante went on to experience a dozen more UFO sightings, thus becoming an expert on them not only by his own estimation, but in the eyes of others, especially local boys of a certain impressionable age, myself among them. By ourselves or in the company of others we'd visit him at his woodworking shop, on the roof of which Dante had erected a large white cross and, alongside it, a billboard featuring a graphic depiction of the infamous wing-shaped object. Spread across the billboard under the drawing, in large red letters, one read:

> **WELCOME all PEOPLE**
> **from OTHER PLANETS**
> **to BETHEL, CT. U.S.A.**

In the back room of that building, when not spinning legs for tables or milling dovetail joints, Dante worked on his flying saucer. No one was supposed to know about it, so we'd been given to believe, though we all did, at least every Bethel boy of a certain age, its maker having taken us, one by one or in small groups or pairs, into his confidence and shown us the thing, peeling back a sawdust-covered tarp to offer us a tantalizing glimpse of smooth rounded wood. Yes, *wood*. Sometimes, there being nothing else for us to sit on in that back room, he'd have us sit on the edge of the thing; it made a surprisingly comfortable bench. There, in his quasi-secret UFO command post, the walls of which were plastered with photographs, newspaper clippings, and other evidence of extraterrestrial activity sent to him by UFO enthusiasts all over the country, between sips of the hot Ovaltine he would brew for us ("the food drink for rocket power"), Dante would acquaint his privileged young visitors with the Roswell Files, ionized air, electro-magnetic propulsion, 'G' forces, and coronas of bluish-white flame.

I've now passed through part of the town, past what used to be Mulanney's newsstand, and what used to be Jerome's Five and Dime store, and what used to be the Old English Drug Company, and what used to be the Doughboy Diner. I'm on my old street, Wooster Street, in my old neighborhood, passing Terry Devendorf's house. This fall my high school graduating class plans to hold a reunion, its thirty-fifth. I won't be going. I have an aversion to reunions of all sorts. Ghoulish undertakings, nights of the living dead.

As for the nonliving dead, already several of my classmates have made the transition, including Terry Deifendorf, who, in exchange for ice-cold bottles of Yoo-hoo, used to lure me into doing his paper route for him. Terry, who must have been kept back a grade or two, was two years older than I. His was (is: it's still there) one of those nondescript one-story rectangular tract houses that sprang up all over the Northeast in the mid-1960's, with a one-car garage tucked

under one side. In Terry's garage we'd sip Yoo-hoos and he would show off his model Corvette collection. I looked up to Terry. He was older than I, and wore crisp white Hanes T-shirts and cuffed Levis. Terry was an all-American boy, something I decidedly was not. He'd hand me a bound stack of *Bethel Home News,* and, with one or two instructions and his blessing, send me off to do his paper route for him. He'd even let me use his bicycle; in fact, Terry insisted on it. It was a green Schwinn Sting-Ray with a banana seat, butterfly handlebars and custom extended sissy-bar. On frozen-sweltering days, with his benediction ("Take it easy, Selg.") Terry would consign me to a hell of shabby roads, delinquent customers, and fierce, unchained dogs. Once, chased by a rabid terrier, I rode Terry's Sting-Ray into a ditch, scratching the handlebars. Terry's disappointment knew no bounds. "I can't trust you with anything, can I, Selg?" More often, though, Terry seemed pleased with my performance. "Nice work, Selg," he'd say, patting my back on my return, and then—like Ali Baba proffering a jewel-encrusted vessel from his cave—hand me a sweaty can of Yoo-hoo from the garage refrigerator. This, combined with the privilege of riding Terry's green Sting-Ray, constituted payment in full for services rendered. But my real payment was having Terry like me; being embraced—or anyway tolerated—by this all-American boy. Once, when we were horsing around in a dirt lot whose owner had aborted the construction of yet another small rectangular house,

Terry, popping a wheelie, rammed his Sting-Ray into me. The threaded shaft of its front hub gouged a wad of fatty flesh the size of a garden slug out of my left calf. Mr. Deifendorf drove me to the emergency room. I still have the scar: the glossy white ghost of a garden slug.

We used to poke fun at Terry and his passion for Chevrolets. If one of us so much as paid a compliment to a Ford, he'd grab us by the scruffs, march us to the powder-blue convertible Corvette parked in the bicycle-seat factory lot, force us to our knees before its front grill and have us bow and repeat, "Hail Chevy! Hail Chevy! Hail Chevy!"

Now Terry Deifendorf is dead. He died two years ago. I suspect heart issues. The low-resolution black-and-white photograph accompanying his obituary, which I found online, was of a man whose obesity had done away by and large with his neck, who wore glasses and whose hairline had receded but who was nevertheless and without question Terry Deifendorf. The obituary went on to say that he'd "retired as a captain with the Bethel Volunteer Fire Department" and was the owner of something called "Ironclad Spray-on Linings." And yet as far as I'm concerned Terry remains in his garage, tinkering with his model cars, sipping his Yoo-hoos. I want him alive in his T-shirt and cuffed Levis, calling me "Selg," telling me to "hop on" (or off) his green Sting-Ray. I want him to have survived. Instead Terry is the one survived: by a father, a wife, a son, a sister, a brother, a father-in-law, a sister-in-law, two grandchildren, sundry nieces and nephews. And by me.

Though I can't honestly say that I liked Terry, I liked him enough to choke up a bit as I sat at my computer, my insomnia having woken me at two a.m. It seemed to me suddenly that all the Terry Deifendorfs in the world were dead, popping wheelies in heaven or hell. And so was I; I was dead, too, only I'd been too busy dreaming up this *other* life, the one where, by some miracle, I remained untouched by time, forever innocent, a child in a world of dying and dead old men. Let me say it just once: *I don't want to die.*

❖

I'm coming up to my old house now, 75-rear (or 75 ½) Wooster Street. The house sits far back from the road, at the end of the long driveway once lined with weeping willows, though the willows, I can see as I drive past, are gone now, every one of them. Before they would have hidden both the house and the structure at the bottom of the hill that was my father's laboratory. Having turned right up the road of a development that runs parallel to the driveway, I have a clear view of both structures. My father's laboratory (the Building, we used to call it) has been left to rot. Its roof sags; the windows are boarded, and what used to be something of a lawn next to it has gone to brambles. The adjoining barn has collapsed. Unlike Mr. Ives's house, it most emphatically qualifies as a ruin. Why this should anger and sadden me, I'm not sure, since like many people I usually *like* ruins. I used to especially love the ruins of hat factories that were so much a part of my childhood landscape, with their crumbling brick walls and chimneys. My inventor father and I would go out of our way to explore the remains of trestles, mills, and foundries. On our first visit together to my hometown after her birth, I carried my infant daughter, still in a swaddling blanket, up the steep path to what's left of Hearthstone Castle, the former summer residence of E. Starr Sanford, an affluent New York City photographer. The three-story stone structure once had seventeen rooms, including nine bedrooms, a library, a billiards room, and an eleven-foot verandah. The castle produced its own electricity, I've been told. Now it's a ghostly shell on the brow of a hill in Tarrywile Park, taken over by the city, which has consigned it to the forces of nature. Against her mother's better judgment, I carried Audrey up there, thinking it might impress her. And though she dozed through the ordeal, *I* was impressed. There is something beautiful about ruins, something melancholy and sublime in how, while disintegrating, they pay tribute to that which no longer is. This is what the artist Piranesi captures so well in his etchings of Roman ruins, the dream of a present in which the past is alive and transparent, heightened and even glorified in its disintegration. The beauty of  ruins—and what are memories if not the ruins of experience?—lies in this paradox: that they glorify the past by underscoring its absence. Ruskin, an early advocate for the preservation of ruins, was among the first to appreciate their transcendent power:

> A broken stone has necessarily more various forms in it than a whole one; a bent roof has more various curves in it than a straight one; every excrescence or cleft involves some additional complexity of light and shade, and every stain of moss on eaves or wall adds to the delightfulness of colour ... This sublimity, belonging in a parasitical manner to the building, renders it, in the usual sense of the word, "picturesque."[1]

But when the ruin is that of your own past, it's more grotesque than picturesque, and in the rotting hulk of my father's former laboratory

---

1. The value of ruins has been so greatly admired that architects like Albert Speer proposed to erect buildings such that, in a thousand years when they fell to ruin, they would make on whoever saw them a favorable impression of the men who built them and the time in which they were built. They were *meant* to become ruins. Some have even speculated that the Great Pyramids of Egypt, along with the ruins of Macchu Picchu, Stonehenge, and other megaliths of Neolithic builders, were built with this intention: not to impress the men or gods of their ages, but to awe those of the future. Perhaps the Danbury Mall was built with the same ulterior motive, to force time's hand, the way sculptors apply a patina to their bronze statues, or forgers treat their fake Rembrandts with a special dust to make them look old.

I find little to admire.

As for the house at the top of the driveway, I'm afraid to look up at it, but do. It's still there. I see the garage where I kept my first car, a rust-bucket MG convertible with four different-sized tires, and the porch where on muggy summer days we ate poached chicken with  my mother's homemade mayonnaise as the louvered draw fan at the top of the stairs sucked air in through the screened windows. In winter the porch was off-limits. A rolled towel shoved under its door kept the cold from leaking into the rest of the house. My mother kept the liquor there, ancient bottles of vermouth, creme de cacao, and kirschwasser, all wearing furry gray mantles of dust (my parents didn't drink much), and a filigreed Arabian tea set that now adorns my brother's Georgia home, as do most of the good antiques we grew up with. If our mother ventured into the porch on winter days, it was to toss breadcrumbs to the wild turkeys that visited her once a day, gathering by the dogwood tree. Now the porch is boarded up with sheets of plywood, the memories of those years boarded up with it. A gutter hangs. The antenna sprouting from the chimney is bent at ninety degrees. The three stately maple trees that engulfed the house are all gone, including one that I made a feeble attempt to cut down with a toy saw at age six. As for the white picket fence leading to the mulberry tree, two-thirds of the pickets are gone. A half dozen beat-up cars are parked in the driveway. No doubt a commune of paperless day laborers lives here now.

I've seen enough. I pull away, vowing not to say a word of what I've seen to my mother, who would rather not know. It would break her heart. Who knows, it might just kill her.

I decide to skip breakfast; I've lost my appetite. Besides, I no longer care to see the town. I don't care to visit Tony's Food Market, or whatever has taken its place. Ditto Noe's, the five-and-dime, the hardware store. I've had enough of haunting and being haunted. Instead I turn around and head toward Germantown, to the doctor's office. I'll tell him I've been losing sleep (true) and that I've been visited recently by vaguely suicidal thoughts (also true, though less frequently so).

But what really bothers me is the sadness, this crushing weight of nostalgia bearing down on me, dragging me under. At least I assume that nostalgia is the culprit, though I may be wrong. Since making my appointment, I came across a newspaper item about a study conducted not long ago by psychologists at the University of Southampton. According to it, since nostalgics tend to have more positive feelings about their pasts, they feel a greater sense of continuity and meaning in their lives. Therefore, the study suggests, nostalgia may increase one's self-esteem while making one feel more loved and protected. It may even improve a person's physical health. "[Nostalgia]," writes theologian and philosopher Ralph Harper, "is the soul's natural way of fighting sickness and despair." This may apply in particular to older people, who suffer especially from feelings of neglect and isolation. "Nostalgia is now emerging as a fundamental human strength," the study's authors go on to say, before concluding—with no apparent irony: "[It] has an exciting future."

As for me, I'm less than convinced. Though it may give succor to the aged and infirm, and provide material and inspiration to poets (Rilke continually refers his young poet to the "treasure house of childhood"), for a healthy not-yet-old man, looking backward is about as helpful as looking down to a tightrope walker.

Anyway, it makes me sad.

❖

Though still on Sandpit Road, Dr. Jerome's office isn't where it used to be; it's just down the street, in a shiny new complex of medical office buildings once occupied by a small park, with a shallow wading pool that my mother used to take my brother and me to. In the sumptuous waiting room there's a directory on the wall with photographs of all the physicians serving the private clinic. From a distance I try to tell which of a dozen gray heads belongs to Dr. Jerome, but my nearsightedness defeats me. At last I give up and approach the poster, to find that my mother's doctor has indeed grown older, advanced (degenerated?) from middle to old age. I'm reminded of another article I read once, about another doctor, Samuel Johnson, how distressed he was when in middle age he returned to his Litchfield roots only to find his "play-fellows" all grown old, forcing him to suspect himself of no longer being young. According to the photo at least, Dr. Jerome still wears a bow tie. That comforts me.

Forty minutes pass before I'm seen.

"Mr. T—Pinuccia's son?" Dr. Jerome says, and I nod. He gives me the once-over. "How old are you?" he wonders, squinting.

I tell him.

"Well," he says, "for a start I'd say you're suffering from a serious failure to age properly. Must run in the family. Come with me."

He leads me to the examination room where he checks my vitals, and where we exchange small talk. He asks me what I've been up to. I keep it simple. "You're the artistic one, right?" he says.

"Something like that."

"So—what can I do for you today?"

"I don't know," I say. "I guess I've just feel kinda crummy."

"Kinda crummy, huh?" He presses his stethoscope to my chest. "Hmm, I don't know that there's any cure for 'kinda crummy.' You sure you don't have gout? Gout I can cure. Or scurvy? Have you got scurvy? I can cure scurvy."

It occurs to me that a physician who wears a bow tie will crack jokes. I grin and bear it. "What's the matter, really?" he says when I fail to laugh. "Talk to me."

"I guess I'm just depressed," I answer with a shrug.

"What are you depressed about?"

"Nostalgia."

"You're feeling homesick? But you're home now, aren't you?"

"Yes," I say, "and no," and I refuse to elaborate. Instead I say, "You know it used to be a disease."

"Nostalgia? Is that so?"

"Among Swiss mercenaries. They used to bleed people for it."

"We don't do that here."

He tells me to stand. "You have children?"

"A daughter," I say. "Sixteen months."

I didn't plan to be a father. Certainly I didn't plan to become one at fifty-two. In fact I'd made the opposite vow: that I would never visit upon my own child the Curse of the Older Father. Don't misunderstand; I adored my father who was forty-seven when he had me. Yet I suffered from his being older than other fathers, from his unwillingness to throw balls or run or jump into bodies of water. "I can't; I'm too *old!*" How often I endured that refrain! Yes, we did other things; we went to museums; we rode the funicular up Mt. Beacon. But I wanted a baseball-throwing father, a father who would join with me in body and spirit. At the height of my frustration I took my silent oath. But passion and biology had other things to say about the matter. And so at fifty-two I became the father of a healthy fetus, one that I begged its mother, over a plate of rapidly congealing fettuccini at a tavern in Gramercy Park, to destroy. Outside, it rained. I remember us walking across the park at Union Square, her mind firmly made up, my arguments exhausted, sharing an umbrella. I could no more imagine myself a father at fifty-two than I could picture myself walking in space. My biggest worry, apart from financial concerns, was that I wouldn't love this fruit of my own flesh. Suddenly the same future that I'd long doubted and distrusted, that bleary nebula, had hardened into a solid mass of tissue sharing my DNA. Not only was I forced to accept it; I had to bear the responsibility for it. When a friend of a friend got the news, she remarked, "I guess Peter finally decided to grow up." In fact by then I had resigned myself, but the golf-ball-sized thing growing in my lover's womb was more a cause for fear than of affection. I felt not as a father feels toward his child, but as a son toward a father who wields absolute power and authority and whose verdict is final. She (by then we knew it was a girl) commanded *my* fate. Despite all that, I wanted to be a good father and especially to overcome, or at least make up for, the curse I'd handed down to her. When she grew up, I promised both of us, I'd throw balls, I'd jump into lakes, I'd run and play with her. I hadn't counted on the fickleness of an academic career, on visiting posts spread far and wide, or on my partner's determination to complete her graduate degree in poetry at a university in the middle of Nowhere, Illinois. I hadn't counted on feeling so cut off—not just from the future, but from my past and from myself.

It was around then that I began dreaming of Bethel, of Tony's and Noe's, of a driveway lined with elephantine weeping willows, of the white picket fence leading to a mulberry tree.

"Congratulations," says Dr. Jerome, probing my scrotum. "Has she got a name, this daughter of yours?"

"Audrey."

"Like Audrey Hepburn. Very nice." He snaps my undershorts back on.

"She's in Illinois," I add, "with her mother."

"Oh," says Dr. Jerome.

"Mom's in graduate school, and I've got a one-year visiting appointment at Saint Lawrence University."

"I see." He leads me to the scale. "How long since you've seen her?"

"Six—no, seven weeks." A tear tugs at the corner of my eye.

"No wonder you're feeling nostalgic. You must miss her terribly."

"I do," I say and for the first time I feel the weight of this truth.

"Are you taking anything? For depression?" the doctor asks.

I shake my head.

"Would you care to?"

"I'm game if you are."

He writes me a prescription for Lexapro, a month's supply.

I still have all thirty pills.

I've been reading up on bioluminescence, the phenomenon of living things giving off light. While the kinds of lights that we normally see (the sun, a lamp, a candleflame) come from high-density energy sources (heat, in other words), bioluminescence is the product of low-energy systems with no significant changes in temperature involved. The light emitted by fungi growing on rotting wood is one form of bioluminescence; fireflies, algae, bacteria, and plankton as well as some types of jellyfish, coral and other invertebrate animals have all been known to generate it. The term comes from the Greek *bio* for "living" and the Latin *lumen* for "light."

This is nonfiction, but it interests me. I'm especially intrigued by something called foxfire, also known as "will-o'-the-wisp," "corpse-candle," "spook-light" and "friar's lantern": the faint glow of light seen by hunters and others who find themselves in the woods after dark, arising from patches of leaf-covered ground or from old stumps and decaying wood. Thought to be supernatural, these "cold" fires were the source of speculation, folktales and myths concerning elves, ghosts, and forest sprites. Since the odd light emanated from dying things, before its true source was learned many assumed that the process of decay *was* the cause, that it was the light of death that they were seeing, the essence of mortality, of impermanence.

Nostalgia gives off a similar glow, and may be just as misunderstood, since what gives the past its glow isn't that it's dead or dying, but that new things and ideas, new hopes, spring from it. Where I've looked to the future and seen devastation, others see a blooming garden. That is the healthy way of looking at things. Now and then, with Audrey in mind, I've shared this vision or something close to it, with my daughter as the single bright bloom growing out of a ravished landscape, and me standing there holding my little watering can that feels (mostly) half empty, in search of a spigot, or a well, aware that I must nourish and nurture; that's my job. Though it is accompanied by a hefty dose of anxiety, how can I not be grateful for this image?

Nostalgia is a form of irony, of feigned ignorance. It therefore can never be taken at face value. It alters its object; it is not *of* its object, though it is often confused with its object, *which does not really exist*.

I have ceased playing that game in bed at night where I revisit my hometown and haunt my own past. I no longer heed the siren call of that particular Circe's island, with its treacherous lullabies. Let the broken hourglass spill its sand!

At Saint Lawrence, in my library carrel, on the otherwise bare white wall above my computer, I kept a photograph of my daughter sitting in her little rubber chair. In Old English *Audrey* means "noble strength": what we all need to look forward, to face the future. As for what to look forward to, in a few days, before I pack up and leave here, I'll see her again, my daughter whose face lights my way as surely as any will-o'-the-wisp. She is my bioluminescence: and I the stump from which she grows. I'll take her for a walk into town, share a muffin with her at the local greasy spoon, watch with a father's pride as she insists on forcing the blue square peg into the red round hole: so like her papa!

And from here on, when Audrey's not around, after tucking myself into bed at night, rather than go back to Bethel in my dreams, I'll picture the two of us, my daughter and I, together, riding that creaky wooden funicular up Mount Beacon, to that gay pavilion at its summit where, I am told, people once danced.

❖ *Black Bubbles*

"Dr. Numbnuts," we called him. His real name was Trimpert, Dr. Albert Trimpert. He was the Town Medical Examiner, but my friends and I called him Dr. Numbnuts owing to how he'd examine us during routine physicals at the Middle School. We lined up in our gym shorts. When the time came, one by one we'd step up to him and hold our breaths as he yanked our shorts down and examined us, pulling our dicks up and down, back and forth, gazing into the little hole on top as if into the eyepiece of a microscope. Then: the *coup de grace*. Using the knuckles of the first two fingers of his left hand, Dr. Trimpert would perform a swift painful test, jamming them up into our scrotums from below. What he was testing us for I don't recall, and may not have known at the time. But anyway to us for this reason he was and always would be Dr. Numbnuts.

From over the tops of his bifocals, across his desk in his little room in the back of the police station, looking me straight in the eyes, Dr. Numbnuts said: "You'll have to live with this for the rest of your life. You realize that, now, don't you, son?"

Dr. Numbnuts had said more or less this same thing to me already several times, and a few times I'd already given him the same automatic response, though the truth was that I didn't know, could not possibly have known then, what I would or would not have to live with for the rest of my life. I only knew that I was scared and tired and hungry and wanting as badly as I'd ever wanted anything to be home with my mother and brother and father having dinner and watching television.

"Well?" Dr. Numbnuts said. "Well, do you?"

From a corner of the Medical Examiner's office Sergeant Steiner kept looking at me, then looking away. I think the Sergeant may have felt as awkward and uncomfortable as I did., or maybe he just wanted to go home, too. It was past six o'clock, and though the blinds were drawn in the office I could tell that it was starting to get dark outside already, and people were home with their families, sitting and passing food around different kinds of tables.

"Yes," I said. "Yes, yes: I realize it."

That morning my friend Chris Rowland and I had volunteered at the dog pound as we did every Saturday morning. It was an unusually warm late September day. The dog pound was by the town reservoir, right next to the dam, a squat cinderblock building with a fenced in incinerator behind it. When I arrived, Chris's bike was there already, leaning against the chain-link fence enclosing the incinerator. I pulled my bicycle up alongside it. The K-9 Patrol Van wasn't parked there. Canine Control Sergeant Steiner was out on patrol. We had the pound all to ourselves, how we liked it.

A faint smell of dog shit clung to the humid air. I went in the back door, which wasn't locked. It opened to a clamorous smelly tunnel of caged dogs. Through their yappings and mewlings I made my way to Sergeant Steiner's office up front. There was Chris, sitting in the Sergeant's chair behind his formica and metal desk on which the Sergeant's citizen band radio spluttered. On the wall behind it a map of the town bristled with pushpins of different bright colors. White pushpins stood for animals (Sergeant Steiner never called them "dogs") that had been reported for excessive barking. Yellow pushpins were for those that had been reported for other unwanted behaviors (crapping on neighbor's lawns, digging up flower beds, excessive growling and so on). Blue pushpins were for animals cited for having bitten people. Red pushpins were for animals guilty of two or more prior assaults. Black pushpins stood for known or suspected rabies cases.

We started out with the hosing. First we had to transfer the dogs to their outer cages. Each cage had an indoor and outdoor area, separated by a guillotine-style door controlled by a rope and pulley system. With the dogs in their outdoor cages we hosed the indoor areas, and vice-versa. I enjoyed running the hose. I liked watching the water eddy and swirl as it pried up bits of dog shit and other matter and sent them scuttling down into the slop hole, which we would eventually have to open up and clean, and that, opened, exuded a remarkable stench of fermented dog food and doo.

After cleaning the cages and feeding all of the dogs, we'd mop up the Isolation Room, otherwise known as the ICO, the room where unwanted "animals" were put to sleep by the town veterinarian, Mr. Conklin, who dropped by usually on Thursday afternoons. Afterwards he would cram the bodies into burlap bags and carry them out back to the incinerator, which turned them into dog ashes and dust.

With the dogs all fed and their cages hosed we put our favorites on leashes and, with us holding three or four leashes apiece, walked them across the top of the dam toward the reservoir pumping house. Freed from their stuffy cages, the dogs displayed a contagious exuberance. By a vortex of swirling paws and baying snouts they'd all but drag us across the dam. Some days the red door to the pump house would be open, in which case we'd find Mr. Sanchez, the pump house attendant, there, wearing his red bandana tied around his sunburned neck. He kept a dartboard on the inside of the red door. Mr. Sanchez would let us play some darts and show us his latest nudie calendar.

But that day the pump house door was closed. We turned around and headed back to the pound.

By then it was about two in the afternoon. There were hardly any clouds in the sky, and the day had gotten very hot. We sealed the dogs back inside their cages, locked the pound up, and climbed the grassy mound back up to the top of the dam, where we took off our clothes. Chris and I were good swimmers, though of the two of us I was better. Chris favored the sidestroke, while I preferred the Aussie crawl. Since we'd started volunteering at the pound Chris and I had been swimming in the reservoir. We weren't supposed to swim in there, we knew that. In case we didn't, there were signs posted all over the place saying so. But we saw it as our reward for volunteering at the pound.

There is something about swimming in a reservoir that makes it superior to other forms of swimming. The water is clean and clear and beautiful, unsullied by power boats and people. We could have drunk the water, probably, if we'd wanted to. There were no houses around, just water and dam and trees — lots of trees. We heard the breeze sighing through the trees as we untied our sneakers. That swimming in a reservoir was illegal made it all the more enticing. There is increased pleasure in things forbidden, in the illicit. It adds an erotic component. I can't speak for him, but my guess is Chris felt the same way.

We took off our clothes and got into the water, plunging headfirst in unison off of the top of the dam. We swam out about twenty yards, then across to the other shore, where we caught our breaths. Then we swam back the way we had come.

We were catching our breaths when we saw the boat. I was the first to see it, though what I saw was a blinding glimmer of light as something metallic entered and caught the sun. It took a few moments more to register it as a rowboat, and still more time to see the two people in it. We watched as it swung out from behind a stand of pine trees and into the open area in front of the dam where we'd been swimming.

The boat drifted, putting the sun behind it and its two passengers in silhouette — boys, judging by their sizes, though with the sun behind them we couldn't see their faces. Against the dazzling play of sunlight on water I construed the curves of two fishing poles, their metal eyelets flashing. As the boat drifted closer we realized that the two people in the boat weren't boys at all. Chris and I both recognized their similarly convex faces, their protruding brows, the crooked noses, the buckteeth and stiff dirty crew cuts performed, by the looks of it, with blunt kindergarten scissors.

"Veachs," one of us said.

Everyone in Bethel knew the Veachs. It was hard not to, since they were always visible walking around town with their weird half-loping, half-hopping walks, dressed always in undershirts with no sleeves in summer, or, in winter, in bulky coats with filthy fake fur collars. How many Veachs there were, exactly, no one could say, since they were all men and they all looked about the same. During winter they stood by the roadside selling slapdash Christmas wreathes; in the summer they sold apples stolen from the local orchard. Or they went door to door cleaning gutters, pulling weeds, shoveling snow, picking up sticks. When you saw a Veach coming up your driveway, your first instinct was to pretend not to be home, or to give them a few bucks and be rid of them as quickly and quietly as possible. Veachs were dumb. They stank. They were bad luck and not to be trusted.

Chris may have waved at them. I don't remember. He was less predisposed against the Veachs than I. We watched them both fish for a while, wondering what sort of fish were in the reservoir, if they were worth catching, and if the Veachs would try to sell them as they tried to sell most things that they got their hands on. Then we jumped back in and splashed around and swam some more.

I'm not sure how long we'd been swimming and horsing around when one of us heard something, a loud splash. We turned to see that one of the two Veachs had jumped off the boat into the water.

"Idiots," I said. "They'll get us in trouble."

The other Veach sat in the rowboat, laughing his odd, throaty laugh without his shirt on. He was very skinny. You could see his ribs through his dirt-colored skin. As his brother thrashed away at the water with a hodge-podge of strokes, his laughter echoed across the reservoir. From the shallows where we stood Chris and I watched.

Suddenly the Veach in the boat yelled:

"Help! Help!"

We stood there watching with curious smiles.

"Help! Help!" the Veach in the boat yelled again. "My brother — he's drowning!"

Chris and I both looked at each other. Was this some sort of joke? Was he joking? We both looked for the other Veach, who'd suddenly disappeared. Meanwhile the Veach in the rowboat continued to gesture and yell. "Help, oh God, please help!"

Still we couldn't be sure it wasn't some sort of joke, that the other Veach was not hidden safely behind the rowboat, suppressing his titters as his brother hammed it up, wailing and pointing and panicking. For a few more seconds we stood there, watching. Then I said, "Damn it," and took off swimming toward the rowboat.

In movies and TV shows when people drown and someone leaps into the water to rescue them (usually a muscle-bound lifeguard in fluorescent orange swim trunks) the lifeguard never runs out of breath. That was not my experience. In the twenty or so strokes it took me to get to where I had last seen the Veach brother swimming I used up every last ounce of air in my lungs. I had to stop and tread water and catch my breath. Meanwhile the Veach in the boat kept wailing and pointing and crying. By then I knew this was no joke. There was no other Veach holding in his titters behind that rowboat, beside himself with mischievous mirth as I tried in vain to rescue him. Chris, meanwhile, less good a swimmer than me, made his way toward us, his trademark sidestroke taking him forever, so it seemed. He was less than halfway there when I took a deep breath and dove under.

Though the water in that reservoir was exceedingly clear, still, I couldn't see very much, since there was very little to see. Only water and more water: dark green here, lighter there, darker the further down I went. I remembered when I first learned to swim, taking lessons on Sunday mornings at Meckhauer Park, how on the last day of lessons they made you dive off one of the park's twin floats and swim to the bottom, about fifteen feet. Those who came up with a fistful of dripping mud passed the swimming test and earned their certificate; those who didn't could try again, or give up. I tried two, three, four times. After four or five times I gave up. I couldn't do it. I never got my certificate. Though good on the surface, I couldn't handle the depths.

Something like that has been pretty much true of me ever since.

As I dove down, some part of me was back there, back at Meckauer Park diving for that elusive fistful of mud, aware that watching me from one of two identical floats were the swimming instructor and all my fellow swimmers, aware that I would emerge either to cheers or lamentations, victorious or an abject failure. Now, of course, there was far more at stake than a certificate or a fistful of mud.

The deeper I dove, the darker the water grew, until all I saw was blackness punctuated by bubbles. Were the bubbles my own or those of a drowning Veach? I couldn't tell. I couldn't tell if the bubbles rose up from somewhere under me, or were they my own carbon dioxide escaping my mouth and nostrils? At that depth of water everything is confusing. I couldn't tell which way was up or down. My ears filled with pressure, my lungs cringed. I started to panic. With a series of stiff kicks I thrust myself upwards through layers of increasingly pale green water till I broke the surface, gasping.

"Did you see anything?" Chris asked.

I spluttered, shook my head. I turned and looked at the other Veach, the one still in the rowboat. By then he'd stopped pointing and shouting. He sat there making quiet little gasping sounds—as if he, not I, had just risen from the black depths of the reservoir. As if he, too, were drowning.

I took another stiff breath and went under again. And again. By the fourth dive I knew it was futile, just as I had known, years before, that I'd never come up with that fistful of mud. Each successive dive left me with less lung capacity. By the fourth dive I couldn't stay down for more than a few seconds. It was over. I would not get my certificate.

Sergeant Steiner knew about our swimming. He'd caught us a few times and had warned us, as nicely as possible, to stay out of the reservoir. As we dressed, I said to Chris, "Let's say it was just me swimming, okay? There's no point in both of us getting in trouble."

Back in the Sergeant's office, with me watching and the Veach brother waiting for us outside, Chris tried to reach Sergeant Steiner on the CB radio. When that didn't work, he phoned the Sergeant at home. No answer. Reluctantly, he called the police. The Sergeant's desk phone had a speaker. Chris switched it on so we both could hear.

"Officer Steiner's out on patrol," said the officer who answered.

"Please have him call us immediately, okay?" Chris said.

"What's the problem?"

"Never mind. Just please have him call."

A few moments later the CB radio spluttered. Chris told Sergeant Steiner what had happened, more or less.

"You boys wait there," Sergeant Steiner said.

It took ten minutes for the police and fire department to arrive, along with Sergeant Steiner in the K-9 Control Van. From the dam Chris and I watched as two men put on wet suits and scuba gear and went into the water. We had already told Sergeant Steiner our version of what had happened. Afterwards we watched anxiously as he spoke to the surviving Veach, hoping our stories would not clash. When Sergeant

Steiner returned, he told Chris, "You can go home now, son." Then, to me with a sad disappointed look: "Not you. You wait here."

As he turned and started walking toward the pound, I followed the Sergeant for a few steps, asking him, as casually as I could with a forced little laugh, what he thought would happen to me.

"I've no idea," Sergeant Steiner answered grimly.

It took over an hour for the two divers to find the body. What they dragged out of the reservoir wasn't a Veach anymore. It was something not human, something wet and gray and unnatural out of its liquid environment. As I watched them put the body on a stretcher, I remembered something that happened to me when I was twelve or thirteen. I had been having these spontaneous, random, devilish thoughts. I'd see an old man or woman walking down the sidewalk with a cane, or someone pushed in a wheelchair, and say to myself, "What if I ran up to that old man or woman and kicked the cane out from under them? What if I knocked over that wheelchair, or grabbed it and sent it rolling down a hill?"

It bothered me that I had these thoughts. It bothered me so much that, one day, I decided to ask Chris' mother, Mrs. Rowland, about it. Mrs. Rowland was a small woman with big red hair. She suffered from a crippling bone ailment and, as it happens, spent most of her time in a wheelchair. A church-going Yankee puritan, she had been cooking something in a big iron stew pot in her kitchen, a soup of some kind, when I explained to her about my devilish fantasies. "Are thoughts like that normal, Mrs. Rowland?" I asked her. While stirring the soup from her wheelchair, not looking at me, without any change of expression on her face, she shook her head and said, simply, "No." I waited for her to elaborate, but she didn't.

That was the end of our discussion.

I thought of it as I watched the divers put the drowned Veach body in the stretcher and carry it up the embankment to the waiting ambulance.

❖

When they brought me to the police station it was about five thirty. I sat in a waiting area, with cops milling around, walking past me with mugs of coffee, oblivious of me as they went about their business. Sergeant Steiner had phoned my parents. My father was out of town; my mother didn't drive after dark and dusk had already fallen. I imagined how that conversation must have gone. At last I was escorted to the Medical Examiner's — Dr. Numbnuts' — office. As soon as I saw him, I wondered if Dr. Numbnuts would jab my nuts with his knuckles, if that would be my punishment. Instead of his knuckles, Dr. Numbnuts jabbed me with my own conscience.

"*If not for you,*" he said, "*that boy might still be alive. You realize that, don't you, son?*"

It took a while, but at last I started crying. I felt my throat go achy and dry and numb as tears tugged at the corners of my eyes. This, I knew, was what Dr. Numbnuts really wanted: not a confession of guilt or even a verbal response to his questions, but an emotional one. He was jabbing my emotional testicles to see if they functioned properly.

But what set off the waterworks wasn't Dr. Numbnut's inquiry, it was my memory of that afternoon in Mrs. Rowland's kitchen. Leaving the Rowland's house that afternoon, for the first time in my life I had the sense that I might not be what I had always assumed myself to be: a normal, good, decent person. Hell, I thought, I might just be a monster. If that was true, I speculated, if I'm a monster, then the world must be full of monsters, of people at least as bad or worse than me. It must be a truly monstrous place.

Since then I'd kept this bit of news to myself, tucked somewhere deep, deep in the dark, hidden away from everyone, including me.

There, in Dr. Numbnuts' office, with night seeping in through the venetian blinds and Sergeant Steiner standing a few feet behind me, I let the memory of that time with Mrs. Rowland wash over me.

"All right," Dr. Numbnuts said, seeing my tears. "Let him go."

In the K-9 patrol van Sergeant Steiner drove me home. My bicycle was still at the dog pound. Lights burned warmly in houses that we passed. Sergeant Steiner lit his corncob pipe and smoked as he drove. We sat in smoke-filled silence, me staring through the van's windshield. In place of the silhouettes of lit houses as the van rumbled on I saw black bubbles coming at me through the darkness.

And though I didn't realize it then, Dr. Numbnuts was right. I would have to live with "it" for the rest of my life. What exactly "it" was, I could not have said then, and still don't know to this day, but whatever it is, I've been living with it, of that much I'm sure.

I'm living with it here, now, forty-one years later, in the quiet room where I've written these words.

❖ *The Muffin Man*

> *Do you know the muffin man,*
> *The muffin man, the muffin man,*
> *Do you know the muffin man,*
> *He lives on Drury Lane?*

YES, I KNOW—OR I KNEW—the Muffin Man, though I'm not sure I knew his street address, or, if I did know it, that I had any idea where Drury Lane was.[1] I learned of him from Pam Albert. She lived in a silver house down the street with a pond in the front yard that we called Pollywog Pond, since it was full of tadpoles.

From when we were two until we were seven, the three Albert sisters—Pam, Peggy, and Sally—babysat for my twin brother George

---

1. Drury Lane is a street in Covent Garden, London. And at least one muffin man really did live there, according to this passage from the collected writings of English dramatist and author Douglas Jerrold:

> Follow a Cockney to Paris. See! he is in the garden of the Tuileries! What can he be doing near the statue of Diana? Ha! the sentry calls to him, and the Cockney, with thunder in his brow, looks savagely at the foreigner. Our indignant countryman is, however, ordered away, and, swelling with national greatness, he moves on. What could he be doing at this statue? Les us see. Oh, here it is! The Cockney—poor fellow, it is an amiable weakness, he cannot help it—the Cockney has written in pencil his address in full on the right leg of Diana: here it is, "John Wiggins, *Muffin*-maker, Wild Street, Drury Lane, was here on the *20th of July, 1839.*"

Incidentally, several of Jerrold's plays were produced in what is now the Theatre Royal on Drury Lane.

and me. From them we learned about pollywogs and tadpoles, daddy long legs and inchworms, cattails and milkweed, the Milky Way and the Big Dipper. The Alberts all but adopted us. When we got lost in the woods behind our house, Mr. Albert, who cleaned and repaired furnaces for a living, lead the search party.

Though I loved all three Albert sisters, Pam was my favorite. She taught me the Muffin Man song, the first song I ever learned. Thanks to that song for me the Muffin Man rose to a position of mythic stature equal to that of Santa Claus and the Tooth Fairy, while the simple lyric planted firmly and forever in my child's mind the image of a plump man in a white smock with matching puffy cap peddling his cart piled with steaming golden muffins, plump as their maker, down the street at dawn, ringing a bell with which he roused his customers from the depths of their sleep. As with most fairytale characters, there was something equal parts reassuring and foreboding about The Muffin Man, something to be desired mixed with something to be feared.[2]

When I first heard the song I'd never seen, let alone eaten, a muffin. My Italian parents were still coming to grips with sliced Wonder Bread, and so the odds of a muffin materializing in the Selgin household were nil. Yet I could taste them in my mind, and even imagined their smell wafting through my bedroom window as the Muffin Man pushed his cart from house to house. Other children woke up craving waffles and Maypo; I woke up craving muffin.

---

2. According to a *NY Times* article of November 5, 1934, to at least one woman living in Westminister, London, the Muffin Man was a mixed blessing. She pressed charges against him for "using a noisy instrument"— his handbell. "Fortunately," the story goes on to say, "the magistrate was a man of feeling for good customs. He said to the constable: 'You are not going to try and stop the muffin bell, are you? It is one of the most familiar sounds I have heard in London for forty-five years. Was the defendant ringing excessively?' Constable: 'He was ringing it fairly often.' Magistrate: 'I thought this was one of the cries of London.'" In the end the muffin man was told not to ring his bell "when there is a policeman about" and dismissed with a caution.

❖

Back then, in the early 1960's, muffins were much less common than they are today. Until late in the 19th century, what we today call a muffin didn't exist at all. The first recipe for a muffin occurring in print dates back only to 1879. It can be found in a book titled *Housekeeping in Old Virginia*, a recipe calling for a batter "the consistency of pound cake [baked] in snow-ball cups as soon as possible."[3] As for the word "muffin," it dates back only as far as 1703, its origins uncertain, deriving most probably from the low German *moofin, muffen,* or *muffe,* meaning "small cake," though etymologists also suspect a connection to the Old French "moufflet," meaning "soft."

Though for a time nothing distinguished the American muffin from its English equivalent, as the two nations parted ways so did their recipes, with the English muffin remaining a flat, round, spongy, air-filled concoction prepared with yeast-leavened dough and cooked on a griddle, while its American cousin evolved into a sort of "quick bread" prepared from a sweet batter and baked in individual molds.

If anyone deserves credit for the American muffin, it should probably go to Professor Eben Horsford and George Wilson, who invented baking powder in 1854. Before then housewives had to rely on much slower potash. Thanks to baking soda, muffins could be made quickly and easily, and thus became an ideal breakfast food. Unfortunately, as quickly as they were made they grew stale, and hence were rarely seen outside of private kitchens until preservatives appeared in the 1950's. These early muffins were made from common grains — corn, oat, wheat bran — with nuts, raisins, and apple slices sometimes added to the batter. By the turn of the century, muffins

---

3. That's if you don't count the recipes agricultural writer Solon Robinson's submitted to the American Agriculturalist in May of 1849, one of which was for something called "Louisiana Muffin *Bread*."

had grown so popular in her *1898 Boston Cooking School Cook Book* Fannie Farmer provided no fewer than 15 recipes for them.[4] By then baking pans with multiple lozenge-shaped molds were often used, pans rendered obsolete in the 1950's when paper muffin cups were invented. The paper cups in turn gave way to Teflon and other types of non-stick pans, some in elaborate shapes. Around the same time, packaged muffin mixes became popular,[5] making the easy muffin even easier.

Meanwhile a handful of entrepreneurs sought for muffins the franchise food eminence enjoyed by doughnuts and French fries. It was not to be.[6] Though muffins never attained the dubious distinction of World's Most Popular Fast Food, by the time Pam Albert taught me the Muffin Man song every diner in America featured an array of bran, corn, and blueberry muffins under a glass pastry dome. In diners muffins were as obligatory as ketchup bottles.

---

4. A recipe from the *New York Times,* September 13, 1908: "The following recipe makes a rich muffin for either breakfast or luncheon. As the fashion for eating cold bread and toast does not prevail as much as it did all hot breads are restored to favor. ¶ To make these muffins, use one cup of cornmeal, one of wheat flower, half a cup of white sugar, two tablespoonfuls of butter, two eggs, one cup of milk, two small teaspoonfuls of baking powder, one saltspoonful of salt. ¶ Rub butter and sugar together, add the beaten eggs, the milk, and at last the corn meal and flour, with which have been sifted the salt and baking powder. ¶ This quantity will make about a dozen muffins. The method can be changed by using a cup of cream in place of the milk, and omitting the butter and using only one egg."
5. Including the still popular Jiffy Baking Mix, invented in 1930 by Mabel White Holmes.
6. At least not until 1980, when Dunkin' Donuts became the first chain to offer muffins baked on the premises. In the same year, Winchell's Donut Houses tried out a muffin recipe in several of its Los Angeles stores, while at its home base in Utah Mrs. Fields Cookies did likewise.

THE KUHREIHEN MELODY ❖ 51

My first muffin is more memorable to me than my first non-innocent kiss (in fact I've forgotten my first kiss). It was at Caldor's department store, the 1960's answer to K-mart. At the front of the store was a long counter where you could get sandwiches, ice cream sundaes, and other snacks. We were on our way out, my mother and my brother and I, when I saw it there, glowing under a glass dome: a single lonesome corn muffin. It was late afternoon. The bright counter was deserted, the man behind it rinsing a stainless milkshake tumbler while wearing his conical paper cap. I tugged at the sleeve of my mother's blouse. She shook her head, claiming it would spoil my appetite for dinner. Please, I begged. At last my mother relented. Out of the bargain my brother finagled a hot dog.

The counterman offered to warm the muffin for me, but I couldn't wait. Before I could stop him, he cut it in half—not from the top down, but sideways, creating two hockey-puck like wafers. He served it to me on a small round plate edged with green pinstripes. Even allowing for having been split in two, in shape it was unlike today's muffins. For starters it far more modest in size, three inches across at most and maybe two inches high, and lacking the bulbous, mushroom-like caps of current muffins. Instead, this muffin was nearly flat on top, with the subtlest rise at its center, and an even more subtle gradation forming a flange at its circumference. From top to bottom it was a perfectly even, golden ochre, and spongy in texture.[7] Not wanting to undermine its flavor with Coca-Cola or chocolate milk, I ate it with a glass of water,

---

7. "What is a good muffin? The best specimen is so light that you are surprised when you pick it up that anything of its size could weigh so little. The top is slightly rounded, with a rather rough surface having cauliflower-like bumps and a somewhat shiny appearance. The volume is good, the grain or "holes" of medium size and the texture tender. By way of contrast, a poor muffin has a peaked or pointed, rather than rounded, top, with a smooth and dull surface instead of one rough and shiny."
—from "Muffins, the Good and the Bad," *NY Times*, April 9, 1945.

ignoring the knife and fork the counterman had given me, choosing instead to tear it into bite-sized bits with my naked fingers. Its grease coated my fingertips, so I was forced, *forced* to lick them following every bite. I ate with Zen slowness, wanting to savor every morsel, to prolong the experience, picking up crumbs and licking them one by one like flecks of gold off glossy, greasy fingers. At last my mother could no longer contain her impatience. She yanked me off the stool and dragged me—still licking my fingers—through the store's automatic doors and into the parking lot, where her boat-like black Mercury waited. All this time the Muffin Man's song ran through my head.

Years later, when I was a struggling artist in New York City, muffins became my all-purpose food. I ate them for breakfast, lunch, and sometimes even for dinner. Corn muffins were my favorite. They were the perfect "starving artist" food: tasty, inexpensive, and filling—not terribly healthy, but not that unhealthy, either.[8] And muffins offered something more than nutrition: they were a source of comfort, too. Their very shape suggests maternal comfort: round and soft, like a mother's breast. Add warmth and sweetness and you get the full package.[9] Other foods might have done more for me by way of vitamins and other nutrients, but few offered more solace. On my worst days, days when it became clear to me that my talents were insufficient to my ambitions, days permeated with self-doubt and gloom, I'd step

---

8. The healthful qualities of true muffins should not be exaggerated, nor should they be overlooked. A scientific study done in 1988 found bran muffins to be a healthier choice than other pastries and most breakfast cereals. However the same study also found them higher in calories—but mainly due to their enormous sizes. But back in 1937—long before calorie counting became a national pastime—the health benefits of muffins were already recognized. "A Muffin A Day Keeps Cathartics Away," read the headline in the Herald-Journal: true enough, provided the muffin is a *bran* muffin.

9. "Muffin" is a recent pejorative slang term indicating the fleshy overflow or "love handle" caused by a plump woman's wearing tight pants. It is also slang for the female genitalia.

into a coffee shop, sit at the counter, and order a corn muffin toasted lightly with butter and coffee. No sooner would it be placed before me than the gloom would dissipate, replaced by something warm and reassuring, the sense that somehow things would be all right after all. How doomed can a world be with corn muffins in it?

Eventually my source of comfort turned against me. Having spent the better part of a decade eating practically nothing but corn muffins, I developed an allergy to them that left me bloated and feverish and gave rise to epic headaches. I spent the next decade avoiding all foods with corn or corn syrup in them, meaning just about everything from pickles to powdered coffee creamer.

Just as I was foregoing my beloved muffins, the rest of the country developed a mania for them.[10] Suddenly, like the mushrooms they so resemble in shape, muffins sprang up everywhere: and not just in diners, but in cafes, health food stores, even in posh restaurants. And just as suddenly they went from being a humble, working-class food to being trendy, gaudy and huge, pumped up to grapefruit size on muffin steroids.[11] And where once muffins were simple creations of whole grain augmented with a sprinkling of raisins or nuts, suddenly they were made of all things: from zucchinis to sour cream, from peanut butter

---

10. To where, by the late 1980's, even politicians were feeling the pressure. In August of 1987 Governor Cuomo signed into law a bill declaring the apple muffin New York's official muffin. Two years later, Merrill and Kenosha fourth graders lobbied for a similar bill to claim the cranberry muffin for Wisconsin.

11. In the same era that brought SUVs to prominence muffins grew so large the tops alone sufficed for a full meal. Indeed, there were even attempts to design baking trays that would produce "all top" muffins. The notion worked its way into an episode of the TV sitcom *Seinfeld* ("The Muffin Tops"), in which the character Elaine Benes goes partners in a bakery named "Top of the Muffin to You" that sells only the tops of muffins. Since every action produces an equal and opposite reaction, it was only a matter of time before mini-muffins became fashionable.

to avocados.[12] Granola muffins, cappuccino muffins, strudel muffins, pumpkin, blueberry, applesauce, yogurt, oatmeal, and chocolate chip muffins—muffins whose entire purpose in life seemed to be nothing more or less than denying their muffinhood.

And just what, I ask you, distinguishes a so-called chocolate muffin from what, back in my day, we used to call a *cupcake?* Take away the whole grains, add more sugar and a drizzle of frosting, and what have you got if not a cake by some other name? A good muffin may be many things, but a cupcake isn't one of them. The distinction isn't semantic. Muffins are—or were—less sweet than cake; some have even been savory. They were meant to exist in the continuum between cake and bread. Still, I'd bear no grudge against postmodern muffins if within their teeming ranks one could still find a classic corn or bran muffin. In fact those are the two types of muffins one is least likely to find these days. Except in diners (themselves a vanishing species), one isn't likely to find corn muffins at all. That the purveyors of so-called "gourmet" muffins show such ignorance of—contempt for?—the archetypes should annoy more people. It's one thing to arrive at variations on a classic theme; it's another to do away with the tried-and-true original in the process. To those who prefer chocolate muffins I say by all means let them eat cupcakes. Only let me have my corn muffin, too.

Like most cries in the dark this one will go unanswered. Times change, and so must muffins, I suppose. Some day soon my beloved corn muffins will have gone the way of typewriters, locomotives, and other quaint relics of the past, to be resurrected every now and then as museum pieces or curiosities for the sake of a handful of nostalgic geezers. The future belongs to the young. And the future of muffins

---

12. In Fort Lauderdale In the late 1970's Danny Cangemi opened the first of his muffin shops, each of which offered 28 flavors of muffins. "I figured if Howard Johnson could do it with 28 flavors of ice cream and an orange roof, I could do it with 28 flavors of muffins," he told the *Lakeland Ledger*.

belongs, apparently, to cake eaters.

Meanwhile I still eat corn muffins whenever I can find them. I even sometimes bake my own. And whenever I'm troubled by this changing world, I take solace in them and in the lyrics of a song my babysitter once taught me.

Do I know the Muffin Man? Indeed I do.

❖ Eagle Electric

ON THE QUEENS SIDE OF THE 59ᵀᴴ STREET BRIDGE, above a windowless industrial building, a barge-sized neon sign winked on and off, on and off, all night long, floating the motto of the Eagle Electric Manufacturing Company, reminding all within eyeshot that

PERFECTION IS NOT A ACCIDENT

Above these words loomed an imposing tin eagle, its silhouetted wings spread across the dusky Manhattan skyline. From my window its talons seemed to claw at the tops of skyscrapers.

This is where I lived with Dwaine[1] for some months starting in the late winter of 1977. Jimmy Carter was President. Abe Beame was Mayor. Pay phones cost a dime. Postage stamps needed to be licked. Subway tokens were quarter-sized brass coins with a Y-shaped hole in the center and cost fifty cents. New York City was broke, lawless, bohemian, dissolute, and dangerous.

Our apartment building was a block away from the Pepsi-Cola bottling plant on a side street named Extra Alley, as if there had been just the right number of alleys in the vicinity and it had been thrown in for good measure. For its short, wavering length the alley paralleled the No. 7 Flushing Line elevated, so close that, from the same window of mine that looked out over the Eagle Electric Company sign, I could read the lips of commuters as they careened by amid showers of sparks and squeals of tortured iron.

---

1. Names have been changed

Everyone has a crazy-friend-they-met-in-college story, I suppose, though mine may be different than most. I lived with and watched my friend go more and more crazy, up to the day I walked him in the rain to the Veteran's Administration Medical Center on 23rd Street off 1st Avenue, where he admitted himself into the psychiatric ward there. Dwaine would spend the next five years in and out of "loony bins," some on hospital grounds as picture-perfect as Ivy League campuses, others less picturesque.

But when we first met I didn't think Dwaine was crazy at all, just artistic and original and eccentric and filled with the manic energy that went with being an artistic genius.

We met as students at the Pratt Institute in Brooklyn, where I'd been an illustration and painting major, until Dwaine (a name that in Irish means "the dark, mysterious one") asked me to act in a short film he was making about a heroin dealer. I was sharing a table with him in the Pratt snack bar when he framed me with his thumbs.

"That's a good face you've got," he said.

"I do?"

"A touch of DeNiro; a hint of Pacino. Ever done any acting?"

"A little," I lied.

"Take off your jacket. Roll up your sleeve."

"What for?"

"I want to see your arm."

"What do you need to see my arm for?"

"Would you mind just rolling up your damn sleeve, please?"

I took off my jacket; I rolled up my sleeve. He looked at my arm. "What are you doing first thing tomorrow?"

I shrugged. "Nothing much."

"Congratulations, you got the part."

He scribbled something on a corner of his notebook page, tore it off and handed it to me. "Be there at six thirty a.m., sharp."

Our first film—the one about the junkie—was titled "It's So Good Don't Even Try it Once." Like all of Dwaine's movies, it featured a dream sequence. In it the hero, me, is pursued through the twilit streets of Bedford Stuyvesant by a three-hundred pound, gas-mask wearing, machete-wielding Mr. Softee ice cream vendor.

After that we made about a dozen more films, each more twisted and violent than the last, with the character I played always being shot or stabbed or lobotomized or jumping off of buildings or bridges. We went through buckets of fake blood (which looked much redder than the real stuff) and dozens of "squibs"—button-sized, fake-blood-filled devices sewn into clothing and detonated off-camera to produce gorily realistic bullet holes.

Why all of Dwaine's movies were so violent I could only guess, though I was pretty sure it had something to do with his having been a soldier in Vietnam. I knew he'd been a combat medic there. I tried to find out more, but every time I asked him about the war he'd either shrug or ignore me completely or blow a smoke ring past my face and say something cryptic like:

"Which war, babe? There've been *so* many."

Our apartment had three rooms, including the kitchen, in the center of which a shoe-shaped bathtub floated on a pond of cracked, sewage-colored linoleum. There was no bathroom, just a cramped closet with a toilet. In summer the window sashes swelled and in winter they shriveled, dropping chunks of pale putty and plaster like the droppings of constipated birds. What little heat the landlady provided radiated from a silver painted pipe that climbed up one corner of the kitchen, and that, though hot enough at times to cause third-degree burns, failed to heat the place properly.

There were more than a few things I had to get used to in my new home. For a start it was the noisiest place I'd ever lived. There were those elevated trains rumbling tunnels through my sleep, and garbage trucks bleeping and growling, and the caterwauls of coital cats, and stray dogs barking endless streams of monomaniacal Morse code, and radios blaring, and car alarms wailing, and the hissings of that silver pipe, so loud at times it sounded like a rocket ship trying to blast off. Grumbling under all of those other sounds was the steady drumroll of Dwaine's Promethean snores.

Then there were the nightmares, Dwaine's nightmares, the ones that typically ended in blood-curdling screams, screams that woke me up thinking that he'd been stabbed to death in his sleep. I'd rush into his room to find him sitting wide-eyed up in his bed, his face glowing with each flash of the Eagle Electric sign.

"It's okay, it's okay," I'd say, holding him, stroking him. "You had a bad nightmare, that's all. It's okay; it's okay . . ." When his breathing returned to normal, I'd settle him back down into his bed, wondering what sort of nightmares made him scream like that, and if the flashing neon bloodied his dreams.

Don't misunderstand: living with Dwaine wasn't all darkness and nightmares. Having had a relatively quiet childhood, brought up by Italian immigrants in a dreary Connecticut former hat factory town, having him as a friend was an adventure comparable to living in New York itself, a city I came to equate with Dwaine, as though he and it were one, and in ways they were. Back in our early filmmaking days, he'd take me with him on what he called "location scouting" tours of the city. From Battery Park to the city's northernmost tip—where, as Dwain pointed out, the city remained a natural forest as the Reckgawawanc Indians had known it—we explored the world's most famous island. He showed me the rusty swing bridge by which New York Central line trains crossed from the Bronx to Manhattan over the

Spuyten Duyvil Creek. In Brooklyn, in the Arabic shops along Atlantic Avenue, we sampled sticky halvah and fat figs encrusted with sugar. From there we rode the A-line to its terminus, to watch snowy egrets soar over the mudflats of Jamaica Bay. For Dwaine the city where he'd been born was like his back yard, while for me it remained as dauntingly exotic as the control room of a nuclear submarine. As though it were a confection he had spent his life concocting he shared the city with me. He taught me to savor its seasonal garlands of scent. From dry cleaner chemicals to shoe polish, from Xerox toner to doughnuts, from roasted chestnuts to the smells of money, anticipation, and fear wafting off subway riders' bodies, Dwaine had a nose for every city odor. Walking down lower Broadway, eyes closed, nostrils flared, he could name just about every shop and business on every block.

Dwaine believed it was every artist's duty to sharpen his senses and to keep them sharp. At the Russian baths on 10th Street, we doused each other with buckets of ice water and flailed each other's backs with dried oak branches. While doing so, I noticed for the first time the two quarter-sized fatty cysts on Dwaine's back. His "Lucky Lumps," he called them. We studied the patterns made by torn bill postings on the sides of garbage dumpsters and construction fences, the striped shadows hurled against a brick wall by a fire escape railing, the film-noir moodiness of streetlamp's reflection in a rain puddle.

The cameras in our heads never stopped rolling.

But Dwaine's lessons weren't strictly visual, olfactory, or geographical. Above all he wanted me, his tutee, to appreciate the fact that artists hold a unique place in society, a place of privilege exempt from the conventions and restrictions imposed on other mere mortals. To prove this point, while we were crossing Queens Boulevard against a murderous onslaught of traffic, he admonished me for slowing my pace to let a Metropolitan transit bus roar by.

"Babe," he said, "if you're going to walk with me, please do me a favor and do it like you own the fucking street, okay?"

I protested. "Did you see the look on that bus driver's face? The guy had a hard-on! He would have run me over!"

"In that case, you'd have died with dignity, at least." He smiled. The point, babe, is to never to let the motherfuckers see you sweat."

Still, and though I appreciated the things Dwaine had to teach me, living with him did pose certain challenges. Like those nightmares, for instance, and his mystery walks, excursions he undertook alone almost every night after dinner, usually not returning until after midnight, if at all. When I'd ask him where he was going, he would respond either with steely silence or vaguely, saying he had personal matters to attend to. And no: I could not come with him.

Was it pure curiosity or too many cold nights spent alone that made Dwaine's disappearances all but unbearable to me? Where did he go? To do what? I had to know. I knew so little about him. That he had grown up in New York and was a Yankee fan and had been to Vietnam, that before art school he spent time in the Peace Corps. I knew he smoked marijuana sometimes; I'd come home from my job in Manhattan to an apartment reeking of pot. He drank, too. I'd find the Smirnoff pints hidden behind a glacier of freezer frost, or empty on the floor by his serape-covered futon next to his latest journal, one of dozens of hardbound black notebooks he kept, and that, occasionally, when he wasn't around, I'd read parts of, hoping to learn something more from those pages jammed with handwriting as swift and jagged as an endless series of lightning bolts, and no more legible. He kept the notebooks stacked on an aluminum trunk by his bed, with others like it tucked away inside. And though in time I'd read all of them, from their pages I learned very little, the writing was so frenzied and cryptic.

Out of frustration as much as anything, one night when he'd gone out on one of his mystery walks, I tried to follow him. I waited until he was down in the street, spying on him through my window to see in which direction he turned. Then I hurried down the apartment buildings' ill-lit and loosely treaded stairs, reaching the street just as Dwaine's shadow swung around the corner.

It was winter still. Dwaine walked with both of his hands deep in the pockets of his army surplus pea coat, his cigarette weaving a trail of smoke for me to follow. Through a series of increasingly dismal neighborhoods I shadowed him, past sleeping subway sheds and low buildings squatting beneath a cave-like sky. Once he turned and nearly caught me, and my heart dropped like an anchor into my guts. But then he kept walking, shoulders hunched, heading for the expressway overpass where, among a sea of concrete pillars, I lost him.

As I stood there feeling more lonely and miserable than ever, wondering where my best friend had gone, suddenly he leapt out from behind a pillar, startling me so I fell back-first onto the icy sidewalk. Dwaine wasn't that big. He was my height, about five-foot-nine, a bit on the short side, if anything. Still, as he stood there, in silhouette, he loomed larger than life, his face lit from below as in a horror movie.

"Sorry about that, babe," he said, helping me to my feet and even brushing me off a little. "I meant to scare you, but not that much."

"It's okay," I said.

"Good," he said. "I'm glad it's okay. Now supposing you tell me why you were following me?"

"I wasn't —," I began.

"Don't lie to me, babe. Obviously you were. The question is: why?"

I bit my lip. I was nineteen, but at that moment I felt much younger. "To find out where you were going?" I asked.

Dwaine's smile lit the dark. "Good answer," he said. "I appreciate your honesty. But don't follow me again, okay?"

To let me know there were no hard feelings, he jiggled his false front tooth at me. He'd lost the real one in a hockey game when a puck caught him square in the face. It had been replaced by a single-tooth bridge that was removable and could be worked up and down with the tip of his tongue to chilling or hysterical effect, depending on the given context. Then he turned and kept walking, disappearing through the tall iron gates of Calvary Cemetery.

The bathtub was the center of life in our apartment, the Acropolis of our fourth-floor Athens. It was where we soaked and scrubbed ourselves, and where—using a salvaged door as a tabletop—we broke bread together and had most of our dinner conversations, which revolved, as always, around movies. Dwaine did most of the talking, as garrulous when it came to movies as he was reticent when it came to almost everything else in his life, advancing his feelings and opinions as if they were facts, with me challenging him only when the things he said struck me as completely absurd. One evening, for instance, he insisted that every time you see an orange in *The Godfather* it means someone is about to get rubbed out, that Francis Ford Coppola actually *planned* it that way, that the bright citrus fruits symbolized violent death. When I dared to infer that it was probably just a coincidence, Dwaine gave me a sideways look as if to say *of course it's a coincidence, nitwit, can't you see I'm yanking you're fucking chain, as usual?* On another occasion, he theorized that in *North by Northwest,* when Cary Grant stands waiting at that dusty bus stop in the middle of nowhere—before the crop duster scene—the lack of any scenery (aside from a withered corn field) or background music was meant to express the barren void that lies "at the center of our nation's collective conscience." This I doubted as much as I doubted his "Godfather orange theory," only this time I didn't argue with him, feeling that he was in earnest—though with Dwaine you never could tell.

The 16-millimeter that we'd used at Pratt having been stolen during an afternoon mugging, we no longer had a movie camera, but that didn't stop us from making what Dwaine called "Tibetan Sand Movies," with Dwaine shooting away behind an imaginary camera, and me acting out our carefully scripted scenarios. Though I longed for us to get back to making real movies, for Dwaine, who had had his fill of ten and fifteen minute shorts, that prospect held little appeal. "The next movie you and I make is either going to be feature length, or forget it," he said. "I'm done making dippy-ass movies."

Though we no longer made our own movies, whenever we could we still watched them, old ones, usually, at revival houses — the Thalia, St. Marks, Bleecker Street ...

Watching movies with Dwaine was a mixed blessing. On the one hand, you benefited from his extraordinary knowledge and enthusiasm. On the other hand you had to put up with his elbow-nudgings as well as a steady stream of critical commentary such as is provided on DVDs today. Did I know that, when making *The Train*, Burt Lancaster injured his knee while playing golf between scenes, explaining why he limps through the whole last reel of the film? — things like that. The rest of the movie-going public hardly welcomed Dwaine's erudition, and shushed him extravagantly to no avail.

From those revivals we'd ride the subway home with lines of dialogue etched in our brains, tossing them back and forth to each other like Frisbees. The movie lines that struck us as particularly apt or memorable we would — using a thick black marker — commit to the wall between the refrigerator and the kitchen stove, which we dubbed "the Pertinent Movie Quote Wall." Whoever soaked in the tub dictated while the other person transcribed. We kept a gallon of cheap white paint handy to paint over the quotes when we grew tired of them. Some quotes ("It's lamb on a stick, you should try it!" — *Panic in the Streets*) lasted only a matter of days; while others ("I can't help myself!" — Peter Lorre, *M.)* survived all tests of time.

Dwaine did most of the cooking, bringing home bleeding steaks,

London broils that he would season with pepper and garlic and panfry on our stove. To watch Dwaine cook was an intense experience, like love or war. Fork and peppershaker in hand, he presided over the frying pan like a priest presiding over the liturgy of the Eucharist. There was something coded and regimented about him when involved in any act demanding concentration, stiff as a soldier at attention, until he'd burst out laughing or jiggle his front tooth and destroy the effect.

One night, Dwaine brought home a large bag of fortune cookies he'd found in a dumpster outside a fortune cookie factory, at least a hundred of them. We sat side by side at the tub/table, smashing them like walnuts with our fists, reading the fortunes out loud to each other, adding the phrase "in an insane asylum" after each, giggling like schoolboys. The fortunes that most captured our imagination we taped to the refrigerator door. The others we set on fire using Dwaine's lighter, turning the pale paper slips into tiny writhing angels of colorless ash.

That Christmas I went home. I owed my parents, whom I hadn't seen in over a year, a visit. To be honest I'd been feeling homesick. I asked Dwaine if he wanted to come with me. He demurred.

"No Chaldean rune worship for me," he said. "Besides, babe, I hate Christmas so much I'm sure I'd spoil it for your entire family."

I took the train from Grand Central, a bunch of wind-up toys I'd bought for Christmas presents riding on the baize seat with me, the winter landscape flashing by beyond the green-shaded window like frames in a movie. To the train's rhythmic *kachumps* my mind flashed its own mental movie images: of Dwaine dangling from the light fixture in our kitchen, or floating in a tub of cloudy red water. At the time I'd been given no cause to think Dwaine was suicidal, yet for some reason I couldn't stop worrying about him, maybe because I cared for him as much as I did.

I lasted five days in Connecticut. After two years in New York City, I found my home town unbearable. I felt like a ghost wandering its streets — streets that reeked of the past: a moldy, dusty smell. I didn't even bother to look up any of my old friends. What for, when every cell in my body had changed? Compared to those of New York, the streets of Bethel, Connecticut looked gutted and radioactive, as if a nuclear bomb had fallen there. There was *nothing* worth filming. The few faces that appeared in the streets looked peevish and frightened. The town's only movie theater, having shown porno flicks for three years, had closed its doors. It astonished me that I, Peter Selgin, best friend of Dwaine Fitzgibbon, had sprung from such humble origins.

Two days after Christmas, I was back on the train again, on the lumpy baize seat watching the green tinted world pass by, rewinding my journey back to Grand Central and Queens and Long Island City and Extra Alley, to our apartment, the gruesome images of Dwaine's untimely self-inflicted death accumulating, drawing closer and sharper, till they hung as clear in my mind as movie stills in a theater lobby.

Instead of a dead body or a suicide note, I found a newspaper-wrapped package waiting for me on the tub/table, adorned with a ribbon of exposed 8 mm film. Inside: a framed photo of Marlon Brando as Terry Malloy in *On the Waterfront*. "*To the second best movie actor in the world*," the attached note read. "*Merry Christmas, Bud.*"

I hadn't gotten Dwaine anything. In a panic I raced to the Strand where, among the dizzying stacks of used books there, I found something I thought Dwaine might appreciate: an oversized coffee table book published by Time-Life and stuffed with pictures of movies and stars, titled *Life Goes to the Movies*.

I left it, gift wrapped, on Dwaine's silver truck.

But Dwaine's real Christmas present to me didn't come wrapped in anything. On New Year's Eve, after we'd eaten a shoplifted steak and drunk half a bottle of cheap champagne, as I was getting ready for bed, expecting him to go off alone on one of his mystery walks, Dwaine stood in my doorway.

"What's up?" he said.

"Going to bed," I answered.

"Get dressed. There's something I want to show you."

As we were passing through the kitchen he pointed to a champagne bottle (*Asti Spumante,* actually) on the tub/table.

"Grab the bubbly, babe."

I had no idea where we were going, and didn't ask, aware that this was a time for blind faith. We wore our twin pea-coats, purchased at Guiseppe's Thrift Emporium, mine with blue plastic buttons, Dwaine's with shiny brass ones embossed with anchors, and marched into the harsh headwind that met us underneath the highway overpass, its whooshing traffic sounds echoing ominously between pylons. Out of the darkness Dwaine told me about his brother, Jack. I didn't even know he *had* a brother; he'd never mentioned having a brother before. As we walked he explained to me that Jack had been one of the biggest narcotics dealers in the country, that he'd owned a huge compound in the Arizona desert, with a fleet of tractor-trailers, four Cessna planes, and a small army of paperless Mexicans employed by him. When Dwaine last saw Jack he had just gotten back from "overseas" (by this I assumed he meant Vietnam). On his way to New York from Oakland he'd stopped in Arizona to pay Jack a visit. Like his parents, Dwaine had been operating under the impression that his brother was an undergraduate philosophy major at the University of Arizona. Instead Dwaine arrived to find the compound patrolled by armed guards and surveillance cameras.

"One of the guards tells me Jack's waiting out back," said Dwaine. "I turn the corner and freeze. There's like a hundred people camped around the biggest damn swimming pool I ever saw, all of 'em naked and smoking swagg. Jack steps out of the cabana hut. He's huge, like three hundred pounds, with a thick beard. He looks like Huffnagel.[2] 'Meet my new family,' Jack says, throwing his arms around me. Just then this little kid with no clothes on walks up to the edge of the pool and pees into it. Jack laughed," said Dwaine. "He found it hysterical."

Dwaine went on to tell me how Jack gave him a tour of the place, including the giant Quonset hut where a crew of paperless workers dried, cut, and packaged cocaine paste, while a smaller group of University of Arizona chemistry majors synthesized Quaaludes and LSD. His brother handed Dwaine a sheet of windowpane acid, hot off the press. "'Take as much as you want,' Jack says to me. 'There's plenty more shit where that came from.'"

As we kept walking, Dwaine lit a cigarette, offered me one. He knew that I didn't smoke, but not wanting to break the air of intimacy that has arisen between us I took it anyway. He even lit it for me, his fingers forming a cup of orange flame under my chin. He told me how, after his visit with Jack, while driving him to the airport, his brother asked Dwaine if he cared to go partners with him.

"What did you say?"

"I said no thanks. Jack looks at me like I'm the dumbest ass ever to walk the face of the earth. I'd never seen such a disgusted look on a face before, not counting my father's face when he found out about my other-than-honorable discharge."

Dwaine fell suddenly silent then, like he'd said too much, or maybe it was just one of those dramatic pauses he was so good at, or maybe he just wanted to get past the sounds of cars avalanching on the expressway overhead as we walked under it. It occurred to me then that he drove my curiosity the way some people drive their cars, flooring it or hitting the brakes, nothing in between. He pulled a shiny silver flask from his pea coat pocket, one I'd never seen before, drank from it

---

2. A heavyset Pratt student who played supporting roles in our films.

and handed it to me. The chilled liquor burned my lips and carved a warm tunnel deep down into my guts.

We jumped a spiked iron fence to land with solid thuds on the frozen cemetery earth, and kept walking, passing the shiny flask back and forth. When he started talking again, I listened the way I always listened to Dwaine, as if every word was a door being opened to let in more of the world. Drug dealers! Compounds in the Arizona desert! To think I knew someone who knew, had known, such criminals; that my best friend's brother had been a world-class drug dealer. Dwaine might have said that he knew John Dillinger personally, or that Al Capone was his brother, or Buffalo Bill. The whole illicit country seemed to have spilled from Dwaine's lips to land in a bright gruesome puddle like vomit at my feet. Only it was *good* vomit; it was All-American outlaw vomit, it was just the sort of vomit I craved, the corrosive kind that could completely dissolve my immigrant son status, that sense of being an alien no one from nowhere.

The sky went from cobalt to Prussian to deep indigo blue. Maybe it was the booze in my belly, but the colors of that night seemed to generate their own light with no help from the mercury and sodium vapor lamps or the moon. Was Dwaine drunk, too? If so he didn't show it; he never did, while I felt every drop sloshing around inside my brain like Shelly Winters in a rowboat.

We crossed an ocean of fancy graves to drift into a bay of plain tombstones bearing mostly Irish names: O'Rourke, O'Connor, Doherty, Doyle, Fitzgerald ... Dwaine picked up speed. Soon we stood before a grave with a Distinguished Service Cross sprouting like a bronze sunflower from it:

> Jonathan Daniel Fitzgibbon
> b: October 15, 1946

d: February 14, 1975
Beloved Son of Sean and Irene

"That's him?" I said.

Dwaine nodded.

"So your brother was in the war, too?"

"Infantry," said Dwaine. "Two tours. Jack got drafted; I didn't. He always believed it was because of the color of his skin. See, he had darker skin than me. Black Irish, some people call it. It made no sense to me, but it did to Jack. I think he held it against me, too, in his way. Jack was that way. When I pissed him off, he'd call me his 'little Irish bitch nigger.' Projection, is what I believe the shrinks call it."

"How did he die?"

Dwaine's face went through at least three transmission shifts there in the dark before he answered: "Narcotics overdose related cardiac arrest"—as if it were something he'd been brainwashed into saying, like Lawrence Harvey in *The Manchurian Candidate*.

Then, unzipping his fly, Dwaine undertook what was presumably the crowning ritual of these graveside vigils, and peed a steady stream onto his dead brother's grave mound.

"'Dwaine,' my brother said to me last time I saw him, 'if I ever overdose, I want you to promise me you'll piss on my grave.' Well ..."

Clouds of steam rose from the wet earth as rivulets formed around Dwaine's boot caps. "A fitting tribute," Dwaine added, zipping his fly, "to a guy who pissed his life away."

As we left Jack's grave, Dwaine said: "Have you ever wondered why so many things starting with the letter D are bad?"

"Like what?" I asked.

"Like Death. Disaster. Despair. Depression. Disease. Denial."

"What about Dreams?" I said. "And Daylight?"

"... Disenchantment, Depravity, Drunkenness, Dishonor ..."
"... Destiny, Delight, Determination—"
"... Destruction, Defoliation ..."
"... Doughnuts? Dominoes?"
"... Destitution, Dogma, Divorce ..."
"... Dogs, Daisies, Dill Pickles?"
"... Dysentery, Dropsy, Defenestration ..."
"... Dolphins? Driftwood?"
"Driftwood?" said Dwaine.
"Driftwood's great! You light beach fires with it. It floats!"
"Sometimes you worry me, babe, you know that?"

The mausoleums were mostly Italian in origin. We gazed through the barred bronze doors at altars glowing in whisky-brown light, at the stained windows depicting the Stations of the Cross.

"You Wops sure know how to die in style, I'll give you that much."

"Wish our apartment were this nice," I said.

We both started laughing then. For the first time I felt that we were on the same level, almost. It gave me a strange mixed feeling, the kind I'd get on Christmas mornings after opening all my presents, only to find that the colorful wrappings had been the best part.

We came upon a freshly dug grave, the raw earth piled underneath a tarpaulin beside it. The hole went at least eight feet down. A metal ladder stretched alongside it. I dared Dwaine.

"Darers go first," he said.

So I climbed down. Being the son of an atheist, I didn't believe in heaven or hell, so had no reason to fear a hole in the ground. As I went down Dwaine made werewolf sounds.

"Very funny," I remarked.

"Not at all. In fact it's pretty *grave*."

I reached the bottom.

"Step off the ladder," Dwaine commanded. I did. He withdrew it.

"Good evening," he said with his hands cupped around his mouth. "We hope that you are enjoying your stay at the Club Inferno. Tonight at midnight we will have bingo in the Seventh Circle Lounge with prizes complimentary to you. Free wailing and gnashing of teeth instructions are available. See Moloch in the cabana."

Suddenly Dwaine stepped out of sight. Still, I wasn't afraid. What was there to be afraid of? In fact I thought it was funny, and started laughing down there despite not having been in so dark a place since my mother locked me in the attic for having smashed a shaving cream pie in the family dog's face. But then my eyes adjusted to the darkness and I saw something sticking out of the dirt beside me, a milled corner casting a silver gleam of moonlight: a coffin's edge. I said, "Dwaine?"

Then I screamed, "*Dwaaaainnne!*"

Dwaine peered down.

"You rang?"

"Get me out of here, fucker!"

"Why, don't you like it down there?"

"There's dead people here!"

"What did you expect, the June Taylor Dancers?"

"*Give me that fucking ladder!*"

My feet hardly touched the rungs as I bounded upwards. When I arrived within arms' reach, Dwaine pulled me out the rest of the way: Hercules pulling Cerberus from the infernal regions. I fell panting against a nearby tombstone.

"*How bold of you,*" Dwaine said, patting my back, "*to descend into the depths where the futile dead live on without their wits.*"

"Fuck off!"

"Come on now, it wasn't *that* bad."

"How do you know?"

"Trust me. I know." He smiled.

❖

From there we rode the subway to Times Square. I'd never been to Times Square on New Year's Eve before. I'd heard the tales of crowds and muggings and of people getting shot and stabbed. Dwaine assured me that crowds wouldn't be our problem.

"Not where we're going," Dwaine said.

As much as Dwaine hated Christmas, he loved New Year's Eve, as if the mere turning of a calendar page could usher in bright prospects while eradicating the unseemly past. Having exited the subway, we shoved our way through the throngs that had already gathered along 42nd Street, passing under the bulky marquees of once illustrious theaters gone to seed, pagan cathedrals where, as Dwaine saw it, people went to be delivered from their dull, pathetic, and often painful lives, and had their prayers answered—if only for an hour and a half. Now half of those theaters were boarded shut, while the other half showed only porn and slasher flicks.

"Such a shame," said Dwaine.

As the crowds grew ominous, Dwaine pulled me off the sidewalk and into the arcade of an office building where a disused subway entrance was blocked by sheets of plywood.

"After you," he said, having pulled back a sheet.

We headed down stairs so dark I couldn't see my hands in front of my face. Dwaine lit his cigarette lighter. It hardly made a dent in the dark. My legs shook.

"Relax, babe," said Dawine. "Pretend you're watching *Beneath the Planet of the Apes*."

At the bottom of the stairs Dwaine put out the lighter, took a flashlight from his pocket, and pointed it at a mildew-covered mosaic. Bite-sized tiles spelled 42nd STREET.

I asked, "How long has this been here?"

"Since 1938. It was built as a crossover station before the Second World War, but never used."

I shivered in my pea coat. En route to other places trains roared through the station. Dwaine looked up and down the platform, then jumped into the tracks, telling me to do likewise, warning me to watch out for the third rail. "They say that one of the most efficient ways to commit suicide is to piss on a third rail," he said as we started walking, headed uptown. A train light appeared, highlighting old newspapers and scampering rats. As the subway roared by we flattened our backs into a maintenance notch. Then Dwaine walked another dozen yards, to where rusted ladder climbed toward a matrix of dusty light. He climbed and I followed him up into a crawlspace under a grating that brought us, on hands and knees, into a chamber about eight feet long by six feet wide by five feet deep. There was a wooden fruit crate there, so coated with wax drippings it looked like something growing at the bottom of the sea, and an old mattress, and a bunch of candles—long, tapered ones. We stretched out on the mattress and looked up through the grate at the lights of Times Square, pulsing away up there like a heavenly pinball machine, tinting the air with bright circus colors.

"The Stonehenge of the New Millennium," said Dwaine, looking up. "Or the asshole of the world, depending on your point of view."

"Is this where you go nights when you don't come home?"

"Sometimes. Now and then."

"Kind of lonely, isn't it?"

Dwaine shrugged in the dark.

"What do you do down here?"

"Do? What do I *do?*"

"Yeah, what do you do?"

"I don't *do* anything, babe. That would defeat the purpose. You're not supposed to *do* anything in a sanctuary, and this place is a sanctuary. I come here to get away from all the crazies up there." He pointed up, then cupped a hand over his ear. "Hear that? That's the OM: the gut-rumble of the New World Order." (I listened; I didn't hear a thing.) "Listen …" He made the sound for me. Then I heard it: a steady hum, like the sound a refrigerator makes. "There's a Moog synthesizer hidden down here somewhere, in the belly of civilization. It gives off a special frequency designed to calm human nerves. They say it's been humming that frequency since 1971, since the day I signed a piece of paper solemnly swearing to defend my country against all enemies foreign and domestic."

I asked him what made him enlist?

"Damned if I know. Because my dad dared me to. Because I was sick of him calling me a pussy. Because I wanted to be like John Wayne. Or maybe it was the OM. Maybe the OM drew me to that recruiting station, you know, like a snake charmer's flute? Listen." We listened. "They say that OM's the only thing holding this city together. They say if it should ever stop that everyone will go wild, rampaging, screaming naked in the streets, tearing each other's throats out. Someday, babe, for sure it's gonna happen, the other shoe's gonna drop. And when it does, down here—that's where you'll find me."

"What, in this hole?"

"You call it a hole, babe, but when the time comes, trust me, it'll be the closest thing to Paradise on earth."

"Maybe so, but won't it be lonely? I mean—wouldn't it be better to have … you know … some company?"

"No. It wouldn't be better."

"Why not?"

"Because—there are certain things that should be experienced in private, alone. A long walk along a deserted beach is one, a good bowel movement another, *Last Tango in Paris* a third. The end of the world is one of those things. I wouldn't *miss it* for the world, and I won't want to share it with anyone, not even with you, babe. And least of all with all the murderous motherfuckers up there." He pointed with his chin. "As for being lonely, George Orwell said that loneliness is just another word for being part of a very small minority. That's what we are, babe, you and me. Part of a very small minority. We don't fit into the system. We're type-B cells swimming in a type-A bloodstream. Of course we're lonely! Would you want it any other way?"

I shook my head; I wouldn't want it any other way.

The candle spluttered. Through the overhead grate I watched the lights of Times Square shifting like St. Elmo's fire. We lay listening to the OM humming under the sounds of loudspeakers and jubilation floating up above us. Then the countdown began. When the moment of truth arrived, Dwaine took out the bottle of *Asti Spumante* and two Dixie cups from the satchel he'd been carrying.

"To us, babe. To the Two Greatest Artists in New York."

We toasted with cheap bubbly, with me feeling I'd crossed a threshold of some kind, that at last Dwaine and I had entered the sacred space of true brotherhood. Sure, there were things wrong with Dwaine; there were things wrong with everyone, especially with artists; in particular great artists. And I believed that Dwaine was a great artist, or would be someday, soon as he saw fit to generate some art. I needed to believe in his greatness in order to believe that I myself might be great in some way. It beat the hell out of thinking that I was wasting my life.

"This will be our year," Dwaine assured us both. "Count on it." He held up a pinky as in, *We've got more talent in our pinkies than most people have in their whole bodies.*

Later that morning, as I drifted drunkenly off to sleep, Dwaine, naked and reeking of partly metabolized alcohol, climbed under my sheets. At first I thought he was pulling some sort of prank on me.

"What gives?" I said, laughing. "What the hell are you doing?"

Dwaine wasn't laughing. He sat there, smiling in the dark, his features lit fitfully by the neon sign winking across the street. I heard what at first sounded to me like plumbing noises, rumbles and gurgles, until I realized they were coming from Dwaine's stomach, like he was about to get sick.

"Are you okay?" I said.

"I'm fine," said Dwaine, his voice hard to hear. "Fine."

I reached up and switched on my bedside lamp. A mistake. He screamed. "Turn it off! Turn the goddamn fucking light off!"

I did, but not before seeing the erection that Dwaine hadn't had time to cover, its bulbous tip red and glossy. Grabbing the sheet from my bed and wrapping it around himself, he rushed out of my room. By the time I said, *Wait!* he was gone.

For a long time I stood there, feeling all of the bones in my face, all sound — including that of the elevated, which chose that moment to squeal by — edited out of the scene as in a violent sequence where everything turns to silence and slow motion before going black.

There are times in our lives that change us forever, or could have. Had I not been an insecure immigrant child from small-town Connecticut this might have been one of them. Instead I had to switch on that fucking light. Why? I should have let Dwaine get into bed with me; I should have let him do whatever it is that he'd wanted to do. Again, *why?* Because it would have done no harm. Because we were two lonesome creatures burrowing in the dark, seeking warmth, comfort. Because life is short and the night, that night especially, was going to be long, very long. And finally because, when you get down to it, apart from changing my whole life, it wouldn't have made any difference.

I stopped feeling the bones in my face and called into the darkness: "Dwaine?"

Stepping into his room, I felt the breeze from his open window against my bare ankles. I climbed the fire escape to the roof, where I found him wrapped in the white sheet, huddled close to the edge, the remains of a dead pigeon like a sacrificial offering at his feet.

He looked up.

"I'm not a homo," he said.

"Neither am I."

"But I am fucked-up."

"No, you're not."

"Yes I am, babe. You bet I am. I'm fucked up and so are you. Only I'm too fucked up, and you're not fucked-up enough."

A subway passed, its roar and lights splashing. High over our heads a police helicopter flut-flutted, the scene lit intermittently by flashes of neon. Dwaine gave a weird laugh then, edging closer to the brink. I dove and grabbed and pulled him toward the stairwell shed, where I held him close and he burst out crying.

"You're my only friend," he said to me through a stream of tears. "My only friend in the whole goddamn world. Funny, isn't it? Don't you think it's funny, babe? I think it's hysterical!"

I held him, feeling the clammy patch of skin between his Lucky Lumps. Had Dwaine been a woman I'd have kissed him then, oh yes, I would have. Instead I silently, secretly prayed to the Eagle Electric manufacturing company sign across the way, wishing it would swoop down and protect us, shield us with its enormous tin wings.

❖ *The Opening Credits to* Rebel Without a Cause

"It came from genius, that's where it came from."
—Dennis Hopper

0:01
A WIDE-ANGLE SHOT OF THE HOLLYWOOD DISTRICT OF LOS ANGELES at night as seen from the Santa Monica Mountains, the city lights stretching like strings of pearls along Hollywood and Sunset Boulevards. You might assume the view is from the famous Hollywood sign, from whose 45-foot tall "H" silent movie actress Millicent Lillian "Peg" Entwistle, despondent over her fall from stardom ("I am afraid, I am a coward. I am sorry for everything. If I had done this a long time ago, it would have saved a lot of pain. P.E.") leapt to her death. In fact it's from the Griffith Observatory, a short distance away. It makes sense, since the observatory is the setting of two key episodes in the movie, and the film's final moment, wherein a briefcase-carrying man in a trench coat, the director, is filmed from above walking toward the observatory entrance as dawn rises. In other ways the film, of which the following opening credits scene is a microcosm, achieves its circular shape, starting (after this opening shot) at dawn, and ending 24-hours later with a high-angle view of the Griffith Observatory.

0:03
When I first saw *Rebel Without a Cause*, I was a freshman at the Pratt Institute in Brooklyn. I was nineteen, five years younger than James

Dean when he starred in the film. This was in 1976—before streaming, before Netflicks, before CD's, VCR and VHS. If you wanted to see a movie, you had to rent it for serious money and screen it using a big, clunky, subject-to-jamming 16-mm projector, or get lucky and catch it on TV.

I had yet to see a James Dean movie. Of the three he made before he died at age 24, I'd heard that "Rebel," about teenage rebellion and delinquency in the 1950's, was the best, though that wasn't my main reason for going.

0.04

We've barely broached the first seconds of this opening, the few dozen frames of celluloid that, at 24 frames-per-second, take us from a dark screen to a view of L.A. at night. No sooner does this happen than the Warner Brothers logo, familiar to my generation from Looney Tunes—a blue shield holding the initials WB in golden deco-style

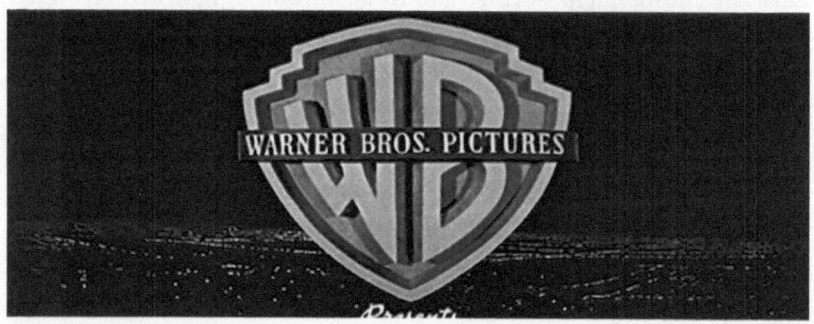

letters, with a dark belt running across it saying WARNER BROS. PICTURES (and, in smaller, script-style letters underneath it, "Presents")—fills the screen.

Nicknamed the "Brain Shield" when first used in silent films of the 1920s, over the next seventy years the logo underwent dozens of transformations, including the short-lived "Zooming Shield" that lurched toward viewers on a backdrop of black-and-white clouds. By 1955, the year *Rebel* was released, common practice superimposed the logo over a backdrop germane to the movie's subject, in this case Los Angeles at night as viewed from the Griffith Observatory.

0:05
Marlon Brando was my hero. In my dorm room next to the mirror before which I did curls and navy lifts with a rusty set of barbells, I'd hung a poster of him in *The Wild One,* leaning over the handlebars of his motorcycle in his leather jacket. On my roommate's stereo to his dismay I played Alex North's theme to *Streetcar* over and over again. I wore one-size-too-small T-shirts, lifted my set of rusty barbells, and did everything else I could to coax some measure of brutish sensuality from my adamantly boyish physique.

0:06
A horn section sounds the first brash notes to Leonard Rosenman's melodramatic score. The percussive notes rise in pitch, with the final note sustained, mimicking the opening (G-G-G-Eb) of Beethoven's 5th Symphony, said to be Death knocking at the door, though this is contentious. Here, since the notes rise rather than fall, the effect is more triumphant than portentous, suggesting that in what follows, though there are tragic elements, the hero will prevail. That said, since the notes coincide with the appearance of the aforementioned brain shield logo, the triumph may be strictly that of a self-aggrandizing motion picture company.

0:07
I was new to Brooklyn and city life. I grew up in a small Connecticut town. Compared to me, with their punk hairdos and French cigarettes, my fellow students seemed much more sophisticated. Like Jim Stark,

the character James Dean plays in *Rebel*, but also like Plato (played by Sal Mineo, who hero-worships him), I was lonesome, having yet to make any real friends. Those who knew me back then tell me I was cocky, arrogant. If so, under that cockiness I was a bundle of insecurity.

0:08
The Warner Brothers' logo and the panorama of Los Angeles at night give way to a street scene viewed from a low angle, just inches above the macadam. The street is North Sierra Bonita Avenue at the intersection of Franklin Boulevard. On the pavement in the near foreground, riding the bottom of the screen, are several pieces of litter: a scrap of wrapping paper with a floral pattern, some gold ribbon, and—at the right side of the screen under a scattered bouquet of lilies—a wind-up toy monkey that, when wound up, bangs a pair of cymbals.

Manufactured by the Japanese firm Daishin C.K. and marketed under the name *Musical Jolly Chimp*, the toy was extremely popular during the 50's and early 1960's. In addition to banging its cymbals, when its head was pressed it screeched and bared its teeth. Following Daishin C.K.'s success, other manufacturers came out with similar toys. The names these knock-offs sold under included *Wind-up Monkey Playing Symbols*, *Pepi Tumbling Monkey*, and *Clockwork Musical Monkey*. Though the monkey toy's cameo in this opening scene looks improvised, the toy was actually written into the screenplay, where it appears soon after a scene (filmed but never used) in which a youth gang assaults a man carrying a package of gifts down "a lonely street full of parked cars" on Easter evening, as evoked by the hymn being sung by children in the distance. Frightened by the delinquent thugs, the man drops a pack of cigarettes. The gangsters wait for him to pick it up. He does, offering one to the leader, Buzz, who says:

> BUZZ
> (smiling, encouraging)
> You smoke it. Smoke it, Dad.

Smiling uncertainly, the MAN puts the cigarette in his mouth. BUZZ, still smiling, takes out a packet of wooden matches.

> BUZZ
> (continuing)
> I'll light it for you, Dad.

BUZZ ignites a match and holds it near the Man's face for a second, searching it. Then he ignites the whole box under his nose. The MAN shrieks, and his packages fall. BUZZ slaps him sharply, his smile gone.

The camera pans away as the figures enclose him, and holds on a small mechanical monkey which has dropped from its wrappings. It begins to dance madly on the pavement, then runs down.

Several evangelistic viewers have claimed that the toy monkey symbolizes the Death of Darwinism. Although the drama does take place during Easter and is replete with Christian motifs and images, I still call that a stretch.

0:09

For now, though, we have a male of indeterminate age, seen only from the waist-down, stumbling in leather shoes, dark slacks, and a dark sport coat along a littered street. In the background to his left and slightly out of focus is a barricade blocking the street. Look closer and you'll see the word "DANGER" on a white signboard posted to the barricade, with "KEEP OUT" under it, and some other words—too blurry to read—in between:

> **DANGER**
> (blurry words)
> **KEEP OUT**

What the danger is and why the road has been blocked off isn't clear. Or are we to interpret this as a symbol of the dangerous period in which the film is set, the dawn of the Atomic Age, the era of fallout shelters and duck-and-cover drills. Public school children of all ages were instructed to get on the ground and hide under a table (or, if no table was available, next to a wall) and assume a "prone position," covering their exposed body parts with loose clothes or their hands? Is it a coincidence that the house seen glowing in the background bears an uncanny resemblance to the White House?

A street map holds some answers. Though technically North Sierra Bonita Avenue ends at the intersection with Franklin, the driveway of the big house, the one that looks like the White House and whose white columns are discernible behind and to the right of the man stumbling toward the camera, follows the avenue's trajectory, such that an absent-minded or drunk driver might mistake it for the road and barrel through. Hence the "DANGER/KEEP OUT" sign, a precaution dispensed with a few years after "Rebel" was made, when a cast-iron gate was added to the driveway.

As for the house, according to a real estate listing dated January 2004, it is a "Southern Colonial Hollywood Grande Dame" built in 1912, sits on a 10,498 square-foot lot, and features a formal dining room, a "grand" living room, a remodeled kitchen w/ new range & hood, a den, a library, an office, a "sleeping porch," a gym/exercise room

w/steam shower, a pool with a fountain, an unfinished attic, no common walls (detached), and a composite roof. It has 5 bedrooms and 3.5 baths and a total usable interior space of 4,398 square feet. The lot is zoned LARE9 (sub-dividable to 9,000 square foot lots). On the market for 70 days, it sold in January of 2005. List price: $2,195,000.00.

The listing says nothing about the home's cameo in *Rebel Without a Cause*. Still, it gave a "glowing" performance—radiating warmth, comfort, and security, in contrast to the dire warnings at the opposite side of the screen, from which this symbolic "white house" ostensibly offered protection.

0:10

I went to the screening hoping to find T. Shirley there. The "T" stood for Terry, which was short for Theresa. T was a painting major, a talented one. Strawberry blond, with a dash of freckles around her nose. She lived in Bensonhurst and took figure drawing class with me. Like every heterosexual male in my class, I had a crush on T. Shirley. When I heard about the film showing, I screwed up my courage and asked if she'd care to watch it with me. To my surprise she said yes. My plan was to watch the movie with her, then ask her to walk with me to *Junior's*, a mile away on Flatbush Avenue, for a cup of coffee.

0:12

As the anonymous figure stumbles toward us the brassy overture ends. A tremulous sax takes over, its jazzy, warbled notes snaking into the soundtrack as the man, as if about to do some push-ups, falls hands-first on the pavement where the monkey beats its cymbals. The man, or boy (he's neither one nor the other, but a blend, or nullification, of both) is Jim Stark, though we know him as James Dean. In case we don't, in a practice known as "above-title billing" (the film's title having yet to appear), JAMES DEAN spreads across the screen in bright red Small-Caps, with the letters J and D larger than the other letters, and the star's iconic face watching the wind-up monkey from underneath the D and E in "DEAN." As warbling saxophone is superseded by sneering trumpet, we simultaneously see *and* read "JAMES DEAN."

0:13
As students shuffled into the auditorium I searched for T. Shirley. It was midwinter, late February. I stood near the back, gazing over the rows of heads as boys and girls in groups and pairs—their heavy clothes exuding wooly winter odors—jostled by in search of seats. T. Shirley had to be somewhere in that packed auditorium. But where? I

kept on searching. As the houselights dimmed, I grabbed one of the last remaining seats just in time to see the man/boy stumbling into the picture frame. No sooner did I first set eyes on him than I wished I were Dean/Stark.

0:14
Must I trot out all the usual trivia concerning this "cultural icon of teenage rebellion"? That he was born in Indiana, but moved to

California when he was six, only to return to his birth state, to Fairmont, to live with his aunt and her husband on their farm? That he had an "intense" relationship with his pastor, the Reverend James DeWeerd, and may have been sexually abused by him? That from an early age he was fascinated by bullfighting and car racing? How, after graduating from high school, he moved back to California, where, after majoring in pre-law for a year, he transferred to UCLA to study acting? How, following several bit TV roles, he moved to New York City, joined the Actors Studio, and studied the Method under Lee Strasburg? How his big break came when director Elia Kazan, seeking another Brando, cast him as emotionally disturbed Cal Trask in *East of Eden*? How his next role, that of troubled teenager Jim Stark in *Rebel Without a Cause*, would cement the public's image of him as the poster boy of rebellious youth? That on September 30, 1955, soon after completing *Giant,* his third film, while driving the Porsche 550 Spyder he nicknamed "Little Bastard" west on Route 466 toward Paso Robles, with his mechanic Rolf Wütherich in the passenger seat, at the junction to Route 41 he crashed head-on into a black-and-white Forde coupe driven by Donald Turnupspeed, and died shortly afterwards? That his last words were *"That guy's gotta stop. He'll see us!"*? That while filming *Giant* he made a short Pubic Service film for the National Safety Council. In it, speaking to actor Gig Young on the subject of reckless driving, he advised viewers to drive more slowly, adding, "The life you might save might be mine!"? That for his role in *Giant* he was awarded a posthumous Oscar? That his legend was born almost immediately with his death? That despite what may have been a publicity stunt love affair with actress Pier Angeli, he was bisexual, if not gay? I need only say "James Dean" for most of this to be understood as clearly and instantly as the imperative on the stop sign at the intersection of Routes 446 and 41.

0:16
Still no sign of T. Shirley.

0:20
As "JAMES DEAN" fades, the movie's title takes it place, broken into three lines and tilted diagonally across the screen, the letters staggered like those of the HOLLYWOOD sign (from which Peg Entwistle leapt to her death). The font used resembles a heavy, box-shadowed Franklin Gothic, a popular sans-serif typeface designed by Morris Fuller Benton in 1902 and used often for billboards and other display purposes. But the middle bar of the uppercase "E" (as in REBEL) is too short. Avant Garde Gothic Heavy is also a contender, but the bar in the uppercase "A" in CAUSE on the screen is centered, whereas the Avant Garde "A" has a lower bar. The letters were most likely hand-cut based on Franklin Gothic or a similar typeface, with the box shadows added. In any event the title, in quotation marks, takes up the entire screen, covering James Dean's face and the rest of his body while leaving room for the wrapping paper, the toy monkey, and the brightly lit house with the columns rising behind a hedge in the background.

0:21
The color chosen for the titles is an aggressive bright red, the color of fire apparatus ("Fire Engine Red," hex triplet color coordinate #CE2029, CMYK blend 0-C, 89-M, 80-Y, 19K; Hue = 357°, Saturation = 89%, Value = 81%), or a bullfighter's capote.

Red plays a significant role in the film. It's one reason why, having started filming in black-and-white, the director switched to color. The toy monkey's cap, Jim Stark's tie, his signature windbreaker, Natalie Wood's lipstick, the mismatched sock worn by Plato in his death scene —all are red. Res is the color of blood, also of courage, sacrifice and martyrdom, as reflected by the film's three main dramatic events, with

Dean/Stark's participation in a "chickie run" (a contest wherein the first person to jump out of a car speeding toward a cliff's edge is a "chicken") indicative of his courage, and the themes of martyrdom and sacrifice

played out, respectively, in Dean/Stark's cloaking his disciple (Plato) in the mantle of his windbreaker, and Plato's subsequent death. Red also connotes rage ("seeing red"), as when Dean/Stark cries, "You're... Tearing... Me... *Appaaaart!*" in the police station with his parents, and later when he attacks his ineffectual, apron-wearing father (Jim Backus), pitching him over his armchair as his domineering mother looks on ("You want to kill your father!").

Red is also associated with romantic love (valentines) and with sexual passion, though there's little of the latter in this film in which the lead seems less enamored of Judy/Wood than of himself. Then again there is Plato/Mineo's passionate hero worship of Stark/Dean, a love best characterized as adulation, or—according to Merriam-Webster) —"excessive or slavish admiration of flattery." The word "adulation" has an interesting derivation, from the Latin *adulari,* meaning "to fawn on," and applied mainly to the affectionate behavior of dogs toward their masters. From just about the moment he meets Stark/Dean, Plato/Mineo pants after his new master, following him everywhere on his backfiring motor scooter. So infatuated is Plato that, as adulators will, on behalf of his idol he first sacrifices his own identity, then, ultimately, his life. "Puppy love" is another term that accurately describes the adulation Plato feels toward Dean/Stark.

0:22
"Puppy Love" also accurately described my feelings for T. Shirley—feelings that weren't sexual, quite, at least not in the overt gamy way I had felt toward other women, for whom I didn't care nearly as much and with whom, for that reason perhaps, I'd had more success. Maybe it was those wholesome freckles, or her harp-shaped lips, or the strawberry blonde hair, or that she was such a talented painter. In T. Shirley's presence I felt something approaching awe. Deep inside I suspected that she was too good for me, which is why I had to win her and why I was doomed to fail. I was her fawning Plato/Sal Mineo.

0:23
Finally, red is a warning, a sign urging us to proceed with caution, or to stop *("That guy's gotta stop—he'll see us.")*. It is also the color equated with Communism, perceived during the period when *Rebel* was filmed as a dangerous threat and referred to by some as the "red scare" or "menace." Communism embraces the ideal of the classless society as defined by Plato (not Sal Mineo's Plato, but the Greek philosopher) in his *Republic*:

> The private and individual is altogether banished from life and things which are by nature private, such as eyes and ears and hands, have become common, and in some way see and hear and act in common, and all men express praise and feel joy and sorrow on the same occasions.

What can be more private and personal than adulation? On the other hand what could be more public?

But the vivid reds may all be there for a much simpler reason: They looked good in the new color film stock that Warner Bros. was using.

0:25
The movie's title (which appears now, spreading diagonally across the screen) was taken from the psychiatrist Robert Lindner's 1944 nonfiction bestseller. Subtitled "The Hypnoanalysis of a Criminal Psychopath," Lindner's book transcribes forty-six analytical sessions with "Harold," a juvenile inmate in a Pennsylvania penitentiary, presenting those traumatic events from his infancy, childhood, and adolescence that (presumably) propelled him toward his life of petty crime. Though Lindner sold the rights to his book to Hollywood for $5,000, and though both his book and the film that took its title share the subject of juvenile delinquency, they have nothing else in common.

Following the sale, the project kicked around the studio for over a decade, morphing through several treatments, including one by Lindner himself, none of which got further than a five-minute 1947 screen test in which twenty-four-year-old Marlon Brando tried out for the role of the troubled teenager. (You can watch it on YouTube.)

Seven years after that project was shelved, Nick Ray approached Warner Brothers with a story about middle-class kids in trouble. Warners liked Ray's idea, but didn't care for his working title, *The Blind Run*. Since they already owned it, along with their blessing the studio gave Ray the title *Rebel Without a Cause*.

The rest of Lindner's book they threw away.

0:26
By now I'd given up all hope of seeing—let alone sitting next to and walking arm-in-arm to *Junior's* for late night coffee with—T. Shirley, who (I concluded miserably) was either somewhere in that auditorium watching *Rebel Without a Cause* with some other guy, or making out with said other guy back in his dorm room.

0:27

Snarling trumpet and swaggering brass notes give way to syrupy violins as the leading co-stars' names appear, with Natalie Wood ("Also Starring") getting top billing, followed by ("with") Jim Backus "and" sixteen-year-old Sal Mineo.

At first Nick Ray was unimpressed with Mineo's audition. But after watching him interact with Dean he offered him the role, saying, "Every once in a while a director has to gamble. I'm taking a chance. You're Plato."

For Jim Backus (best known to most as Thurston Howell III, the ostentatious Yankee millionaire stranded—with a cast of equally silly characters—on a desert island in the heavily syndicated 1960's sitcom *Gilligan's Island)*, the role of Jim Stark's father represented a rare dramatic turn. By then Backus was already famous as the voice of cartoon character Quincy Magoo: a wealthy, short, elderly gentleman who engenders a series of comical disasters as a result of his severe nearsightedness. At one point in the film, Backus' cartoon analogue makes an appearance in the form of Stark/Dean imitating him during the scene in the abandoned mansion. In the same mansion scene, Dean, Wood, and Mineo form a symbolic family. At one point, Jim and Judy pretend to be newlyweds interested in buying the home, with Plato as real estate agent. Asked by them if children are permitted, Plato/Mineo responds, "We really don't encourage them. They're noisy and troublesome, don't you agree?" In  the voice of Mr. Magoo to the problem of unwanted children Dean/Stark offers this modest proposal: "Heh, drown 'em like puppies, heh." Backus himself taught Dean how to do Magoo's voice.

0:28
When it came to casting sixteen-year-old Natalie Wood as gang leader Buzz's squeeze (who, after Buzz dies in the "chickie run," falls in love with Stark/Dean), here too Nicholas Ray had his doubts. Could doe-eyed, tree-climbing, pet-loving, virginally adorable Wood pull off a gangster's moll? In the end not only did Ray cast her, the forty-three-year-old director seduced her. So Dennis Hopper, another actor cast as a member of Buzz's gang, discovered on arriving unannounced at Bungalow 2 of the Chateau Marmont, Ray's hotel suite. Having found Ray and Wood in bed together there, an infuriated Hopper wondered if Ray's casting of the young starlet owed less to her acting ability than to her charming her way into Ray's boudoir.

0:29
As for James Dean, there had never been any doubt. Had Brando been available for the role he wouldn't have served it as well. By then Marlon was too old to play a teenager. Also, he lacked Dean's essential quality, his vulnerability, the same vulnerability I felt sitting in that dark auditorium watching Dean/Stark while wondering where—and with whom—T. Shirley was. The Brando style brutish sensuality I'd labored away at for months, the muscles and tough-guy poses, all melted away, replaced by Dean/Stark's heroic vulnerability as the music swells and he rewinds the toy monkey which has ceased beating its cymbals.

0:30
As Dean/Stark winds the toy monkey, the score's main theme is introduced, a melody suggestive of romantic splendor, with its heavy emphasis on strings. Now the watch on Dean/Stark's wrist is clearly visible, an insignificant detail except insofar as it serves as a reminder that the story we're about to see takes place in twenty-four hours, from

dawn to dawn, offering a good example of a modern drama wherein the Aristotelian unities are observed:

1) *Unity of Action:* a drama should follow one main action with few if any subplots;

2) *Unity of Place:* a drama should occur in a single setting and should not attempt to compress geography, nor should the stage represent more than one place; and

3) *Unity of Time:* the drama should take place over no more than 24 hours.

Considering that it's a movie and not a play, *Rebel* does an admirable job of observing these unities. Even with respect to #3, it keeps locations to a minimum: the police station, the Stark residence, the planetarium, the cliffside venue of the chickie run, the abandoned mansion, and, finally, a return to the planetarium for the climactic scene in which all the principle characters are united.

Indeed, there's a claustrophobic staginess to *Rebel Without a Cause,* a sense that all the events of the story take place not in a real world or city, but under an artificial dome—like that of the planetarium in which the end of the world is enacted, with Plato/Mineo cowering under his seat as Stark/Dean offers assurances ("It's all over; the world ended.").

0:31

Like Plato, I cowered in my seat, feeling that my world had come to an end, or had ended, while I was being reborn into another world, a world in which for the next few months I would be Dean/Stark. I would play that role to and for myself and anyone else who cared to watch. The misunderstood loner, the rebel outsider, the angry sensitive young artist chafing against the status quo. I'd be unique, abstract. I'd live fast, die young, and leave a beautiful corpse.

0:32

By now Dean/Stark's jacket—one of two jackets he wears in the film, the other being the famous red (blood, danger, passion, warning) windbreaker that he offers to Plato in the last scene—has come into focus. At first the jacket, a sport coat, looks black, but later on in the movie it appears to be of white-accented black tweed. In fact the sport coat is brown with white and orange speckles, or, in vintage clothing store argot, "atomic flecked."

The coat (which still exists) was designed by Sy Devore, the "Tailor to the Stars," and bears his label on the inner chest pocket under the Warner Brothers wardrobe label (*"3-18-55, Prod. 821 (Rebel without a Cause), Name: James Dean, 5797M"*). According to the catalogue copy for Saban Theater of Beverly Hills' May, 2011 Auction #44

> This highly identifiable screen-worn artifact was filled at one time by one of the most enigmatic and iconic cult figures of Hollywood history, James Dean, in what is without question his most memorable screen role as troubled teenager Jim Stark in Nicholas Ray's *Rebel Without a Cause*. Dean wears this particular jacket for most of the first half of the film, when he then switches for the "chicken [sic] run" to the more thuggish red jacket. After production wrapped, co-star Nick Adams obtained the jacket and, some years later, having befriended Elvis Presley and learning of Presley's fascination with Dean, gifted it to him as a thank-you for shirts Elvis had given Adams. ... After cherishing it for some years, Elvis gifted the jacket to his uncle, Vester Presley, who describes the history of these transactions in a signed LOA [letter of authenticity], accompanied by another signed LOA from Presley's hairdresser, who was present at both exchanges. Easily one of the most significant original wardrobe articles to be offered from the silver age of Hollywood.

At auction Dean/Stark's "atomic fleck" jacket sold for $63,250, testifying to its status as a cultural artifact. In *Rebel* the sport coat has a different significance, as does the red (danger, passion, blood, warning) windbreaker, as do jackets generally. They function as mantels—like the Seamless Robe of Jesus, which, according to both Western and Eastern Orthodox tradition, was divided among the soldiers after his crucifixion. After the credits end, in the next scene, when Dean/Stark encounters a shivering Plato in the police station where he's been booked as drunk and disorderly, he offers him his jacket ("It's warm"), an offer Plato refuses (recall Peter's denial of Christ following *his* arrest: "Before the rooster crows you shall deny me thrice"). Later, in the chickie run scene, Buzz dies when the strap of *his* leather jacket gets caught on the door handle of the jalopy he's supposed to jump out of, trapping him as it hurls over the cliff. In the final planetarium scene, where once again Dean/Stark offers Plato his jacket (now the red windbreaker), this time Plato accepts it. Later on when, wearing it, Plato is shot by a policeman, at first Jim Stark's father assumes that his son has been gunned down.

At the movie's final moments, in a last display of paternal love for his fallen disciple, Dean/Stark cover's Plato's corpse with the (blood) red windbreaker. A few seconds later Dean/Stark's entry into adulthood is marked by his ineffectual father wrapping *his* jacket over his son's shoulders, saying, "Whatever comes we'll face it together. I'll try to be as strong as you want me to be." The adulator (Plato/Mineo) becomes the hero/martyr; son becomes father.

Yes, it's all rather heavy-handed, but this was the 1950's. Movies had embraced Freud and Christianity with a vengeance.

0:33

Later on, with the movie over and the house lights flickering on, while joining the students shuffling toward the exit doors, I'll see T. Shirley inching along with them, walking hand in hand with a tall fellow I'll recognize as one of the nude figure models from life drawing class.

0:34
But now we're still watching the opening credits. As Dean/Stark winds the monkey toy the names of the supporting players appear. Though it would cease by the 1970's, the practice of billing cast and crewmembers in opening credits was still common in the 1950's. Before 1970 most films had no closing credits at all, nor did they take half as long as the movie, and list every gopher, crew member, and caterer. One forgets that these actors did other things, too, had careers, families, hobbies, interests, struggles, illnesses, etc., that their lives weren't completely given over to playing bit roles in movies.

Among first-tier supporting players are William and Dennis Hopper; the first (who plays Judy/Wood's Oedipally hamstrung father) is best known as Paul Drake, Perry Mason's trusty assistant on the eponymous TV show. As for Dennis Hopper, William's cousin, my generation knows him best as the sleazy hippy biker in *Easy Rider*. The first name on the list, Ann Doran (Dean/Stark's domineering mother) appeared in over 500 films. Having played minor roles before and after *Rebel*, Corey Allen (Buzz) turned to directing, winning an Emmy for an episode of *Hill Street Blues*. Ed Platt, the juvenile counselor whose desk Dean/Stark pummels with his fists, played the Chief in *Get Smart*, a sixties TV spy spoof created by Mel Brooks and starring Don Adams as bungling secret agent Maxwell Smart. Less well-known is Platt for producing the first independent color movie shot on videotape, or for having suffered from depression, a condition that, along with the actor's financial woes, led to his suicide in 1974 following two earlier attempts on his own life. Platt's ashes were scattered in the Pacific. Marietta Canty, who plays Plato's nanny, and who stopped acting in 1951 to become a nurse at the Terry Steam Corporation in Hartford,

Connecticut, where the house she lived in bears both a plaque and an entry in Wikipedia ("The Marietta Canty House"), though the former actress herself rates no entry. The last name in the opening credits, Virginia Brissac, plays Dean/Stark's stern-faced, authoritarian grandmother whose portrait he kicks a hole in. Brissac made a career of playing stern-faced, authoritarian figures.

0:36
Of the second-tier supporting cast members one rates special mention: Nick Adams, who, following his bit role in "Rebel," became a poor man's James Dean and would eventually star in his own Civil War-based TV drama titled—coincidentally—*The Rebel*. While filming *Rebel* Adams had a crush on the film's star.

Like Plato/Mineo, Adams sacrificed his identity through adulation; he never shook the "poor man's James Dean" mantle. He died of an overdose in 1968. He was thirty-six years old.

0:38
As the last of the supporting actor's names fade, Dean/Stark snatches the toy monkey into his grip.

0:43
A few days after watching the movie, at an army surplus store on Canal Street, I bought a secondhand red vinyl windbreaker. I wore it half-zippered over a white undershirt, baggy Levis, and cowboy boots poorly suited to New York City winters. Because my curly hair refused to submit to a Deanish pompadour, I went into a barbershop and asked for a crew cut. With my hair shorn, dressed like Stark/Dean, for several weeks I operated under the assumption that my pretense wasn't as obvious as a shaving cream pie in the face.

Near the end of April, shivering in my out-of-season windbreaker, pacing the subway platform at Clinton-Washington while waiting for the train, next to my signature on a cartoon I'd doodled weeks earlier on an add for Bacardi Rum, someone had scrawled:

Formerly James Dean, presently Crew-Cut Charlie.

Who had written those words next to my name? A friend? An enemy? My roommate? Might T. Shirley herself have written them? Was she letting me know that she had seen through my pretense? Was she letting it be known to me and the entire subway riding world that I was a fool? Or had she, by virtue of having acknowledged my existence down there on that frigid subway platform, paid me an anonymous, underhanded compliment? Before I could decide, the graffiti-slathered subway train roared into the station.

0:47
The movie we are seeing has, we are told, been filmed in CINEMA-SCOPE and WARNERCOLOR, the word "CinemaScope" splayed across the screen, its letters iceasing in size as they spread out from the center, giving the phrase a panoramic quality.

The first process employed an anamorphic camera lens, one that "stretched" the image to project movies across a wide screen, shifting the aspect ratio from the industry standard of 1.37:1 to 2.66:1, thereby nearly doubling its horizontal width. The process was invented by Henri Chrétian, a French astronomer, and used from 1953 to 1967, when it was abandoned in favor of Panavision, a technology that employed two anamorphic elements instead of one, making it possible to keep the focal plane at a constant ratio of 2X, correcting the

so called "mumps" effect that stretched actor's faces in close-ups. However flawed, CinemaScope could not have found better use than in this opening scene, whose horizontal emphasis—Dean stretched across the pavement—is emphatic to begin with.

The inspiration for the scene wasn't CinemaScope; it was Édouard Manet's painting *Incident in a Bullfight*, known also as *The Dead Toreador*. First exhibited in the Salon of 1864, the painting aroused such derision that, according to the artist's friend Antonin Proust, Manet "boldly took a knife and cut out the figure of the dead toreador." In fact the cutting took place in the artist's studio after the Salon's rejection. Concurring with critics that the painting's perspective was off (the bull was too large) and its composition clumsy, Manet sliced the original painting into two sections and reworked them both, with *The Dead Toreador* resurrected from the lower two-thirds of the original.

The painting shows its subject splayed on his back on the ground, one lifeless hand bent around the sword on his chest, the other faintly gripping his magenta capote, a thin trickle of blood oozing from his left shoulder toward the bottom of the canvas. Among its most striking qualities are its proportions, 60 inches wide by 30 inches tall: a ratio of 2 to 1, inviting comparison with CinemaScope's aspect ratio of 2.66:1— especially if you allow for the fact that in most movie theaters in 1955 the actual dimensions of the screen were cut shorter, so what people usually saw was closer to the proportion of Manet's painting.

None of this was evident to James Dean, who liked *The Dead Toreador* for its subject matter, not its dimensions. Gang leader Buzz's nickname for Dean/Stark is "Toreador" ("What you waiting on, Toreador?"): an allusion to Dean's obsession with bullfighting and justified by Dean/Stark's calling out "Moo!" during the planetarium scene when the image of a bull is projected over the constellation Taurus. Afterwards, during the knife fight scene, Buzz refers to his rival as "Moo."

0:48
Why this pronounced, delayed, desperate need for heroes, i.e. to be someone—anyone—other than myself? Because I'm a twin? Because my parents fought? Because my father spanked me? Because I once saw my mother naked at the top of the stairs? Or was it the straightforward need to escape my own boundaries and not be stuck playing the severely limited role of "me" in which I'd been typecast since birth?

0:50
WarnerColor was the Warner Brothers brand name applied to the new "monopack" color stock produced by Eastman Kodak starting in the '50s. Unlike Technicolor, the color process that reigned supreme from the late 30s *(Gone With the Wind, The Wizard of Oz)* through the 1940's, and that required three separate strips of celluloid (cyan,

magenta, yellow), Eastmancolor and its derivatives kept all the colors on one strip. This and the fact that Technicolor took much longer to process and cost far more resulted in the latter's extinction from 1950 until 1972, when Francis Ford Coppola revived it for the first of the *Godfather* films, the last American films to use the system.

What Technicolor and WarnerColor shared is the surreal vividness of saturated hues, especially the reds (blood, warning, passion, danger) and greens, a vividness closer to dreams (for those who dream in color) than ordinary life, likened to the aftermath of cataract surgery.

Both processes also have in common the chemical instability that results in those vivid colors fading and turning blue, a problem that resulted in the degeneration of many classic films and would persist until 1983, when Eastman addressed it in its conservation methods.

0:51
As the violins soar to a fever pitch the screenwriters are credited, with "Screen Play by Stewart Stern" larger on top, and "Adaptation by Irving Schulman" and "From a Story by Nicholas Ray" in smaller type below.

In fact the "story," a sheaf of notes that Ray wrote and Schulman developed into a treatment, has nothing in common with the movie or even the final shooting script, which was largely inspired by Stern's friendship with James Dean. According to Stern, when he and Dean first met, "We were sitting there, just the two of us, and Jimmy started mooing like a cow. We went back and forth mooing." It was their "mooing" together that inspired the planetarium scene, the one where Dean/Stark moos at the constellation Taurus.

For conceiving the "original story" of *Rebel,* Nicholas Ray was nominated for an Academy Award. Subsequent appeals to Ray by Stern to credit him retrospectively went with the director—who died in 1979—to his grave.

0:58
The word *hero* comes from the Greek ἥρως (*hērōs*), "hero, warrior," particularly one with a divine ancestry. *Heros* shares its meaning with the Latin word *seruāre,* whose prefix, *ser,* means "to safeguard or protect." A hero is one who protects, a protector.

Who was I protecting if not myself *from* myself?

1:02
Another jacket plays its role in the film, another "mantle": the scrap of gift wrapping paper with which, as the credits continue to roll, Dean/Stark covers the monkey, turning it into a child that he tucks into bed (or into the fallout shelter, as the duck-and-cover films would have instructed him, arranging it in "a prone like position" and covering its exposed areas). Soon Dean/Stark and the toy monkey lie sprawled on the pavement together, huddled between DANGER and SECURITY.

1:03
A week after reading those words on the subway wall, coming home hours after midnight after a long day of shooting scenes for short subject film with a friend majoring in filmmaking, I was mugged by a street gang. They surrounded me, a dozen kids of different ages. I was

carrying a bag of Super 8 film stock and the movie camera. They beat me to the ground and pummeled my head and stomach as I lay there covering my face. One took my wallet from my pants. Then they ran off. For a while I lay there, in my red windbreaker, still clutching the movie camera, with the torn bag and rolls of exposed Super-8 film scattered around me.

To the opening theme music from *Rebel Without a Cause,* I put the camera down on the pavement and proceeded to cover it, protectively, with the torn paper bag.

1:05
Having covered the toy monkey, Dean/Stark pats its gift-wrapped belly. He tucks the gold ribbon under its head for a pillow. As the names of the Director of Photography, the Art Director, the Film Editor, the Sound Designer, the Set Director, the Costume Designer, the Makeup Supervisor, the Dialogue Supervisor, and the two Assistant Directors appear, Dean/Stark tucks *himself* in, curled up next to the doll with his hands ("exposed parts") tucked under his chin first before tucking them fetally between his knees.

1:06
Dangling from the fine print at the bottom of the screen, like baubles from a Christmas tree, are the logos of the International Alliance of Theatrical Stage Employees (I.A.T.S.E.), the Motion Picture Association of America (MPAA), and the Radio Corporation of America (RCA). These are soon usurped by the names of the Composer (for whom the violins screech extra loudly), the Producer, and, finally, the Director.

About director Nicholas Ray the less said the better. He's been given the last word, so to speak, after all. A talented director of whom Godard famously pronounced, "Le cinéma, c'est Nicholas Ray!", Ray was also an alcoholic depressive, a prescription drug addict, a compulsive gambler, and a bisexual misogynist as notorious for his afternoon trysts with underage actresses at his Hollywood bungalow as for the powerful films he directed.

1:08
After her freshman year T. Shirley left Pratt. No one seemed to know where she went. Like the warmer colors in those old Technicolor movies, with time my feelings for her faded, only to return full-force when, after ten years, I saw her again.

One winter afternoon, in the company of some friends I walked into the bar at One Fifth Avenue, where I found her shucking oysters. She wore a blue apron and gripped the shucking knife by its bulbous handle. She hadn't changed. The strawberry blonde hair, the bow-shaped lips, the dash of freckles ("atomic flecked"). I was no longer James Dean. I'd grown up, a bit.

I asked her: was she still painting? She pursed her bow-shaped lips and shook her head. She didn't elaborate. I waited for her to ask me what I'd been up to. She didn't. She went back to shucking oysters and

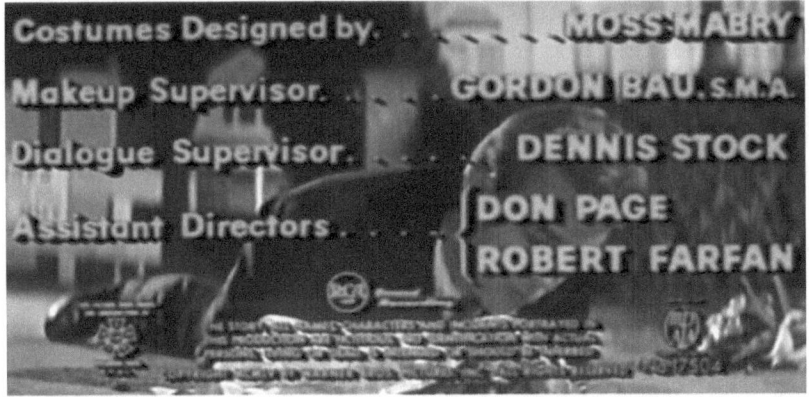

I re-joined my friends at the table where the hostess had seated them. On our way out of the restaurant, when I looked her way T. Shirley

was still shucking oysters. Either she didn't notice me leaving or she didn't care. Anyway, that was the last time I saw her.

1:12
Directorial credit for the opening scene should really go to James Dean, who, after 24 straight hours of shooting the scripted opening, with the cast and crew dead on its feet, approached Nick Ray with an idea. He had Ray put the cameramen down on the ground. Then he did the scene. According to actress Steffi Sidney (one of the members of Buzz' gang), it took Dean a dozen takes to get it right.

"He didn't go into the fetal position to begin with," she explained. "He just looked at the monkey."

Beverly Long, another cast member present that night (morning, actually, since they'd shot through the night) who watched the scene unfold from a few feet away, said, "We all sat there with tears in our eyes. It was so beautiful."

Dennis Hopper, also there, wondered, "Where did that come from?" only to answer his own question:

"It came from genius, that's where it came from."

1:22
In time I would shed my fixation with Dean and other movie heroes. I'd seek and find role models elsewhere, in writers and artists, mainly, and not so much in them as in their work. I'd take my inspiration from the dance rather than from the dancer. I'd come to realize that true heroes are defined by their actions, not their images.

Still, to this day whenever I see a poster or a movie still from *Rebel Without a Cause,* I'm back in New York City, back in Brooklyn. It's winter again, and I'm still in love with T. Shirley. I'm Dean/Stark shivering in my uninsulated scarlet windbreaker: the suffering, broken-hearted young man, mistaking his longing to forgive and accept himself for the need to be understood and accepted by others.

1:23
The credits role, violins soar, the Cold War rages. Before an invisible exhausted film crew on a chilly May morning pretending to be Easter a handsome twenty-four-year-old movie star sprawls on the pavement at Franklin and North Sierra Bonita, a wind-up monkey close at hand. His suffering is palpable as is his yearning for love. Cold and alone, in embracing himself he embraces us all.
   Total running time: One minute and twenty-four seconds.

❖ *Some Field Notes on Setting*

I write this at a café in the Piazza del Pantheon, Rome, on a dreary winter's day. Clouds hang low over Hadrian's temple to the Gods, that ancient granite eyeball open to the skies. I'm thinking of setting, of how it not only informs and colors our lives as well as those of fictional characters, it helps to create them. No wine without the glass, they say. And no story without a setting.

Even this essay has its setting, the café where I sit writing these words at a small round table veiled in blue and yellow linens, the yellow like butter, the blue of an evening sky. From the gaping mouths of stone fish spew the waters of the fountain in front of the Pantheon—one of the fountains in the slapdash oil paintings my father, a skillful and dedicated Sunday painter, did, and that lined the walls of my childhood home.

Setting follows us everywhere, a tune so catchy it hums us.

I have planted myself here with the resoluteness of a weed. You can do that in Roman cafés. I've come here with no idea what, exactly, I intend to write.

Whatever I write, it will be informed by this wobbly table; by these linens; by the lingering sweetness of the cappuccino I drank a little while ago, its residue brown and crusty and clinging to the cup; by the Pantheon's blackened columns; and by the fountain whose waters, on this grim, damp day, feel redundant. I write with the sense that I have been and will be here forever, glued to this spot, as fixed to it as the columns of the Pantheon to theirs: ancient and inviolate.

I grew up in two countries, the Europe inside my childhood home and the America outside of it. Inside were dusty books in foreign languages crammed onto shelves, along with my father's slapdash paintings of fountains and statues. Outside were baseball diamonds, white picket fences, and woods. Inside was the dust of the Old World (not that my mother failed to keep a clean and tidy house; this was the dust of centuries that no amount of Pledge could eradicate); outside were five-and-dime stores and the ruins of hat factories.

Tucked into a corner of the house, Nonnie, my grandmother, my father's mother (Giulia Senigalia, née Treves), kept her own equivalent of an apartment. There the essence of old Europe was even more distinct, a heady compound of naphthalene from the mothballs rolling around in her linen drawers, lavender, and dried cat urine (a mystery since Nonnie kept no cats). As if to prove that this was Europe and not North America, Nonnie kept a bronze miniature statue of Romulus and Remus, the twin founders of Rome. My brother George and I are twins. *"Questo e Giorgio, e questo e Piero,"* Nonnie would say, pointing to each of us in turn and to the twins sucking at the she-wolf's teats.

In a sense the city of Rome founded me. It and Italy, the country that went with it, the country where both of my parents were from, coursed through my blood. I was eight when we crossed the Atlantic by passenger ship and finally got to see the place. Though too young to appreciate much beyond *gelato nocciola,* the filigreed labels on tall bottles of *acqua minerale,* and bicycles with convoluted handlebars, still, I stood transfixed before the cortiles (courtyards) of Piacenza, gazing through their locked iron gates at weeping-willow trees and marble Venus statues—some real, others painted on walls. Through those barred gates the courtyards stretched infinitely toward some dreamy Elysium, simultaneously promising and withholding heaven. In Italy, every surface was cracked and pitted or burnished smooth as if kissed by an infinite series of lips. Voices bounded off those broken walls like organ notes off a cathedral's vaulted ceiling. Even the doves sounded different, cooing in Italian, saying, *"Ma basta, ma basta"* (translation: "Cut it out!"). Birds, trees, bicycles, flowers, bricks, doves: all seemed happier here. And I loved that everything was ancient and wise and dusty, like my grandmother.

Back home, environment exerted its own influences. The house I grew up in sat on a Connecticut hillside with its back to the woods. I spent a lot of time in those woods. They were dark and Dante-esque, but they were also my best friend, always willing to play with me. I'd hike up to the bald patch of rocks we called Eagle's Nest. From there you could see the whole town, a valley packed with abandoned hat factories, their smokestacks pointing like brick fingers into the sky. I'd take a deep breath and as run fast as I could down the mountainside, leaping like a gazelle over rocks and fallen trees: it's a miracle I didn't break my neck. Like Peter Pan, I could fly, but only downhill in the woods. As soon as my feet crossed the property line into our back yard, my magical powers evaporated. Those woods, they were my real home, as was the Italy annexed in Nonnie's corner room.

I think of Saul Bellow's beloved New York and Chicago, of the skyscrapers he described as "monuments of [men's] mystery," of his transit buses spewing poisonous bouquets of vapors. Bellow's descriptive prowess was such that he could render a kitchen sink so well you could pour water into the description. No writer has done more justice to America's cities than Bellow, who faithfully translated their magnificence and their meanness, their generosity and cruelty. A Chicago morning, Bellow-style, from *Dangling Man,* his first novel:

> In the upper light there were small fair heads of cloud turning. The streets, in contrast, looked burnt-out; the chimneys pointed heavenward in openmouthed exhaustion. The turf, intersected by sidewalk, was bedraggled with the whole winter's deposit of deadwood, match cards, cigarettes, dogmire, rubble. The grass behind the palings and wrought-iron frills was still yellow, although in many places the sun had already succeeded in shaking it into a livelier green. And the houses, their doors and windows open, drawing in the freshness, were like old drunkards or consumptives taking a cure.

In Saul Bellow's hands, like patients on a tuberculosis ward the opened windows of a tenement yawn in great gulps of tainted air. A clump of weeds rising from a rubbled lot invites as much pity as any foundling in Dickens. In most if not all great descriptions, the pathetic fallacy is courted if not engaged outright, with cities in particular having always been comparable to the people who crowd them, with all their charms, aspirations, flaws and blemishes.

A flashing neon Schlitz or Blatz sign in a bar window draws sympathy from Nelson Algren. His blinking neons bleed. In Algren's hands even shadows and air have feelings:

> There through the starless night or the thunderous noon, sunlight or rain or windless cold, she would sit till the tenement's long shadows moved all the way down from the fourth floor rear, slid silently under her door and drifted across her lap, to tremble one moment at still finding her there and then lie comforted and still. While all the air hung wearily.

Sometimes interior and exterior landscapes are so inextricably linked it's hard to say which is more real. Is the Mexico in *Under the Volcano,* Malcolm Lowry's phantasmagorical masterpiece, the setting of the drunken consul's deliriums, or the result of them?

In Joyce's *Ulysses* the characters live in cities of thought, with the map of Dublin identical to that of Leopold Bloom's brain. The plot of that novel couldn't be simpler: two men of different pedigrees and generations crossing a city in opposite directions, meeting halfway. Yet the inventory of sensual phenomena borne by their dual streams-of-consciousness could not be more exhaustive. Joyce didn't plot his masterpiece so much as he connived it as a means of recovering the Dublin he'd turned his back on as a young man, and which he spent much of the rest of his life reconstructing, pub by paving stone, using words. With the possible exception of Faulkner and his Yoknapatawpha County, no author ever made a setting more completely his own.

Compare Joyce to Dostoevsky, whose novels are so wanting for atmosphere that—while his characters beat each other's Slavic brows—one searches in vain for a piece of furniture to sit on. With Dostoevsky, talk isn't cheap, but it is in infinite supply, and readers in search of a breeze or a sofa may as well search for oxygen on Mars.

(A Vespa splutters by, its driver clutched by his lover who clings to him from behind. A busload of tourists gathers to be photographed in front of the Pantheon's skyward-facing marble eyeball. The jacketed waiter brings me another cappuccino, my third ...)

The same atmospheric stinginess has a paradoxical effect in Hemingway's stories and novels. The less lush his descriptions, the greater their impact. How did Hemingway do it? If he washes a freshly-caught trout in a clear rushing stream, you feel the water so frigid your fingertips grow numb. In *A Moveable Feast,* when at Le Select (his favorite Parisian café) he drinks down oysters with ice-cold wine, you feel the cold against the back of your throat:

> As I ate the oysters with their strong taste of the sea and their faint metallic taste that the cold wine washed away, leaving only the sea taste and the succulent texture, and as I drank their cold liquid from each shell and washed it down with the crisp taste of the wine, I lost the empty feeling and began to be happy and to make plans.

In this passage from a mean-spirited posthumous memoir that happens to hold some of Papa's best prose, atmosphere is so well evoked it can give you an ice-cream headache. Yet the feelings are evoked by things themselves, not by an author's wish to sanctify or glorify them. Like all good writers, Hemingway avoids sentimentality, privledging concrete experiences over feelings.

Great stories are joined to their settings. The fogged-in London of Bleak House, Marjorie Kinnan Rawling's creeks and bayous, the Marabar Caves in *A Passage to India,* the coffin-shaped gondolas in *Death in Venice,* the bureaucratic metropolis of Kafka's unfinished *The Trial* ... Were he writing his speculative fictions now that we've torn the lids off both inner and outer space, what sort of settings would Jules Verne choose?

As a whole, settings are an endangered species: Forests burn; glaciers melt. Aside from its tattoo and pizza parlors, small-town America is no more, replaced by one great mall as in Nicholson Baker's *The Mezzanine,* where several hundred pages are given to a voyage up an escalator. The last few decades have served up a slew of minimalist fictions exploring nihilism and ennui, fictions in which settings are distilled down to and codified by brand names of clothing and burger franchises. It's not the writers style that have gone generic, but the world: McSetting. In such sandy soil can great stories survive, let alone thrive?

The streets of my hometown were equal parts dangerous and drowsy, heavy with boredom, suspicion, and conformity. We Bethel boys pedaled our bikes endlessly, ducking into the town hall to slurp ice-cold water from the drinking fountain there, around which we converged like truth seekers around an oracle. Or we'd sit atop May Hill, the cliff overlooking a former hat factory that had been converted into a bicycle-seat company, breaking off chunks of cheesy limestone and hurling them onto the reject shed's corrugated tin roof, forcing the security guard to exit his little white shack and shake his fist up at us, thus temporarily relieving our abysmal boredom. God, were we bored! Bored and Bethel. They were synonyms. We longed for the coming Apocalypse, for the fuel oil storage tanks arrayed along the railroad tracks to ignite and suck the whole town into a fireball. We'd set imaginary C-4 (plastic) explosives along the railroad tracks and do the job ourselves—like Burt Lancaster in *The Train*, or William Holden in *The Bridge on the River Kwai*. To the promise of heaven held out by those dreamy Piacentine courtyards, my hometown's landscape of violence-inducing boredom stood in severe contrast. Such were the dual landscapes of my divided nature: destructive and contemplative, deadly and dreamy, bountifully bored.

In her essay entitled "The Nature and Aim of Fiction," Flannery O'Connor writes, "The writer operates at a peculiar crossroads where time and place and eternity somehow meet. His problem is to find the location." Where and when would my dueling landscapes feel at home?

For a time the jumble of foreign accents and bumpy cobbled streets of New York City came closest. As a child, I'd visit there with my papa on his so-called "business" trips; only years later would I learn that he kept more than one mistress there. We stayed at the Hotel Paris on West 96th, where the elevator operator let me man the controls. The city was modern and old, its hydrants and fireboxes layered with thick coats of grimy time, its skyscrapers leaping into the future, the subway's roar as fierce, damp, and rank as a lion's, the Empire State Building lit up at night like a Christmas tree, filling me with a child's categorical delight. And yet—though New York was where I'd live for thirty-six years and where I've felt the most at home—it no more qualifies as the "peculiar crossroads" of which O'Connor speaks than the Rome I'm sitting in now, at this café fronting the Pantheon, writing these words that you are reading.

Whether or not we are writers, each of us in his or her own way is searching for that ultimate setting—not just the setting of our stories, but one for our souls, for a place to hang our existential hats. Maybe that crossroads doesn't exist; maybe it never existed, not in physical time and space, anyway. Maybe that setting can't be pinned down by degrees of longitude and latitude. Maybe it can only be pinned down with a pencil or pen (or their equivalent).

It may be, too, that the only place a writer can ever safely feel at home is the place where dreams and ideas meet, where thoughts turn into words, sentences, paragraphs and scenes, where moods, inspirations, and feelings are as fixed as the stars in the firmament:

A sheet of paper, the ultimate setting for all our stories.

❖ *The Bones of Love*

"To be taken in everywhere is to see the inside of everything. It is the hospitality of circumstance." —G.K. Chesterton

BEFORE THE FLOOD, BEFORE THE HURRICANE, before AIDS and Katrina … before iPhones and iPads … before stem cells and global warming … before that vast polluted well of human knowledge known as the Internet … before the Twin Towers crumpled to dust and the polar caps melted and the world picked up its heretofore plodding pace toward doom … when cross-country hitchhiking was still possible however not recommended, you stood by the highway. The James Dean type, your personal manager opined, "but with an Italian twist." The same manager suggested that you change your surname, offering alternatives to the one on your driver's license, an instrument of Connecticut issue gone now along with your wallet and backpack. You made the hitchhiker's semaphore. Behind you a green sign wavered in the swampy air:

New Orleans: 68 mi.

You hadn't meant to go to New Orleans. You hadn't meant to go anywhere, in particular. Shortly after your twenty-second birthday, having quit New York and along with it your so-called acting career, you moved back into your parents' home in Connecticut, where you spent your days running circles around the high school track, and evenings watching reruns of *Hawaii Five-O* and *M*A*S*H*. Two months of this and you realized you would have to do something with your life, or end it. So you hit the road.

Along with your backpack—the one the smoke alarm salesman from Oswego drove off with while you emptied your bladder at a Dixie

Truck Stop—you carried a phrase, a mantra bestowed upon you by a recurrent dream: *Be at life's mercy.* You carried it all the way from Norwalk, where you gained your first ride, to beyond Baton Rouge, where you stood now in the heat-undulated air. You carried it the way some people carry their hopes, fears, and regrets. It came with its own music, this mantra, this earworm: Mahler's *Kindertotenleider* played on a scratchy record. *Be at life's mercy ... Be at life's mercy ...*

A retired pediatrician driving a rusted Cutlass conveyed you to the French Quarter where, on a side street off Canal, your found a hotel. The bulky neon sign spelled "LeDale" in broken neon tubes and peeling paint. To get to what passed for a lobby, you had to step over several prone bodies. The human blowfish behind the Plexiglas check-in booth informed you that a room cost ten dollars per night, a bunk bed half as much. Out of a last twenty rolled into your left sock you paid for a bunk, then left to partake of the sights.

At sundown the French Quarter was just coming alive. You added yourself to the tourist throngs on Bourbon Street. With its carnival-colored lights and shops selling trinkets and sexual paraphernalia, the Quarter put you in mind of a toy-scale Times Square, stirring up in you a nostalgia for the city you once called home and the dreams of glory you'd abandoned there. In the threshold of a jazz joint you stood letting the wailing notes of a saxophone squirm over you. Your reflection in the neon-tinted glass did indeed put you in mind of James Dean, a comparison reinforced by the catcalls that rained down from the fancy wrought iron grillwork overhead and that in your egoism you supposed were meant for you. If you searched for yourself in mirrors, it was only because you failed to find yourself there.

Back at the LeDale, a quartet of bare bulbs cast their subaqueous glow across two rows of bunk beds. A standing fan shoved swelter and boozesweat from wall to wall. As you pried off your cowboy boots and socks, the man in the bunk next to yours slid open one bloodshot eye and smiled. A cockroach skittered over your toes.

No sooner did you fall sleep than you dreamed "the dream." You stood atop a mountain, but not really. Really you were in the living room of a garish Hell's Kitchen apartment, its walls flocked with red velvet *fleurs-de-lis*. A rumbling Teutonic voice instructed you to imagine a canopy of stars. The same voice urged you to reach for one star, the brightest, nearest, and dearest of them. *Hyoo ken, hyoo ken, hyoo ken!* ... How you tried to touch that nearest and brightest of stars! But you couldn't; you failed. You were a disappointment, a bad boy, a very bad boy. You had to be punished ... you needed to be punished. From the dream you awoke drenched in sweat for which the hot night bore only part of the blame.

Be at life's mercy ... Be at life's mercy ...

It took you less than an hour to land a job. The Café du Monde was one of several cafes fronting the Mississippi, with marble-topped tables, wrought-iron chairs, and stucco walls that melted, or seemed to, like vanilla ice cream under the tropical sun. Long ago someone had dubbed it the Cafe Doomed. Ever since its employees referred to it by its proper name only when the owners were within earshot.

Curly, the headwaiter, his skull crowned with a sprig of red hair, showed you the ropes. The waiters collected their orders of beignets (airy doughnuts shaped like pillows, sprinkled with powdered sugar) on plastic trays, then paid the cashier from their own pockets before filling cups with thick, chicory-laced coffee and steamed milk, and carrying them to their customers, who reimbursed them.

"That way," said Curly, "anyone bolts, you're out of luck."

Three hours into your first shift, you took your first break. You sat at an empty corner table, about to bite into a free beignet, when another waiter sat down opposite you: a short, skinny man with a tall glossy forehead and an imposing handlebar mustache.

"Curly says you hitched all the way from Connecticut," he said. You nodded.

"Lord, you could've gotten yourself killed — what with that innocent face of yours!"

The skinny waiter sniggered. With his drooping mustache and a gold hoop earring in one ear he put you in mind of a shrunken pirate. In the mirror of his glossy forehead a ceiling fan twirled.

He lit a Gauloises. "You wouldn't by any chance be in need of a place to *shtay?*" A gap between his front teeth made him sound drunk, which, in retrospect, he probably was. "I'm looking for a roommate. I gave the old one the boot." His sniggers broke into coughs.

There were times — this being one of them — when you wished you were less attractive to homosexual men. You gazed up at a ceiling fan.

"My place is no Taj Mahal, but it sure as hell beats the LeDale."

You wondered how the shrunken pirate learned you were staying there, then remembered having scrawled "Hotel LeDale" next to the word "address" on the job application.

"The rent's only twenty a week. If that's not too much for you."

It was half what they were charging for a bunk among hacking, sweaty, toothless, sordid strangers.

"My name is Donald, but most everyone calls me Don." He held out a small, damp, tentative hand. "If you're interested, I can show you my place after work."

Like wet marbles the pirate's beady eyes skidded off yours.

With a nod from Curly your break ended.

At dusk you and Don left the cafe. As you passed the register Curly grabbed you by the sleeve of your white waiter's uniform.

"Watch out for Sherman," he said sotto-voce.

Before Curly could say anything more, Don said, "Mind your own business!" and pulled you the rest of the way out of the cafe.

An afternoon shower had left the streets steaming. Cobblestones gleamed. The air reeked of tidal muck and dead fish. Flowing to your left, the Mississippi looked remarkably like the *cafe au lait* you'd been serving all day. Downriver on the Natchez wharf the calliope played. "Sounds like a drunken teakettle," Don said with a snigger. You passed a series of cast iron gates, each gate locking in its miseries and mysteries. In front of a narrow green one Don fished out his keys.

"I always make sure to keep this gate locked," he said. "There's a certain element that I've been trying to discourage."

You followed him down an alleyway lined with tin pans piled with mostly chicken bones. "The landlord's daughter," Don explained. "She's always feeding the neighborhood strays. I tell her don't feed 'em chicken bones, only she won't listen. More cats have died of her generosity than of all natural causes combined."

The alley opened to a courtyard bounded by cracked stucco walls decked with drooping geraniums in earthenware pots. There was an umbrella shade table minus its umbrella. Everywhere air conditioners thrummed and wheezed, the sound of New Orleans breathing. A set of wooden stairs mounted to a bruise-colored door sealed with a padlock.

"I always try to keep this door locked, too," Don said, unlocking it. "Even when I'm at home. I lock it from the outside, then climb back in through the balcony window. Just an added precaution."

The bruise-colored door released a chilled ectoplasm of soap, tea, and vinegar: clean, domestic smells. You stood in a room scarcely large enough to hold a folding table and two chairs. There was a small refrigerator and a two-burner hotplate. A towel lay neatly draped over the faucet. The counter sparkled. A colorful curtain of Mardi Gras beads divided the kitchen from the bedroom. With a flourish Don parted it.

"*Shtep* through my rainbow!"

The bedroom was entirely taken up by one queen-sized bed. You looked down at it, then up at Don.

"It's true," Don said. "There's just the one bed. But it's big and I'm small. I'm sure we'll both fit."

To have left then would have made perfect sense. To have shouted one or several colorful oaths and stormed out, slamming the bruise-colored door, would have been entirely understandable under the circumstances. Instead, you weighed your options. There were arguments of substance for not rejecting the shrunken pirate's offer out of hand. The LeDale was by no means more prepossessing than the shrunken pirate's dwelling. Multiplied by bunks, it was at least a dozen times as dreary, dirty, and dangerous. Your one night there, you'd hardly slept. When not dreaming of mountains and stars you lay awake imagining a series of rusty razor blades being dragged across your throat. Here at least you would know what you were up against. And the shrunken pirate looked harmless. Worse come to worst, you could easily fend him off. You tested the mattress. It yielded softly to your touch.

"Well?" said the shrunken pirate. "What do ya say?"

Be at life's mercy ... Be at life's mercy ...

No sooner did your head touch the pillow that Don put in a fresh case and plumped for you than you dreamed the dream. Once again the Teutonic voice exhorted: *Hyoo ken, hyoo ken, hyoo ken can!* From the dream you opened your eyes to the shrunken pirate's head bobbing in the gloom above your groin. "God*dammit!*" you said, shoving him so hard he fell into the crack between bed and wall.

"I am *sho, sho shorry,*" Don spoke from the crack as you searched for your socks. "Please—forgive me."

"Where are my socks? What the heck did you do with them?"

"I gave them a wash. Your blue jeans, too. They're hanging on the shower rod. I didn't think you would mind."

As the air conditioner thrummed and you struggled to put on the damp socks, Don said, "I dreamed that you were my very own private angel fallen out of the clear blue sky. White wings you had—like a swan's. One of your wings was broken. I tried to mend it for you. Then I tucked you in bed and lied down next to you, and then—well, I guess you already know what happened next." All this he said from down there in the crack. You told him to get out of there.

"I'd like to, but I'm afraid I'm stuck."

You helped him out. "Please," he said as you did. "Don't leave. I'll *die* if you leave. I swear I won't ever touch you again. I won't lay a finger on you. You can knock all my teeth out if I do. I'll insist on it."

Raindrops snapped against the air conditioner's casing.

"All right," you said, getting back into bed. "But don't try anything funny again. I mean it."

"Thank you, Lord," said Don to his ceiling.

From there on things improved. As if to make up for his transgression Don darned your socks, laundered your clothes, cooked meals for you—hash and eggs, chili con carne, ravioli and baked beans from a can. You'd come home from the café to his notes on the kitchen table:

Dear Peter,
  I put the toilet tissue in the bathroom. The bottle of Joy is on the sink, the bottle of Pinesol is under the kitchen sink & so are the trash bags in case you want to use them for a laundry bag but double them up for your laundry because they're a little thin. I didn't have time to wash the rugs today so another day won't hurt them. The outside light and the tv doesn't work so please do not plug them in. ok? Also don't forget there is a nice steak in the freezer if you want to have it before I get home. See you tonight at about 11:30 or so?

  —Donald

Don refused to let you pay rent, insisting that you save it toward a plane ticket home when the time came. "Over my dead body will I let you hitchhike again. I'm just glad to have you here with me, is all. You're the best roommate I ever had." He said it with a twinkle in his eyes and a grin on his face that broke through his droopy mustache.

In return for his hospitality, Don asked only that you observe the farcical ritual of keeping the door padlocked from outside. You would climb through the bedroom window onto the balcony, replace the padlock, then reenter through the bedroom window, closing it behind you so that the air conditioner could do its job.

"Just who are you expecting, anyway?" you asked.

"Please, just do as I ask. It's my one request."

"It doesn't make much sense. I mean whoever this person is, sooner or later he'll figure out that you're home."

"Humor me, please."

"Okay, but if you ask me it's ridiculous."

"Friend, you're not in Connecticut anymore."

On the cork wall behind the bed were tacked postcards, napkin drawings, and photographs, among them a faded snapshot of a boy, age eight or so. It might have been Don as a boy, but you didn't think so. He was too nice-looking, and the photo didn't seem old enough.

Don insisted that you write home to your parents. "Drop them a postcard now and then, at least." He even furnished the cards, touristic ones of Bourbon Street all lit up at night, and stamps to go with them. Though you complied, you resented this reminder of the past that you had gone to such great lengths to forget, a past that shamed you, that existed for no greater purpose than to tie you to your failings and remind you that, despite all those years of struggling in New York City, you were still a naïve, vulnerable, sensitive kid from Connecticut. No wonder you were never cast in certain roles. You never could play tough guys convincingly. Always your vulnerability got in the way. It didn't help that the one time your father attended one of your plays, a community theater production of *Camelot* in which you'd been cast as Lancelot, to the strains of you singing "If Ever I Would Leave You" his Promethean snores had filled the theater.

And though you got along pretty well with your fellow waiters at the cafe—graying gay men, mostly—you had to endure their ceaseless teasing. Thanks to the cowboy boots that you wore, they christened you "the Connecticut cowboy"—the joke stretched to eight syllables by their exaggerated Southern drawls. An Eden of private schools and white picket fences, such was their notion of your home state, a place as exotic and unreal to them as Oz. Your efforts to explain that you grew up among the ruins abandoned hat factories and attended public school fell on deaf ears. You were their prep-school angel, their great white hope descended from the Connecticut clouds. Though the greatest role you had ever landed had been in an off-Broadway equity waiver production that went straight nowhere, to your fellow waiters at the Cafe Doomed you were a star—albeit a fallen, bruised one.

As the summer days melted one into another, your memories of New York melted with them. New Orleans was your home now. You fell in love with the Quarter. You loved the cobblestone streets and those sudden, fish-stinking afternoon rain showers. You loved the river that snaked through the city, with its coffee and estuary smells. You got to like the shrunken pirate, too, this strange mustached man who treated you so kindly and whom you came to trust and care about.

You'd been working at the Café Doomed for a month when, coming home one evening, you saw the green gate swinging open. The tin pans lining the alley were upset, their chicken bone offerings scattered. In the courtyard you saw Don, shirtless, clutching a wilted geranium in his mouth, tangoing himself from wall to wall. Stepping closer, you saw the dark bruise over his eye, its color matching the front door that, likewise, was flung open. He smiled at you as you stood there, watching him, frozen until, disgusted, you retraced your steps back to the street. You spent the next two hours in a bar, writing in the notebook you'd been keeping and thanks to which you no longer thought of yourself as a failed actor but as a fledgling author. When you returned, Don lay sprawled across the bed covers, one bony arm dangling over its side, its finger pointing at a yellow bead on the floor. Near it was another bead, this one red, and another, green. The floor was strewn with colored beads. The curtain was torn, the rainbow scattered. A trickle of blood ran from Don's nose onto the bedspread.

You shook him awake.

"What happened? Who did this to you?"

"It was an accident. I fell in the shower."

"Bullshit! Someone did this. Who?"

"Mind your own business."

Through the strings that were all that remained of the curtain you entered the kitchen. An empty wine bottle sat on the table next to an equally empty tumbler. Normally, Don tried to hide his drinking from you. You'd waken to the sounds of ice being cracked from a tray, and open your eyes to the shadow-play of him lifting a tumbler projected on the kitchen wall. Some mornings he would be so hungover you'd have to help him into his waiter clothes and half-carry him to the cafe, where you'd ply him with cup after cup of *cafe au lait*. Six hours later, when his shift ended, somehow he'd still be drunk, and you'd have to half-carry him back home.

One evening, as you half-carried your roomate home, a sudden rain shower fell, one of those five-minute jobs that left the Quarter steamy and stinking of mud and fish. As the clouds cleared, in the sky above the river the full moon gleamed, as bright as a Mardi Gras bead. A breeze wrinkled the surface of a puddle.

"Goddamned *shitty*," Don muttered as you helped him along. "Whole place is nothing but a goddamn swamp. Can't even get buried here. They have to put people in mausoleums to keep them from floating away. Not that I blame 'em for trying. ..."

You arrived at the gate and had gotten out your key when Don grabbed hold of your wrist. Together you peered through the bars of the gate. At the far end of the alley, a man straddled the stucco wall. He wore the gray blouse of a Confederate uniform, its sleeves shorn, its shoulders stained with rain. In the dim light you watched him twirl a wooden cane while kicking the heels of his bare feet against stucco. Catching you watching him he smiled.

"Who is that?" you wondered.

"Better let me handle this," said Don.

"Is that the guy? The one you're so afraid of?"

Suddenly sober, Don took your set of keys from you.

"Come back in an hour," he said, looking through the gate.

"You sure?"

Don nodded and kept looking. "I'm sure."

Having nowhere else to go, you went to the café, to find Curly there in the rear entryway, blowing smoke rings into the dim, wet air.

"What gives, Connecticut?"

"I have no idea."

"Something up with Don?"

You explained.

"Warned you."

Curly offered you a cigarette. You didn't smoke, but took it anyway. Like most actors you found props irresistible. Together you and the bald headwaiter watched the moon, duller now over the river.

"Don ever tell you his story? How I found him behind the café?"

You shook your head.

"He was living in Detroit. Married. Working for Kaiser Aluminum. On Wednesday nights he played poker with his pals. They weren't his pals. They just liked fleecing him at poker. He wasn't like them, if you catch my drift. Maybe that's why he was so desperate to get them to accept him. One morning after a game his wife, she finds him asleep at the table covered with cards and chips. She lays into him, calling him a brown-nosed loser, and so forth. He starts blubbering. While blubbering he looks up and sees his kid watching him from the bannister."

"Don has a *kid?*"

"Shannon. Must be around your age by now. Anyway that's when he lost it. He hauled off and belted his wife. Broke her nose. She took everything—the house, the car. Shannon. He packed a duffle bag, got on the first bus leaving town, and came here. The LeDale? Your hotel? Don stayed there. Tried to join the Merchant Marine. Practically drank himself to death waiting for his sea card. When his money ran out, he took to sleeping between the pair of dumpsters behind the café. That's where I found him: eating stale beignets, begging cigarettes. I took him home, cleaned him up, gave him a job. Ever since he's hated my guts."

"Sherman—is that... his *son?*"

Curly shook his head. "Shannon's his son. Sherman's his former roommate."

You attempted to blow out a smoke ring. The wavering O ruined its way into the night air. With a cowboy boot heel you smashed the cigarette butt. "I should be getting back," you said.

"I wouldn't if I were you. You can stay at my place tonight."

"I'm not afraid."

"That's because you don't know what's to be afraid of."

"He doesn't look all that dangerous."

"Who, Sherman?" Curly shook his head. "He's not an actor; this isn't an audition. He's already got the part."

❖

You'd walked less than a block when you heard what sounded like distant artillery and turned to see fireworks exploding in chrysanthemum blooms across the river. You'd forgotten it was the Fourth of July.

You found Don asleep. Before getting into bed yourself, you studied the snapshot on the wall. It seemed incredible to you that the beautiful boy could have been Don's son, was *still* Don's son, assuming that he existed. You wondered how long it had been since Don had last seen him? As long as the photo was old, probably. By now its towheaded subject was neither towheaded nor a boy.

As you lay next to Don, having switched off the lamp, you reflected on how much you yourself had changed in the past two months. No longer were you the vulnerable innocent kid from Connecticut, no longer the sweet, sensitive, naïve boy. You were a man now, fit at last to play a hero or a villain. In spite of which when the dream came (and it did; it always did), there you were again, in the casting agent's home, on that imaginary mountaintop, reaching for the brightest and nearest of stars. You were reaching for it when a rapping sound woke you.

Open up, Motherfucker!

Both you and Don sprang up in the bed.

It's raining, goddammit! Lemme in!

Don asked: "Did you put the padlock on the door?"

You shook your head. You had forgotten.

"Lord."

Don got out of bed and put on his jeans. The rapping sound grew louder. Don put on his shirt. You asked:

"What are you doing?"

"Letting him in. What else can I do?"

"Don't!"

"I have to. He'll break the door down."

"Hide," you suggested. "In the bathroom. I'll get rid of him."

"Sherman is not easily gotten rid of."

"Just do it!" The force of conviction in your voice took even you by surprise. A smile wormed its way underneath Don's mustache. "My angel," he said. "Have it your way." With a snigger he stepped into the bathroom and locked it from inside.

In the kitchen drawer you found a paring knife. You shoved it into the pocket of the black waiter's pants you had thrown on. The rapping noise—wood on wood—circled the balcony to the bedroom window, where it ceased. The silence was punctured by a burst of shattering glass. In fear and fascination you watched as, like a very thin snout, the tip of a wooden cane entered, followed by a bare, filthy foot, followed by a rain-soaked, denim-clad leg. Soon all of Sherman stood in the bedroom, in a puddle of broken glass. From the buttons of the Confederate uniform blouse with its sleeves shorn rainwater dripped. He blew a party noisemaker.

"Happy Fourth of Joo-lie!"

You sized up your adversary. Though you were about the same height, his shoulders were broader and less sloped. His thicker forearms were laced with tattoos. In each of his pupils twin gassy stove flames burned. He was dirty; he exuded filth. He smelled of hot buttered popcorn and b.o.. Aside from a pale worm of a scar wriggling from the corner of one eye to the edge of his lip, the rest of his face was the brown of pottery glazed and fired under a Southwestern sun. In his way he, too, resembled James Dean, but a dirty, mean James Dean.

"So—you're Donald's new roommate, huh? From Connecticut? Where'd you meet Donald Fuck, hmm? Cafe? He ask you if you needed a *playsh* to *shtay?*" He hummed a radio frequency from Mars and appeared to be stoned. You felt for the knife in your pocket.

"What is it you want?"

"Where's the motherfucker?"

"Don's not here."

"Motherfucker …" He slid past you and into the kitchen, where he rummaged in the refrigerator. "Fourth of *Joo-lie* and motherfucker's got no fuckin' beer. Hmmmm…"

He settled for Coca-Cola. With his cane propped against a chair he sat down, his bare and bleeding feet on the table. You stood before him, clenching and unclenching your fists. Hands were always a problem; actors never knew what to do with them. Sherman wiped blood off his foot with a finger, brought the finger to his lips, and licked it. As he did, you recalled a scene from *Rebel Without a Cause,* the one at the Griffith observatory, where James Dean is harassed by a gang of switchblade-wielding goons. What happened exactly you couldn't remember, but somehow James Dean prevailed. You pulled the paring knife. As you held it in your grip it Sherman eyed it with the curious contempt of an adolescent boy examining a worm in a terrarium.

"Gonna stick me with that? Huh?"

Having risen from the chair, he hiked up his Confederate blouse, exposing a washboard belly that he brought to within an inch of the knife's blade. "Go on, then: stick me. *Stick me!*"

You stood there.

"That case, put it away, or someone's gonna get hurt. Hmmm …"

He sat down again and lit one of Don's cigarettes. As its fumes filled the kitchen, you felt your insides grow hollow. The hollow feeling penetrated your bones, sucking the marrow from them. A prickly heat washed over you, and with it the memory you had tried unsuccessfully for the better part of a year to suppress. There you were, in the casting agent's living room, standing before him in his satin bathrobe on his white sofa, the red *fleur-de-lis* papered walls engulfing you like a fence made out of burning pitchforks. You had been told to beware of the casting agent, that he was "a slime bucket of the first order." But then you were also told that if he liked you, you'd be made. So, with the heavy drapes drawn, the lights dimmed, and Mahler's *Kindertotenleider* playing on the stereo, with the Teutonic voice coaxing you, you reached for that star—the nearest, the brightest, the most beautiful and alluring of all of the stars in the firmament. *Hyoo ken, hyoo ken, hyoo ken*—But you couldn't; your arms were too short; you were too weak. You had failed. *Hits obeless. You are ze saddest, ze loneliest boy in ze world, a liddle boy at ze merzy of vorces much bigger zan you. Zurrender to zose vorces, put yorzelf at zeir merzy. Be at live's merzy; be at live's merzy ...*

Grabbing his cane, Sherman lurched to the bathroom and pounded its door with it. "Motherfucker, get your skinny fag ass out of there!"

The bathroom door burst open and Don stormed out. Snatching the Gauloises from Sherman's lips he flung it to the floor.

"Stop smoking my cigarettes! Stop bringing me dead flowers!"

"Shut the fuck up, motherfucker!"

"Leave my place alone!"

"Dance with me, shit for brains!"

"No!"

"Shut the fuck up and dance!"

As you stood watching, still gripping the paring knife, with an Apache glare in his eyes Don's former roommate bent him back into a tango, saying: *"Whose your best goddamn roommate, huh, Don?"* Through his droopy mustache he kissed Don roughly. *"Tell the world who your best fucking roommate is!"* As the scene unfolded, you felt yourself dissolving, melting as bit players are wont to into the scenery, becoming as insubstantial as the rain that now fell softly outdoors.

"Do me a favor, would you please, Peter?" you heard Don saying to you, though you might have been in another room, on another planet, in a distant galaxy. "Run out to Sidney's for me and pick me up a jar of pickled pigs feet? Would you do me that favor, Peter, please?"

You felt a tingling in your palm and looked down to see the coins he had deposite there. You looked up to see Don's pleading, shameful, desperate face, then over his shoulder at Sherman, who grinned at you. How you longed then to stand up to your antithesis, to this embodiment of your shadow-self: your tattooed, unwashed shadow, this malicious darkness that you simultaneously coveted and held beyond contempt. Hah! Who were you kidding? You'd be stuck on that mountain forever.

You stepped toward the door.

Then you stopped, turned, and lunged.

Your nemesis offered surprisingly little resistance as together you both fell into the puddle of broken glass. In the following few moments you reclaimed every impulse or instinct ever lost to you during a performance, in rehearsal, at an audition. You pounded away at Sherman's scarred filthy face, snarling:

"Be at life's mercy; be at life's mercy ..."

So caught up were you in your performance you failed to register the cane's first blow. It took several more blows to rouse you. Though you were still on the floor, you felt yourself falling: first from a mountaintop, then from a cloud. You reached up to grab hold of something, anything, only to slice your hands and fingers on the shards of jagged glass left behind in the shattered window. Blind with terror, you stumbled out into the wet, unambiguous night.

It was after dawn when Curly found you between the two dumpsters behind the Cafe Doomed. Hours later, with your bandaged hands in your lap, from your window seat on the Douglas DC-9 you watched the French Quarter turn into a postage stamp.

Meanwhile the plane climbed the sun's rays, hurling you toward that nearest, brightest, and dearest of all possible stars.

❖ *Barber*

Today I'm going to get a haircut. I just decided. There's no barbershop in sight. I don't even know of any barbershops in this neighborhood. The urge to get a haircut has come upon me suddenly, like an early afternoon sun shower. I don't know this part of the city very well, yet already I feel a heavy sense of comfort, a balanced feeling scented with Lilac Vegetal and talcum powder as I drift along in search of a barber pole, one of those red, white, and blue cylinders that whirl 'round and 'round, hypnotizing people into having their ears lowered, as if getting a haircut is the most patriotic thing a person can do, up there with voting, giving blood, and joining the Marines.

As a boy I dreaded getting my hair cut. I dreaded the mechanical white chair, the barber's sneaky saw-toothed smile, the snipping sound his scissors made close to my ears, menacing as the whine of a mosquito, though preferable to the buzz of dog-clippers, as we called them.

There were two barbershops in my hometown. Patsy's and Chris's. My mother took me to Chris's, though to me he wasn't Chris, he was Floyd, the barber on *The Andy Griffith Show*: a short, slope-shouldered, seedy little man with an Adolph Hitler mustache and salt-and-pepper hair combed back in tight curls. And though I liked *The Andy Griffith Show*, I hated Floyd the barber. His hands were too small; so were his teeth. They were the hands and teeth of a burrowing rhodent. Both Chris and Floyd had the same lecherous smile. I imagined them both doing nasty things to kids in mysterious back rooms kept hidden behind a stained blue curtain (where they kept copies of *Playboys* and *Penthouse* and other dirty magazines in a drawer, I guessed).

As with all suspicious persons, you couldn't say where Chris/Floyd was from, somewhere far away, Bulgaria or Romania—one of those places ending in 'ia'. It would not have surprised me to learn that he did taxidermy on the side, or that he practised cannibalism, and that an old-fashioned ice box in his back room brimmed with things floating in Mason jars. Floyd oozed bad breath and spoke in a thin, raspy voice that equalled the sound my father's files, the ones that said "bastard" on them, made when he filed sheets of stainless steel and aluminum with them in his laboratory: a voice dripping perversion and espionage.

On the little table of his barbershop Floyd's real-life equivalent kept a spread of old comic books for customers to engage, their pages foxed with age. Most of the comics had to do with war: flamethrowers, tanks, and U-boats with black leather jacketed *kommandeurs* gritting their teeth while peering through periscopes. The floor of the barbershop was linoleum tiled, with alternating beige and green squares resembling headcheese and creamed spinach. I'd sit in the chrome and vinyl waiting area chair thumbing the same comic I'd thumbed a dozen times before, watching the same Nazi tanks blowing up and flamethrowers spouting and U-boats firing torpedoes at allied ships, feeling as queasily nervous as in the dentist's waiting room, kicking the backs of my P.F. Flyers (guaranteed to make me run faster and jump higher) into the chair's chromium legs, hearing the *snip snip* of Floyd's scissors, seeing tumbleweed-like tufts of dead hair tumble down to the cheese and spinach tiles from the scalp of the customer whose place I would soon be taking. I would take note of the hair tufts falling to the floor, of how many fell on creamed spinach vs. headcheese tiles before Floyd scattered them with the toes of his wing-tips.

Clicksnip. Snipsnip. Zwickzwickzwick.

Most of Floyd's customers lacked sufficient hair to bother cutting, old men with more hair sprouting from their earlobes than from their scalps. As if ashamed to have let their son's crewcuts grow beyond the deignated three-quarters of an inch, fathers brought them in baseball caps. My mother delivered me, abandoning me to Floyd and his sharp little teeth and bad breath while she shopped for groceries at Tony's Market across the street. How I dreaded the moment when the customer would rise from the big complicated chair, hand Floyd two dollars, and wait as, with a *zinnng!* he rang it up on the big silver cash register whose drawer always stuck. Then Floyd would return to the chair (one of three in the shop, the only one that he used), pump it all the way down, snap the seat with his towel, and cast me a lecherous smile over his half-moon glasses. No, no, not yet, I'd say to myself, looking around, hoping by some miracle there would be someone ahead of me who'd been hiding all that time, dreading the barber as much as I did.

Resigned to my fate, I sit in the Death Chair, which Floyd pumps up again. Then he flaps out the striped smock, filling it with air, ridding it of the last customer's dead hair. It billows down over me, soft like a silk parachute. As Floyd tucks it in with tissue his fingers give the back of my neck an inadvertent massage. He glides his skinny black comb through my frizzy hair, not saying a word, not asking me how I want it, tugging the stiff hairs as if to let them know who's boss, seeing how long and reprobate they've grown, sighing and going *tut-tut* with his pointy tongue against his little mole teeth as if to say, *It should never have come to this.* He yanks my hair so hard with his comb my head jerks from side to side; it's all I can do not to say "ouch." Only I don't; I refuse to show the barber my pain. I refuse to succumb to his torture. Instead I stare ahead into the cracked mirror, which Floyd has tried to mend with masking tape, past gleaming green and gold bottles and the tall blue jar of Barbicide with combs floating pickle-like in it, my eyes welling with tears.

Suddenly, with a flick of his wrist, from the breast pocket of Floyd's white jacket the scissors emerge and *snippetysnipsnip* he starts cutting, sending gouges of frizzy hair to the floor, refugees fleeing the country of my head, *swickswitckaswick*, Brillo pad tufts rolling down the front of the striped smock onto the floor tiles: my hair, once upon a time. After a half-dozen or so clumps have fallen, as if to find his tongue he'd had to snip his way through so much hair, Floyd starts talking. Then his bad breath oozes all over me. Don't ask what he talks about; I've no idea: I'm not listening. I'm too busy being horror-stricken by what's happening to my head, counting the frizzy gobs falling like birds shot from the sky, my arms pinned under the striped smock, wanting to catch them, to take them to my lips and kiss them one last time: goodbye.

Talktalk, snipsnip, talktalk.

After a while I can't bear any more. I close my eyes, squeeze them shut, wait for the torture to end, opening them only when Floyd holds the mirror behind my head. However much I deplore what the mirror says, I nod, since there's nothing Floyd can do but cut more hair, right? He can't very well put it back, can he? Besides, I just want to get out of here. The barbershop is a terrible place, a ghoulish place, the place where I have my hair amputated by a foul-breathed Romanian pervert.

But Floyd's not finished. Nossir. It's the old fakeroo! He flaps out the smock and puts it back on me again. It will never end. The barber will go on cutting my hair forever, in perpetuity, for the rest of my life.

But then, after a dozen more *zwicketyzwicks*, Floyd removes the smock again. With a puffy brush dipped in talcum powder he sweeps the back of my neck (which — I have to admit — feels good). With fluid from a tall green bottle he moistens his fingertips and drags them symmetrically across both sides of my head, from under my jaw to behind my ears, leaving a slick shiny trail smelling of lemons, limes, ocean air, pine trees, alchol, and vinegar—which I also have to admit feels pretty good. Then a few more *zwickzwicks*, and, with a decisive snap of his towel, Floyd gives my shoulder a squeaze.

That's it; I'm done. Floyd's finished.

I hand him the two crumpled dollar bills my mother gave me and that I've scrunched and mangled with sweaty fingers, then turn to see her standing there by the door, smiling, right on cue.

It's over. I can breathe again. For another month or so.

Ahead of me down the block a barber pole swirls, blending red, white, and blue: the red of valor, the white of purity, the blue of vigilance and justice, drawing me toward it like a beacon guiding a ship in a storm. With my nose to the plateglass I watch the barber inside at work, a man not much older than I, though watching him turns me into a boy once again. Maybe it's nostalgia — or am I just getting old? — but I long to sit in his complicated chair with filigreed iron plates for the soles of my shoes, for the phalanx of colored bottles, for the mirror mended with masking tape, for the feel of cool wet fingers sliding under my jaw.

A tinkle of bells heralds my entry, the same bells I heard in Chris/Floyd's barbershop. I sit and wait, thrown back to a time when the scariest thing in the world was going to the barber. When it's my turn, I'll sit in the big chair and daydream, nodding off toward sleep without arriving there, existing for twenty minutes in the blissful zone between dreams and reality, the gentle *swickswicketyzwick* of scissors supplying the soundtrack to my reveries.

These days I love the barber: my secular white-frocked priest, a thin black comb and swift scissors his crosier and thurible. I trust him with something no less fragile than my soul: my scalp. In the barber's hands I'm a kid all over again, an innocent boy whose greatest sin is that of having let his hair grow too long.

❖ *Noise*

FOR THE PAST TEN YEARS I've suffered from bilateral tinnitus, sometimes called ringing in the ears, or hissing or buzzing—though in my case those words don't do it justice. Imagine a silver needle of noise threading its way endlessly through your skull from ear to ear, or water coursing under pressure through a pipe lodged in your brain. No one knows for sure what exactly causes tinnitus, something to do with damaged microscopic hair cells in the inner ear. The disease is associated with irritability, fatigue, stress, depression, and a host of other anxiety disorders. It's been known to drive people to suicide.

Luckily, my tinnitus isn't that bad. Anyway I've learned to live with it. Call it a legacy of my days in New York City, that supremely noisy place where I lived for more than three and a half decades, realm of honking horns, rumbling buses, banging trucks, blaring radios, whooping car alarms, and noisy neighbors. The city traumatized me with its noises, chasing me from borough to borough, each with its unique mélange of unwanted sounds, from Holland Tunnel traffic jams to three a.m. garbage trucks to the rhapsodies of street cleaners sweeping the Henry Hudson Bridge at dawn.

Of all the places I lived none was noisier than the Upper West Side, at the corner of 94th and Columbus, where my then-wife and I lived in a second-floor rear two-bedroom foreclosure in a deco building. The apartment had built-in wall sconces, a raised dining alcove, and a sunken living room. We painted it warm colors and filled it with flea market antiques. With each arrival of spring the courtyard dogwood tree bloomed gloriously.

But except for an hour or two in the afternoons the place was as dark as a coal miner's lungs. And it was noisy, terribly noisy. Since we faced the courtyard, traffic wasn't a problem. The problem was the building next door, one of those dilapidated brick highrises commissioned by the Housing Authority under the Wagner administration. An alley divided it from the window of our second bedroom, the studio where I earned my living as an illustrator specializing in caricatures, doing thousands of portraits a year, mostly for corporate clients. There I kept my drafting table and shelves of pens and inks and pencils, along with a stereo unit on which I played jazz, opera, and classical music. There, between cups of espresso, I delved deep into azure grottoes of creative concentration, my idyllic life.

Or it would have been, if not for that building and one particularly noisy resident who played sweet corny songs at top volume all day long, day after day. Concentration shot, bliss destroyed, idyll interrupted.

Noise is sound where you don't want it. Whether it's car alarms or a Mozart requiem doesn't matter. If you don't care to hear it, it's noise. I tried closing my window, turning on the A.C. fan, raising the volume on my music. Still I heard it, the thump-thump of bass notes, the plaintive voices wailing trite lyrics.

I phoned the local precinct.

"We don't consider noise complaints between seven a.m. and midnight to be valid."

"Does that mean I can play 'Ride of the Valkyries' full tilt at a stroke to midnight and no one can do a damn thing about it?"

"That's right," the officer on duty concurred humorlessly.

"Am I to understand that there's no longer such a thing as disturbing the peace?"

"There is—after midnight."

"That cuts it," I announced to my wife after hanging up. "We're moving." Instead I pulled on my jacket and cowboy boots (back then I still wore cowboy boots). In a fever of righteous indignation, against my wife's protests ("Oh, come on, Peter! Don't be an idiot! You'll get yourself killed!") and my own better judgment, marched outdoors.

Security at the building next door wasn't exactly tight. You just had to wait till someone walked in or out to grab the front door before it closed. Once in the lobby, though, I had no idea what buzzer to press. So I went around the side of the building and stood there in the alley, gazing at the culprit's window, through which Stevie Wonder sang, "I just called to say I love you." An air conditioner took up half of the window. Behind a rusty theft grate the other half was cracked open a few inches, the room behind it in total darkness.

"Hey!" I yelled. "You—playing that loud music in there!" The cowboy boots added an inch and a half to my very average height and made me feel tougher than I was, which was not at all. I was still naïve enough then to believe that being right offered one some protection.

I took a quarter from my pocket, reached through the security grate, and rapped it, hard, on the glass. By now you've discerned that I am not the world's easiest-going human being. I'm a perfectionist. One reason why I'm an artist is to achieve—if not perfection—some sense of control over things. However the world isn't a blank canvas or a page subject to editing. One has to deal with imperfect surfaces.

It took a minute of rapping for the music to stop. The silhouette of a head appeared in the window's lower half, black against a paler shade of darkness. A quivering voice said something I could barely make out, the utterance was so raspy.

I said, "Do you have any idea how loud your music is?"

"I'm sorry," the voice said.

"You're disturbing the whole damn neighborhood."

"I'm sorry. I'll turn it down."

"Please do."

Sometimes there's heaven so quickly. I made my way home, cowboy heels sounding confidently against the pavement. When she saw me, my wife shook her head. I smiled, fired up another pot of espresso, and returned to my drafting table, where I plunged blissfully back into my work. Until the music started again.

"Son of a bitch!" Again I pulled on my jacket and boots.

I should have mentioned that it was a lovely October day, just a few clouds in the sky. I didn't need the jacket. Or the boots. Back at the neighbor's window, I rapped on the glass again.

Again the music stopped. Again the rasped apology. This time I saw more of his face. Crew cut. Thin mustache. Around thirty, thirty-five. Gold studs gleaming in both ears.

"If you closed the window it would help," I suggested.

"I can't."

Can't close a window. What was wrong with him? Was he an idiot? He held something up in the darkness, the silver shaft of a crutch, the bent aluminum kind with hinged wrist cuffs. I let the moment of shame pass, then reached in and closed the window for him. His raspy voice said, "Thanks." I wondered what made his voice sound like that. Did he smoke? Was something the matter with his throat? God knew what else was wrong with him.

I was about to go when he said, "You're the artist, right?"

I turned.

"I seen you working."

I didn't cherish the thought of this strange person spying on me through my studio window.

"What sort of art do you do?"

"I'm an illustrator. Portraits, mainly. Caricatures," I said.

"Caricatures, wow! I always wanted to know how to do those."

"It just takes practice," I lied.

"I always wanted to be an artist."

"What's stopping you?"

"Lack of talent."

All this time I could barely see him through the glass, there was so much glare on it. Meanwhile the room remained dark. He asked me my name. I told him.

"Mine's Teddy, as in Theodore. Nice to meet you, Peter."

I smiled, nodded. "Just please keep the music down, okay?"

For the next two days Teddy did, but then it started again. This time, seeing me standing outside his window, he waved me toward the front entrance. "Apartment 1-C," he said.

Christ, I thought, entering the lobby. What the hell am I doing?

For all I knew he was a psycho bent on cutting my organs out and refrigerating them in jars. Or he wanted sexual favors. Damn it, I had an illustration to finish! The lobby smelled of cigarettes and ammonia. Someone had jammed of wad of chewing gum into the buzzer panel. I pressed 1-C and was let in.

I was halfway down the dimly lit corridor when the door opened. A small dog barked. The front of a wheelchair and two pajama-clad legs poked out. "Over here," called Teddy as the dog kept on barking. "Stop it, Ebony! Ebony, stop!"

The place was tidy. What did I expect? One of those junk infested rat holes inhabited by shut-ins like the Collyer Brothers? Illuminated, Teddy looked much younger, maybe twenty-five. He showed me the living room: sofa, TV, books neat on shelves, mostly hardcover novels. A curio cabinet with a porcelain Christ on a cross. A copy of *Speak, Memory* caught my eye, between a hardcover of *Victory*, by Joseph Conrad, and one of *Humbolt's Gift*, by Saul Bellow.

"My father likes to read. Before he quit to teach college, he was a high school English teacher. You like to read?"

I nodded. "You?"

Teddy shook his head. "I'd rather listen to music."

"So I gather."

"That or watch movies." He pointed to an antique rocking chair. "When I'm not in my room, I'm here, in my TV chair." He laughed.

A woman's voice called. "Who is it, Teddy?"

"It's our neighbor Peter."

In the kitchen Teddy introduced me to his mother. Petite, dark, pretty. Hispanic accent. "You live in the yellow building?" she asked. "That's a nice building."

"Thank you."

"Teddy loves artists. He speaks highly of you."

"Want to see my room?" said Teddy.

I followed him down the hallway past a series of framed photographs on the wall, including one of a boy standing with crutches on the steps of a church, grinning.

Teddy showed me his room. Ceiling-high piles of video and cassette tapes and record albums. Amplifiers and an array of large speakers: noise-making equipment. Where not covered with shelves and bookcases, the walls were plastered with posters of movies and musicians. *Dr. Zhivago. Return of the Jedi. Star Trek: The Wrath of Khan.* The air conditioner thrummed. A smaller TV was on next to the bed. Pat Robertson's face filled its screen.

The rest of the room was taken up by an unmade bed, its covers ajumble. A string of rosary beads hung from the bedpost. I sat uncomfortably on the edge of the bed.

Teddy switched the TV off. "I hate that guy," he said. "I hate all self-proclaimed prophets." He pulled his wheelchair up close, so its wheels came past my knees. He handed me a photograph of himself with his arm around a dark-skinned girl. "That's Marisol, my ex-girlfriend," he said. "She's Dominican. My dad's a stern, macho Puerto

Rican. That's why we broke up. Dad said, 'The day you bring a black girl in this house is the day I disown you.' He meant it, too. My dad's a very angry person. Very intelligent and very angry. Dad used to say to me, 'In this world, you play to win or you don't play at all.' 'There's no room in the world for failures and mediocrities,' he said. It's why I don't draw or play music or anything. I'd never be good enough."

"Not as far as your dad is concerned, maybe," I said. "What about being good enough for yourself? Isn't that as important—or more?"

Teddy changed the subject. "So, what do you think?" he said, holding the photo out to me again. "Isn't she beautiful?"

I nodded. "Very." I handed the photograph back.

"I have a favor to ask."

Uh-oh, I thought.

"Will you draw Marisol for me? Her birthday's coming up in two weeks. I want to give it to her. I'll pay you for it."

"I don't know, Teddy, I'm awfully busy."

"Please?"

He handed the photograph back to me.

"I really can't."

"Keep it anyway," he said. "Just in case you get inspired. Besides, I've got another just like it. "

I nodded and said I had to go.

"Okay, but listen to this song first." He put on a CD. "Listen." As the song played he handed me a sheet of paper with the lyrics, which he had written down. "It's called 'Love Education,'" he said. "Listen."

So here I am in solo fashion. I sit alone inside my passion ...

"Like it?"

"Very nice," I lied.

"Here's the part that always makes me cry. Listen."

So there you were, your heart was broken (oh dear)
Burdened with pain, words left unspoken ...

"I really have to go now."

As I rose from the bed Teddy said, "Do you think it's possible to find peace anywhere but with Christ in heaven?"

"Gosh, Teddy, I wouldn't know."

There was a knock on the door. His mother stuck her head in. "Don't forget your two o'clock appointment today, Teddy," she said.

"I won't, Mom."

I left.

Days later the music was back. The pattern was now set: Teddy would blast his music, I'd visit him for a half hour or so, procure a few music-free days, and the cycle would repeat like clockwork. I figured my visits were a small price to pay for some peace and quiet. It beat having to pack up and move.

And Teddy was a nice kid. I grew to like him. He seemed sincere, if sad. And he was obviously sad. Crippled by cerebral palsy, bullied by his macho father, mollycoddled by his devout Christian mother. His father didn't live at the apartment; the details were fuzzy. I never saw the man.

A few times we watched movies in their living room. Mrs. Valdez would bring in a plate of cookies and glasses of milk. Once she made a batch of Jiffy-Pop. I felt like a visiting uncle or cousin.

Though at first she thought it odd, my wife ultimately approved. At least I hadn't gotten myself stabbed to death. Once I brought Teddy home with me. I showed him my studio, my drafting table, my watercolors and mechanical pencils and my collection of crow-quill and Speedball pens. I gave him some pointers on drawing caricatures. "Go for the biggest shapes first," I said. "The shape of the skull is extremely important. Ignore hair and other superficial features. From the skull work your way into the eyes. The eyes are where the essence is located. Get the eyes right and your home free."

I demonstrated, doing a portrait of Teddy. Then I had him do one of me, with me giving him pointers as he drew. The result wasn't half-bad. I rolled it into a tube and snapped a rubber band around it. I gave him a mechanical pencil, some markers, a kneaded eraser, and a pad of Bristol paper. Then I walked him back home.

It went on like that for a few weeks. Then, that November, I landed a big commission: a corporate tombstone for Deloitte & Touche commemorating a billion-dollar bond merger. The finished product would measure four feet by six and feature forty-two portraits in color, bodies included, the twilit Manhattan skyline stretched out behind them. It was my highest-paying commission to date, but it came with a nasty deadline: six weeks during which time I would not only have to do all that drawing but gather photographs of each of the forty-two subjects, who spent most of their time airborne in Lear jets.

Preoccupied with my commission, I forgot about Teddy. It didn't help that he had stopped playing his music. Maybe he'd gone to the Dominican Republic, to elope with Marisol, his forbidden sweetheart. I thought about Teddy with her (when I thought about Teddy at all). But mostly I focused on my work. Then, at seven thirty-one morning, the phone rang. A woman with an Hispanic accent.

"This is Mrs. Valdez, Teddy's mother," she said. "Teddy—who lives next door?"

"Yes, of course, Mrs. Valdez. How are you?"

"I just wanted to let you know that everything's all right. Teddy was checked into Columbia Presbyterian Hospital last night. But everything's okay now."

"What happened?"

"Teddy took some pills, but he's all right now. He's under twenty four-hour supervision. He wanted you to know. He's been talking about you a lot. He really enjoyed your company."

I remembered the caricature of Marisol that I'd done but never gave to him. It sat on my taboret under a pile of sketches and papers. The truth is I'd been avoiding Teddy. It wasn't just the commission; I was afraid he'd started to depend on me. I wasn't big on responsibilities.

"If you'd like to visit ..." Mrs. Valdez said, and then she gave me the information.

"Can I ask you something?" I said. She waited. "Do you have any idea why your son feels so helpless?"

A car alarm went off. As Mrs. Valdez explained about Teddy's break-up with his girlfriend, the hardships he faced owing to his handicap, his constant struggles to adapt to new medications and assistive technologies, I took the phone into the bathroom and shut the door. His mother went on, about the divorce a year ago, about his father moving out, about how she had had to go back to work and leave him alone all day. "My son's been through a lot. It's why he's in therapy. I've been going myself. I try to help him. *Meu querido*, what else can I do?" We both let the question hang. "Please do visit him if you can. He admires you much. God bless and be with you."

I rode the subway to 168th Street and Broadway. Though it was still the middle of winter, it felt like spring. A floral scent filled the air, along with the brine of the Hudson River. The low buildings up there let in wide swatches of sky. It had been a while since I'd ventured that far uptown. In my backpack, tucked between the pages of a sketchbook, I carried the caricature of Marisol, along with a paperback copy of Rilke's *Letters to a Young Poet*.

In the waiting area I sat by a window. Nurses on break smoking cigarettes, gossiping. As I flipped through *Letters to a Young Poet*, my eyes landed on the phrase *love your solitude and try to sing out with the pain*. The sunlight glared off the pages and I felt suddenly tired. When I looked up one of the nurses was looking down at me, pretty, smiling. I smiled back. I'd forgotten where I was, let alone why.

I was reorienting myself when the receptionist called me and directed me to Teddy's room. When I found him, Teddy was on the toilet, finishing up, maneuvering from commode to wheelchair. "Sorry," he said. As he rolled close I saw a few flecks of white in his mustache. The rest of his face was razor-stubbled. Three pimples lit up his forehead. He shook my hand. Teddy had strong hands with oversized thumbs. I hadn't noticed before how big his thumbs were. His earrings were gone.

"Hey, did you ever watch that movie?" he asked. I remembered him handing me the videocassette. I couldn't remember the title. Anyway whatever it was I hadn't watched it.

"You should watch it, it's good."

I promised him that I would.

"This place is like a fishbowl." Teddy nodded toward an orderly standing nearby. "I have no privacy. And the food stinks."

"You were expecting the Four Seasons?"

He laughed. I gave him the Rilke book and the drawing. With a toothy grin stretching from one studded ear to the other he approved of both. I told him about my commission. We chatted. Finally I asked, "Why'd you do it, Teddy?"

He shrugged. "I wish I could be like everyone else."

"No you don't."

"I do."

"Well, forget it. You'll never be like everyone else. No one will ever be like everyone else. Everyone's different, Teddy. Everyone's special, whether they like it or not."

"Being special hurts."

"Being human hurts."

"It's not the first time," he said. "Last time they kept me here for three days. They made me wear a straightjacket put me in a rubber room. I know what it's like to be shackled."

"As options go it doesn't strike me as a very good one."

"You really should watch that movie."

Teddy's mother arrived, carrying a Bible, a paper bag with coffee and bagels, and a rolled-up poster of Jon Gibson, Teddy's favorite singer-songwriter, the man responsible for "Love Education." As Teddy sipped his coffee a nurse took his temperature and blood pressure. His mother asked her why they had taken his earrings. "What could he do with them?"

"He'd probably think of something," the nurse answered.

Teddy's psychiatrist arrived, Dr. Sidney—a handsome, well put-together type, silver goatee and hair, black turtleneck under a pale suit. Teddy showed him the caricature I'd done of Marisol. "Isn't it great?"

"We should get him to do Pastor Bob," said Dr. Sidney.

"Pastor Bob—yeah, that would be great!"

With Teddy's psychiatrist gone, Mrs. Valdez returned. "Mr. Sidney refuses to speak to me," she confided to me. "Can you believe it? His own therapist refuses to speak to me, his mother! As if it's my fault! *Dios mio:* can I help it if he'll always be my baby?"

After leaving the hospital, rather than take the subway I decided to walk downtown. It was a beautiful day, already a lost cause as far as work was concerned. Via Broadway I made my way through Manhattan Valley to Morningside Heights, past Columbia's gates, bookstores, and jammed cafes. Somewhere around 112th Street I heard music playing, drifting down from one of countless pre-war building windows. I imagined as many Teddys hunkered in dark rooms, blasting their music, wanting the world to feel—or anyway to hear—the songs of their distress. I live in a city amplified by anguish, I thought, a realm of lonesome miserable fools abused of the notion that, as long as other others can hear it, no one need suffer in solitude or in silence.

❖

The last time I heard from Teddy was over five years ago. He sent me a Facebook friend request along with a message. By then I'd divorced and moved to Georgia, to the modified A-frame on a lake where I sit writing these words. Teddy's message said that he was doing fine. He had a girlfriend; they were engaged. He earned his living as a graphic designer and had even done some CD covers. He wanted to know if I was still doing caricatures (I was not).

"It's been a rough winter in New York," Teddy wrote. "I bet the weather's better in Georgia." Two or three more messages followed.

Then — as suddenly as they started — the messages stopped.

The city noises that once drove me to despair are gone now, replaced by birds, wind, and boat waves slapping at the pylons of my dock and the sea-wall planks. The few man-made sounds belong mainly to seasonal jet skis and powerboats. I've made my peace with them.

The rest — as Hamlet said — is silence.

Well, not quite. Not long ago I was writing here at my desk when I heard what sounded like rap music. To a person my neighbors are all retirees. I thought: Who the heck's playing *rap* music? Searching for a boat, I looked through one of the big triangular windows facing the lake at water as smooth as glass. I peeled back the curtains of the opposite window, the one facing the street, expecting to see a passing car. Again nothing. I went out on the deck. Nothing. Not a sound.

Huh, I thought, and went back inside and sat down to write again. The noise returned, the same percussive beat, just as loud.

Dammit, I thought, and went through the whole charade again with the same results. Then I realized: It wasn't rap music. It was my own pulse pounding in my ears.

Those two sounds — my tinnitus threading its one long silver note through my skull, and the drumbeat of my pulse—serve to remind me that I once lived in a noisy city, and how now that city is now in my blood, a part of my brain.

I'm reminded too of Teddy, and of how little I understood about life on that lovely noisy day when he and I first met. Since then I've learned that the main lesson life has to teach us is how to lose things. It may be the one and only lesson. Our suffering is all that we really own, and it, too, shall one day pass. All the sounds we hear and make while on this earth are as nothing next to the silence that preceded—and that is sure to follow—them.

❖ *In Praise of Stripes*

TO THE EXTENT THAT THE WORLD IS STRIPED, it is a happy place.

I call your attention to one or more of the following: awnings, beach umbrellas, cabana huts fronting the French Riviera, gondolier's shirts, straw boaters, tigers and zebras, barber poles, candy canes, silk pajamas, Breton sailor shirts, skunk and raccoon tails, flags and bunting, bumble bees, circus tents, popcorn vending machines, race cars, towels and ties, frogs and fish, Edwardian swimming costumes.

Among striped objects it is possible to find things sad or ugly. Prisoners' uniforms come to mind, as do guard houses and crossing gates. There can be something admonishing or even threatening about stripes — an alarm, a shout, a scream. Why do prisoners wear stripes? Do the horizontal bands countermand the vertical bars? Or are (were, the custom having since passed) a prisoner's stripes an attempt to inject some gaiety into their monotonous days? In that case why black and white stripes? Why not red and yellow? Or purple and green?

There was a time when wearing stripes could not only put you out of fashion, but get you killed. According to Michel Pastoureau's "'The Devil's Cloth: A History of Stripes and Striped Fabric," such was the case for an order of Carmelite monks. Inspired by the prophet Elijah, who supposedly sailed off into the sky on a chariot of fire, leaving behind his cloak striped with dark singe marks, these monks' habits were striped brown and white. On their arrival in Palestine in the mid 13th century, the monks soon earned the nickname *"les frères barrés"* — an undesirable nickname, as the term "barré" signified not only stripes but illegitimacy. Ordered by Pope Alexander to surrender their stripes, they refused, incurring twenty-five years of threats and abuse, until Alexander's successor issued a bull banning striped clothing from all religious orders.

Stripes were the trademarks of bandits, whores, cripples, lepers, hangmen, bastards, clowns, jugglers, and Jews (whose *tallits* were striped), and heretics. There was a time when striped animals fared poorly as well, with otherwise innocent zebras ranked among the diabolical creatures in Satan's bestiary. Well into the last half of the 18th century a mythic beast called "the beast of Gévaudan" terrorized French farmers and other country denizens. That the beast was striped should go without saying.

I myself refuse to see stripes in a negative light. Stripes have been good to me. Even when they fail to arouse the patriot in me, the stripes of the American flag give me pleasure. As for barber poles, with their mesmerizing red, white, and blue swirling stripes, you'd think that getting a haircut was the most patriotic thing a boy or man could do, up there with voting, giving blood, and joining the Marines.

I once wrote a story about stripes, about a young man searching for red and gray wide-striped pajamas like the ones his dead father used to wear. I wrote it fifteen years ago. Recently my brother shipped me his Christmas present. I tore it open at once. Inside, a lovely pair of English pajamas: pure silk, with wide red and gray stripes. I put them on right away. They felt so soft, so silkily luxurious. Silkier still for being striped, the alternating vertical lines of color sliding and slithering cool over my flesh. Tell me I don't sleep better in them.

Stripes have had their roles to play in the workplace as well. Sailors aboard their gray ships in striped uniforms, the blue and white stripes meant to symbolize — I assume — the horizon, that ubiquitous line stretching between sky and sea, but also meant to add a note of cheer between bouts of warfare, boredom, and seasickness. The gondolier's striped shirt is emblematic of his masculinity: he can get away with stripes, so he does. His cousin the pizza chef also wears stripes, thin red ones to match his tomato sauce. Butchers too once wore stripes, likewise red, though in that case the color stood for blood. Bankers and ball players wear pinstripes. In all cases a note of joy is attached to servitude. As the gondolier is subservient to his gondola, so the pizza man must whirl his crusts; the butcher wrestles bone and gristle; the banker manipulates money; the ball player pitches in and strikes out; the prisoner serves time. Who wears pajamas is the servant of sleep.

Even awnings and umbrellas serve, reminding us of the bottom line as it pertains to stripes: joyful obeisance, delightful deference. Is it any wonder a sergeant earns his stripes? Or that a tiger cannot change his?

Remember Stripe toothpaste? Invented in 1955 by Leonard Lawrence Marraffino and sold to Lever Brothers in 1957 (the year I was born), the technology consisted of a thin tube with a series of small holes in the front connected to the main toothpaste tube, which contained plain white toothpaste. A connected but separate area in the front of the tube held a relatively small amount of red-colored fluid. When squeezed, the white toothpaste moved down the thin pipe, producing pressure that pulled the red material through the series of small holes to merge with the viscous stream, resulting in a ribbon of white toothpaste with red stripes. For the first two years following its introduction, the brand was popular, capturing a significant eight-percent of the U.S. toothpaste market. But as the novelty wore off (despite a 4.4 million-dollar advertising campaign that included a "rocket balloon" gift for kids with each tube), sales of Stripe plummeted, and by the Winter of 1964 it was off the shelves. A shame. Though it contained a substance called "Hexachlorophene" that was later shown to be toxic, while it lasted Stripe was unquestionably the happiest of toothpastes.

More recently, to the consternation of her neighbors, the owner of a three-story terrace townhouse in a posh neighborhood in Kensington,

South London, painted candy stripes on its façade. Her neighbors sued her, claiming she'd done it to spite them in retaliation for their refusing her permission to demolish the property and replace it with a newer home. The owner claimed on the contrary that she had been moved by a desire to "add to the gaiety of the nation."

"I thought I would do something to cheer myself up and cheer up the street," she said, adding, "Children absolutely love it." The High Court ultimately decided in her favor, with the judge concluding that whether the "garish" color scheme resulted from an owner's eccentricity or her pique, it was not against the law. Chalk up a victory for stripes!

A joyful obeisance is all we can ask of life. It is what the religious prophets called for and what anyone who has lost themselves in service to a higher cause will claim as the source of bliss. I've known the blissful surrender of artistic discipline, joyous surrender, the forces of creativity ranged in bright, regimented rows: inspiration, talent, craft, labor. Stripes are nothing if not organized and enterprising.

And who says stripes are impractical? Zoologists believe that a zebra's black and white stripes help keep it cool by heating up at different rates, generating micro-breezes over its body. As for a tigers' stripes, they are said to help the animals blend into their surroundings, the better for sneaking up on their prey (to which I say phooey! Blake didn't write: *"Tyger Tyger, blending in ... "*).

I've invested in striped sheets, striped socks, striped sweaters and striped shirts, striped tea and coffee mugs, striped bed sheets, striped towels, striped upholstery, pillows and linens. Color my world striped.

Civilization, I say, ought to be striped: brightly disciplined, cheerfully regimented, seriously silly: like Venetian mooring poles and the blazers Tommy Steele wears in *Half a Sixpence*—a lavishly produced but otherwise forgettable motion picture musical.

Imagine how much better a world this would be were more things striped in it. Supposing all police officers wore candy-striped uniforms.

Soldiers, too. What if armaments and weapons were striped? Striped tanks and F-16s and aircraft carriers (see "dazzle camouflage," known also as *razzle dazzle:* a method of camouflage used for ships primarily during World War I, employing complex patterns of stripes and other geometric shapes in contrasting colors designed to confuse more than to conceal, and credited either to an artist or to a zoologist). By decree, institutional buildings, schools, hospitals, and prisons would all be striped. Factories, too. In place of gray, businessmen and women would wear bright, brazen, sassy, silly stripes. Only children would be allowed to wear solid colors, if they choose to do so. Of course they wouldn't.

❖ My New York: a Romance in Eight Parts

> And with the awful realization that New York was a city after all and not a universe, the whole shining edifice that he had reared in his imagination came crashing to the ground.
> —F. Scott Fitzgerald, "My Lost City"

LURCHING THROUGH CYBERSPACE RECENTLY, I chanced upon a luncheon menu from Schraft's, circa 1962. Especially among the city's working women, Schraft's was once New York City's most popular restaurant chain. The menu is an arresting artifact, one that might have been concocted to certify an era's lost innocence—how else account for Jellied Tomato Bouillon, Browned Lamb Hash with Wax Beans, Deviled Tongue and Swiss Cheese Sandwich, Corn Souflé, Minute Tapioca Pudding, Fresh Banana Stuffed with Fruit Salad, Green Apple Pie, and Grapejuice Lemonade? At the top center on the menu: "May We Suggest Bacardi Cocktail 70¢."

My eyes misted over. Here was the New York City I once fell hard for, the city of my childhood and young dreams. And though the menu belonged to a vanished time, still, it was real—as the Hotel Paris had been real, as the passenger ships lined up in their berths had been real. As my innocence, my ambitions, my disappointments and failures and a host of betrayals—mine, my father's, the city's—all had been real.

I. LOVE AT FIRST SIGHT

GAS HEATS BEST. They loomed: black, blocky letters on a yellow field painted on the side of a gargantuan corrugated hatbox. An ad for home heating fuel. But to my six-year-old eyes it might have been God creating Adam in the firmament of the Sistine Chapel.

It was my first trip to New York City with my father. His "business trips," he called them, though someday I would learn that there had been more to them than that. My twin brother George and I took turns, each of us accompanying him every other Friday. The trip took just over an hour, but as far as I was concerned we might have been blasting off to Venus or Mars.

We rode in my father's Simca Chatelaine, an ivory wagon with whitewalls and a split tailgate. I watched him work the gearshift, a thin chrome rod with a pear-shaped knob—an object of fascination that I would secretly commandeer when Papa went into the post office or the bank, my vocal cords imitating the engine's winding RPMs, ignorant of such things as clutches. As Papa backed the Simca past the dying birch tree in the turnaround, I'd see my brother and my mother standing there, my mother waving, my brother crying—as I would cry a week later when it would be George's turn. Why our father took us separately I'm not sure. Maybe because we fought so much.

At the end of the driveway we'd take a right onto Wooster Street and head to Danbury, where we drove past the war memorial and the fairgrounds. On Old Route 6 we'd pass by the Dinosaur Gift & Mineral Shoppe, with its pink stucco tyrannosaurus, headed toward Brewster. Interstate 684 had yet to be built, so we rode on state highways that today would qualify as "back roads," past apple orchards, nurseries, and reservoirs, then down the Saw Mill River Parkway through exotically named places—Croton Falls, Katonah, Armonk, Chappaqua—tallying bridges and groundhogs.

While driving my father hummed: "The Blue Danube," a Maurice Chevalier ditty, his cigarette dangling. He drove with an elbow out the window, preferring his left arm to the Simca's turning signal. The Simca's glove compartment burst with road maps, but my father never consulted them. The city's outskirts were a tangle of parkways, thruways, expressways and turnpikes. That my father could untangle them amazed me, but then they seemed to belong to him, all of those highways, as did everything to do with New York City.

We crossed over the Henry Hudson Bridge. At the tollbooth, Papa tossed a nickel into the perforated yellow basket. We glided under the girders of the George Washington Bridge. Here the city began in earnest. We passed the Cloisters and Grant's Tomb. Among drab shapes in the distance I picked out patches of bright color, reds and blues, the funnels of passenger ships in their berths. To our left as we drove on a skyscraper garden flourished, the Empire State Building sprouting like a deco fountain at its center. Amid this profusion of architecture rose the fuel oil storage tank, the one proclaiming GAS HEATS BEST. This utilitarian structure was no less awe-inspiring to me then than the Queen Elizabeth or the Empire State Building, subjects I'd sketch again and again in Mrs. Decker's kindergarten class.

The elevated ended; the Simca descended into a shadowy jungle of bumpy cobblestone streets. Somewhere along Canal Street we parked. Gripping my hand, Papa led me from one industrial surplus store to another, foraging for plastic and other parts for his inventions, his Rotary Motors, his Color Coders, his Thickness Gauges and Mercury Switches. The sidewalks were crowded, yet somehow to me the people weren't real. They reminded me of baubles on a Christmas tree, each with its unique charms and quirks, but, unlike the buildings surrounding them, insubstantial. There were no dogs and few children. New York was a place for grown-ups.

From Canal Street we walked to Chinatown, where we ducked into shops packed with lacquered trays and jade carvings. Here the streets smelled of fish. In one of those shops my father bought me a carved wooden box (I still have it; it sits on top of the bookcase by the desk where I write). In Chinatown the plethora of street signs, their instructions transformed into adornments by virtue of being illegible, impressed me even more. Snared by a web of utility lines and fire escapes, the enigmatic characters hung butterfly-like in the air.

Then to Greenwich Village, where we entered boutiques lush with beads and trinkets and suffused with the smell of incense, and where one shop window confronted us with a panoply of chessboards with pieces carved from rare woods and exotic minerals. Already I had begun to see the city as a colossal museum, with objects displayed in various galleries according to periods and styles. Beyond displaying its holdings, the city had no discernible purpose. It existed for roughly the same reason as the town park at Lake Candlewood, or the Danbury State Fair: to amuse me.

We lunched at Shraft's, then drove back uptown toward our hotel, stopping on the way at Manganaro's Italian import store, where my father bought a pound of Parmesan cheese—a jagged hunk broken off a great golden wheel. By then the air had dimmed, the better to display the lights of Times Square, where flashing neon signs advertised everything from Pepsi-Cola to Castro Convertibles, and where a giant Phil Silvers as Sergeant Bilko exhaled smoke rings into the electrified dusk. Then up West End Avenue to the Hotel Paris.

Of all parts of the city that hotel was my favorite, a wedding-cake-shaped fortress of garnet-colored bricks topped by a crenellated water tower, with a flagpole reaching even further toward the sky. I recall a lobby of pink marble walls with a mirrored dining room adjacent and a caged, old-fashioned elevator attended by a colored lady (I use the term in keeping with the times) whose beehive of fire-engine-red hair was as imposing as she was diminutive. She let me man the controls, a courtesy for which I will never forget her. You had to pull back on the lever just so or the elevator and the floors wouldn't line up properly. She put her brown hand on top of mine, her warm grip guiding me. At each floor the doors opened to different hallway carpeting, arabesques of blazing color that in their inscrutable intricacies mirrored the teeming metropolis outdoors.

Like all the rooms in the Hotel Paris, ours was small. It reeked of the last occupant's cigarettes, which was okay by me. I accepted the fetid odor as part of the city—my father's city, it seemed to me, as though he had laid every brick and cobblestone and erected every skyscraper and bridge. As he unpacked his suitcase on the bed, I watched, engrossed. A suit jacket, a pair of socks, two pairs of underwear, a can of Desenex foot powder, a safety razor and his battered shaving brush, a shoehorn and a necktie.

The necktie fascinated me most. Though I had seen it often before, often, hanging in his closet back home, here it took on a new aspect. With its yellow paisley drops against a maroon background, it was no longer just my papa's necktie; it was his New York City tie. At that moment, that necktie became the city for me, as the stale cigarette smell in that hotel room became the city, and the gaudy hallway carpeting, and the red-haired elevator operator, and the hunk of Parmesan cheese, and the passenger ships in their berths, and the GAS HEATS BEST sign, and the Groundhogs digging holes in the lawns along the Saw Mill Parkway. It was all my New York back then, courtesy of my father, who'd invented it just for me.

II. PUPPY LOVE

At fifteen, my friend Chris Rowland and I used to visit his neighbor, Clara. A spry, matronly woman in her eighties, Clara lived across the street from the Rowlands in a white-shingled cottage on the curve of a brook. Chris would bring a casserole that his mother made. Clara would thank him and put it away. Then we'd sit in her parlor, Clara in her thronelike wicker chair, eating butter cookies with cider while she sipped tea from a china cup. We assumed it was tea.

New York City was Clara's favorite subject. She still kept her apartment there. She spoke of how, in her younger days, she and a friend opened a teashop in Chelsea, of the Broadway stars who patronized it. "Oh, we had quite a time of it, quite a time," said Clara, fanning herself with a Japanese fan.

One day Clara gave us the keys to her apartment. Chris's father drove us to the train station in Brewster. Through the green-tinted window to the rhythmic clacking of train wheels we watched the familiar world of houses, church steeples, and trees morph into a landscape of buildings, viaducts and bridges. Suddenly the train plunged underground and for a time everything turned black. We stepped out of the train car to find ourselves in a grimy echoing marble cathedral vaulted with sallow stars.

At the newspaper kiosk Chris bought a box of Good & Plenty; I bought a Bit-O-Honey bar. We both chipped in for the *Daily News* and a folding map of the city. We couldn't decide whether to walk to Clara's place or take the subway. Walking, we'd see a lot more, but a subway ride would be more thrilling. We took the subway.

It was late September, but the subway platform still hoarded the summer's heat. The station's dim lighting gleamed off the edges of its innumerable white tiles. A man in a business suit leaned against an iron pillar; others stooped impatiently over the tracks. None said a word. My friend and I obeyed the unwritten law by which New Yorkers pretend to ignore each other. A muffled roar and a breath of fusty air heralded the subway train's arrival. The roar grew deafening until it squealed to a stop and its doors slid open.

We careened under the city, clinging to leather straps as the subterranean world rushed by, a murky blur punctuated by lustrous stations whose waiting passengers could only watch in envy as we roared by on express tracks: 34th Street . . . 28th Street . . . 23rd Street . . . At the place called Union Square, we jumped a set of iron teeth that stretched to fill the gap between subway car and platform. Then up we bounded through a maze of latticed stairways and catwalks into a world of buildings and blinding sunshine.

To judge by our map, Clara's apartment was five blocks east on 18th Street. We passed a Chock Full o' Nuts and a corner fruit stand. We carried our suitcases and walked fast, as though our arrival were not already a thing accomplished—as if by walking any slower we'd dispel the magic of this dream, like those dreams wherein you will yourself successfully to fly. Now and then we faced each other and shared a grin that said we'd gotten away with something or were about to.

Clara's apartment was on the top floor of a tenement. We bounded up three flights. An elaborate series of keys was required for entry. The apartment smelled of mothballs and musk. Should we open a window? Was that allowed? The walls were covered with framed photographs, theatrical posters, and quaint watercolors of Parisian street scenes. A bronze Laocoön graced the fireplace mantel. Even up there with the windows closed we heard the traffic below, the impatient horns of trucks and taxis. While Chris unpacked I studied the photographs, mostly of Clara and a friend, presumably the one with whom she had run the tea shop. In one they both wore fur coats; in another they showed off identical plumed hats. It had never dawned on either of us that Clara might be lesbian. "Oh, I've had many, many beaux," she'd said to us on more than one occasion while sipping whatever from her china cup. Even seeing the photographs the thought didn't occur to me, as it didn't occur to me that someday I would live in New York, that I would engage my ambitions, inflame my desires, commit various acts of ignominy and treachery, and experience a multitude of triumphs, disappointments, sins, failures, and betrayals there.

By noon Chris and I were back out on the street, burdened no longer by our luggage, carrying only the folding map and an eagerness to see everything. Uptown or down? We went down. To the tip of the Battery we walked, passing the still unfinished towers of the World

Trade Center. We stood by a railing watching seagulls wheel over the decks of a ferryboat taking tourists to the Statue of Liberty. From there we walked uptown through the Chinatown that I first came to know with my father; without him guiding me through them its cagey streets seemed less magical. Then up to Little Italy, with its green and red pennants and flags, past the iron-fronted buildings of the Soho and the Bowery to the East Village, where, at the crowded counter of a Ukrainian café, we slurped twin bowls of blood-red borscht. As we were leaving, I gave a quarter to a panhandler. "Don't spend it all in one place," I said, earning a disapproving look from Chris.

Midtown. Rockefeller Center. Radio City. Central Park. The Met. The names arrested me with their authority. At the Guggenheim we balked at the price of admission: three dollars and fifty cents to penetrate a colossal Carvel ice-cream cone. To hell with it! In the district known as Harlem the streets were in every sense browner, its buildings slung low to accommodate a sky brought to its knees by dense, ponderous clouds. We walked faster, the gusts flapping the lapels of our windbreakers, passing a building shaped like the parabolas we learned to draw in algebra class. At every other block a sudden whirlwind whipped grit into our eyes and made us grip our jackets tightly at our throats while hunching forward like old men.

We'd started across town, hungry for Broadway and humanity, eager to arrive at the colossal pinball machine known as Times Square, when the rain caught us. We carried no umbrellas. We'd bought extra tokens, but there were no subway entrances in sight. Taxicabs were prohibitively expensive. Headlong and purblind, we plunged into the monsoon. By the time a subway kiosk arose out of the tempest, we were soaked. We clutched our knees, laughing and coughing as we both caught our breaths.

The subway zoomed us to Times Square, where we emerged into a sea of black umbrellas backlit by blurred neon signs. At an establishment called Nedick's we ordered two "frankfurters" apiece and large, cone-shaped paper cups of orange drink, and ate watching blurry people hurry by in the rain. Even soaking wet, New York was a fabulous place, a wonderful, lewd, sexy, forbidden place. Those trips with my papa had been mere flirtations, as chaste as my grandmother's kisses. Now I was a man, and the city was mine to embrace less innocently.

By the time we left Nedick's the rain had softened to a drizzle. We passed under a succession of marquees featuring slasher and porn films and peep shows for twenty-five cents, a Coney Island of X-rated sex. Had Chris, whose parents were straight-laced Eisenhower Republican WASPs, not been there to shame me, I'd have ducked into one of those seedy theaters. I'd have paid a quarter for a peep show — or two. From the shadows of one theater two women in leopard-skin miniskirts and high heels emerged to offer us a good time. I showed interest; my friend didn't. I had started a conversation with them when, saying, "We're already having a good time, thank you," Chris took my arm and kept us walking.

We got "home" after dark. What a strange feeling, having those apartment keys. "The keys to the city!" one of us joked as the door to Clara's apartment swung open. The musty smell was still there. So was the Laocoön. It wasn't even half past seven, but we were beat. Though the rain had stopped, still, the city seemed less inviting by night, consisting only of bars and brothels and nightclubs and other forbidden and overpriced venues.

Instead we brewed a pot of tea and sat there, in Clara's living room, talking in hushed tired voices to the murmurs of traffic, until our eyelids grew heavy and we slouched to bed, proud of ourselves for having passed, to our own satisfaction, the city's audition. It was the first of many such trials, but I didn't know that then.

❖

III. ROMANCE

The rat was as big as a squirrel. It twitched in a trap next to the walk-in fridge. My boss, a retired New York City transit cop, kept his old service revolver in his office. He took aim, told me to stand back, and blew the thing to furry pink bits, which afterward I scooped into a metal dustpan and carried outdoors to the dumpster.

It was my first job in New York. I'd hoped to be a bartender or a cook, but the owner of the Rozinante Tavern had different plans for me, so I spent most of my time there in the basement, peeling potatoes and cementing cracks in the concrete floor.

It wasn't long before I found a better job just two blocks south, in the oldest building in Soho, a one-time whorehouse with shuttered windows and a pitched roof. To work at the Broome Street Bar you had to be an artist: a painter, writer, architect, dancer, photographer — it didn't matter what kind. I told the owners I was a freshman at Pratt, but that failed to satisfy them. I had to show them some of my sketches before they hired me as a dishwasher.

The bar's owners were two diametrically opposed brothers named Kenn (two n's) and Bob. Short, bow-legged, cigar-smoking Kenn wore blue jeans, cowboy shirts, and belts with enormous buckles. He saw himself as the rough-and-ready type. Bob, on the other hand, was a slender, soft-spoken, effete man with a pale complexion. Their love of artists was the one thing the two brothers shared. While Kenn held forth with the patrons upstairs, Bob spent most of his time at a desk he had arranged by the prep kitchen, keying numbers into an adding machine and chain-smoking Parliaments. He'd take four puffs of a cigarette before snuffing it out, having heard somewhere that the first four puffs contained less nicotine. The floor under his desk squirmed with hardly-smoked cigarettes.

The Broome Street Bar had an open kitchen, with the dishwasher's station facing one end of the bar. I liked washing dishes. I liked the hot, soapy water on my hands and the sense that I was doing something useful. Dishwashing is honorable work, I told myself as the busboys dumped their greasy loads and I flirted with any good-looking woman who sat on the last stool at the bar.

The other workers in the kitchen slung omelets and burgers, sliced sandwiches and cracked jokes. Jimmy, the salad chef, was an architect. Francis, the prep cook, wrote show tunes. Joe Hinkle was supposedly writing a novel.

The waitresses were mostly actresses and dancers. The griddle chef, a guy in his thirties named Bentley, a painter in the manner of Kandinsky, was the funniest and most cynical of the bunch, with a mop of sandy hair that covered his eyes and that he would toss back while flipping his burgers. Somehow, despite his talking a mile a minute in a flat nasal voice with which he cut to the quick anyone he disliked, the ash from Bentley's cigarette never sullied his grill.

The bar was a magnet for artists. John and Yoko were patrons; so were Jasper Johns and Bob Rauschenberg. Among regulars was a sculptor named Bob Bolles. He had a job there, doing what I'm not sure: something to do with either plumbing or beer taps. Mostly he hung out at the bar. Bolles' artistic claim to fame was on permanent (we thought then) display at the "motorcycle triangle," an open area at the intersection of Broome and Watts where bikers parked their crotch-rockets, and where, without permission from municipal authorities, Bolles' jagged iron creations sprouted like rusty weeds, providing windblown papers and coffee cups with crannies to wedge themselves into and neighborhood children objects to skin their knees on. A short guy with an Edgar Allen Poe forehead, Bolles wore hoop earrings and red bandannas and was as much a fixture in Soho as its loading docks and bay doors and freight elevators, as the trucks that barreled over cobblestones to and from the Holland Tunnel. When he died of AIDS in the '80s, Bolles' sculptures fell into ruin. Eventually, under the auspices of a zealous borough parks commissioner, the "dangerous, dilapidated, rusting, falling-apart litter magnets" were carted off to a storage facility on Randall's Island, to make way for a public greenspace to be called Sunshine Park — all pleas to rename it after the dead sculptor having fallen on deaf ears.

Looming over the motorcycle triangle, across the expanse of a windowless building, the words I AM THE BEST ARTIST were spray-painted and signed by one "René." As far as I know, this early example of guerilla art was that artist's only creation, but for me it did the trick. To be the best artist — that was the thing. It was why I had come to the city: to practice my own art, but also to breathe in the atmosphere of artists, to size up and learn all I could from the competition.

Just what sort of artist I would be, I wasn't sure. I had a grandiosity of purpose but no clear vision to go with it. I knew only that I wanted to touch and impress others with my art such that they would someday say of me, "He's the best artist."

Mine was an imperative as inevitable as that GAS HEATS BEST sign that I saw on my first visit to New York with my papa as a child. To impress myself on New York City as it had impressed itself on me: that was my goal, what I wanted, what I yearned for.

Meanwhile I washed dishes.

IV. PROMISCUITY

The Pratt dorm was in a high-rise on Willoughby Avenue, lording it over a neighborhood of tenements and gnarly trees. From there I took a share with a retired church organist named Fletcher on Washington Avenue — or was it Clinton? After that came the sublet on DeKalb and another off Flatbush, just down the street from Junior's where, for the price of a cup of coffee, I'd fill my belly with specimens from the sour-pickle dispenser. From there I moved to a one-year sublet in the East Village, on 7th Street, where the avenues are alphabetized and the women wore orthopedic shoes and drab scarves around their heads. Next came the loft on Broome Street in the summer of '77, the summer the lights went out across the city. By candlelight at the corner tavern they dispensed free lukewarm beer and half-melted ice cream. Then back to Brooklyn, a fifth-floor walkup two blocks south of the Heights, one of those jobs with a claw-foot tub squatting in the kitchen, and cracked, sticky linoleum. Followed by another share, this one in Stuyvesant Town, where they didn't permit air conditioners (fans only) in the casement windows, and where, during the holidays, they strung colored lights around the lampposts. Was this before or after I lived with the crazy lady on Cornelia Street, the one who called me "Leonardo" and vowed to make a star out of me? Through her I auditioned for the singing waiter job on Third Avenue, and for that casting agent in Hell's Kitchen—the one who, wearing a velvet robe in his living room, by means of an exercise called "The Boy on the Mountaintop," lured me over his knees. After the crazy lady threw my things out the window, I moved into the office of the literary agent for whom I'd been working, and who, for a cut in my $100 a week salary, let me sleep on his sofa. After that for a while I left the city, returning to house sit for a lady whose dog mauled me. Then the railroad flat in the area adjoining Soho north of East Houston and that my songwriting partner Mark (I was writing songs then) and I dubbed "So What." The greasy exhaust fumes from the diner downstairs made Mark sick, and so he left the city and me. It was around then that I broke my leg and moved into the Gramercy Hotel. There, lying prone in bed, I could reach out and touch both walls while listening to the echoes of breaking bottles in the airshaft. Then the Greek woman who taught me typography offered to share her place in Astoria, a shag-carpeted, plastic-slipcovered efficiency over a garage a few blocks from Ditmars Boulevard, where the cafes featured excessive chrome and glistening mounds of baklava. After Ourania and I split up, I moved to Sunnyside, to a one-bedroom near Calvary Cemetery, in a neighborhood of dismal pubs with shamrocks on their awnings. Shortly after this I met, proposed to, and moved into a two-bedroom with Tara. The apartment had French doors. I'd step out of the bathroom or the kitchen to see Tara there, through the latticed doors, bent over a Fabriano block, smoking. It was Tara's smoking that put the kibosh on our engagement, so I told myself, though in truth I'd been ambivalent from the start. I hung on in Queens until, with a journalist named Steven, I went in on a rental on 1st Avenue off 14th. It was a one-bedroom; we put up a makeshift wall. We spent a lot of time on the roof there, Steven and I, drinking a brand of cheap red wine called "Gato Negro" and having aggressive philosophical conversations. I stayed there until Paulette, my new girlfriend, and I got tired of squeezing into my captain's bed. She and I rented a floor-through in a brownstone on 101st near West End. In its living room, in the presence of two witnesses, a gay Episcopal priest married us. Six months later we purchased our own place, a foreclosure on 94th and Columbus in an art deco building with a sunken living room and built-in wall sconces. Though on the ground floor and dark it offered a nice view of the dogwood tree in the courtyard. I set up my studio in the master bedroom and decked the walls with my paintings of passenger ships and the Empire State Building at night. In spite of the rap deejay living downstairs, we were happy there, until one morning I awoke from a dream in which, instead of a dogwood tree, our window faced the wide gray-green expanse of the Hudson River. That same morning I boarded a train from Grand Central to the Bronx. At a place called Spuyten Duyvil I detrained. Nothing but weeds, trees, water. Water! How I'd missed it! We lived on an island but rarely saw the stuff. Overhead loomed the blue arch of the Henry Hudson Bridge—the same bridge my father and I crossed into Manhattan in his Simca Chatelaine. Six months later, my wife and I bought a co-op there that we called home for the next twelve years, until we separated and divorced.

I was fifty years old.

V. DISSOLUTION

The dreams of my youth, where had they gone? At the midcentury mark one is entitled to such inquiries. I'd struggled, worked hard, produced, yet there was the nagging sense that I had wasted myself, that I had poured my essence into the city only to see it washed away like so much scum down its storm grates and sewage drains. Another part of me wondered: was it my own damn fault? In abandoning the city (and as any New Yorker will tell you, when you say "the city" you most assuredly do not mean the Bronx or any borough other than Manhattan), had I forsaken my dreams? Had I been as fickle with them as with apartments and women? Had my quest for artistic glory been nothing but one long flirtation—as feeble and hopeless as the flirtations I had engaged in from my dishwashing station in the Broome Street Bar? Had my romance with New York City been nothing more than a prolonged fruitless act of mutual seduction?

The city was a vast repository of passageways and doors, any one of which might lead me to my destiny. To choose one door was to slam all others shut. I remember one day, back when I was still in my thirties, coming home from one of a series of assignations, this one with a woman living in a basement apartment on the Lower East Side. As I walked, the streets seemed to stretch out ahead of me like a cartoon stretched on Silly Putty, growing longer and narrower. Four-thirty in the afternoon. Ruddy, low-pitched sunlight spilled over the tops of buildings that seemed to frown down at me, their cornices furrowed like brows. It might have been my imagination, but the doors of all the buildings seemed to have big padlocks on them and big red-and-yellow signs shouting KEEP OUT and SECURITY ZONE.

The gates were down on all the bodegas. I had to resist the urge to run—a flight toward, or away from, innocence? The woman's name was Greta. Her lobby buzzer didn't work. To gain entry I had to phone from the corner, or stand there, on the sidewalk, hoping she'd see me through the bars of her window. We'd met at a loft party, or a gallery opening, or a play or a poetry reading, somewhere where bad wine and cheese cubes were served. With a pocket full of toothpicks I'd left with her for her place in a taxicab. Her pet cockatoo squawked in its gilded cage. A pachinko machine hung by a mandala poster over her bed. All this is grasping at the past. There was no Greta, or there were dozens of Gretas, each as insubstantial as the photographs in someone else's album, one Greta for each address where I'd lived and for every woman I had loved and ought to have been faithful to. But I was never faithful. I was too circumspect, too terrified of anything even remotely binding. By choosing not to choose, I expunged all choices.

There were times when, on a busy street corner, I'd stand there, frozen, unable to make up my mind which way to cross, other pedestrians jostling me, casting me annoyed looks, cursing me under their breaths though still loud enough for me to hear. I'd learned my way around the city only to find myself directionless there. This lack of impetus led to awkward situations. Late one afternoon the English actor intercepted me on the corner of Eighth and University. He was with the Ol' Vic, he explained, in town for a production of Macbeth. He looked like Richard Basehart, so I believed him. I had no hair; I'd shaved it down to my skull. This attracted homosexual men. Macbeth wondered where "a bloke from out of town could get a good drink." I was still living in Brooklyn at the time and said so. This didn't dissuade him. We went to Chumley's and from there to his place, the borrowed "flat" of some other actor. Having mixed us both screwdrivers, Richard Basehart lay on the floor fondling himself while reciting apt passages from one of Henry Miller's more explicit books. He didn't seem to notice or to care as I stepped over him and out the door.

Another time, during a blizzard that fell on my twenty-third birthday, a former priest who'd taken me to dinner for my birthday offered to let me stay at his place, which offer I accepted, gladly, having always resented those midnight subway expeditions back to whichever miserable borough I happened to be living in at the time. When the ex-priest took me in his mouth I pretended to be elsewhere, with someone else, enjoying the dim ministrations of an altogether different set of tongue and lips. In the morning my host was beside himself. As for me, I couldn't have cared less. What did it matter? Why should I have cared?

Back then I was subject to this recurrent dream, a nightmare that parachuted me into the combat zone amid its vaporous lights and alleyways. Always in the dream I'd end up in a movie theater, one of those sordid venues near Times Square, attached to an unemployed regiment of hunched men in Burberry coats, and where the bodies projected on the screen were always tantalizingly out of focus, looking more like Cézanne's peaches than like men and women engaged in carnal acts. Nevertheless the soundtrack was always clear: a moan is a moan is a moan. As if by my own tumescence I'd be lifted out of my seat and led toward a red sign glowing over the men's room door behind which ultimate depravities lay in wait, tinted with ultraviolet light, perfumed with semen and urine. Debased by my own dreams.

VI. FALLING OUT

The City of New York had become my illicit lover—a woman of the night whose sordid charms I could not resist but to whom I could never entirely give myself. I thought of my father and of his "business trips." Decades passed before I finally accepted that he'd kept a mistress in the city, maybe more than one, though a single name, Berenice (Beh-reh-nee-chay) stood out for me, having surfaced time and again in my parents' frequent fights, such that those four syllables still send their chill up my spine. According to my mother, I once nearly drowned in the Hotel Paris swimming pool, my treacherous papa having left me there to attend to his courtesan upstairs. I refused to believe it. Anyway I never once saw this person, this Berenice, who to this day exists for me on roughly the same plane as Cleopatra or Attila the Hun. My father, too, was unfaithful. The city was his lure, his temptress, his domestic and moral undoing. For New York City he broke faith with his own family, though in the end he returned to us.

But then—as scorned mistresses will—the city avenged itself.

I remember one of the last times Papa visited me there, a year or so before the first of a series of strokes felled him. Paulette and I were still living on the Upper West Side, in the 94th Street deco apartment. My father and I lunched at a diner where he ordered a bowl of vegetable soup. When I asked him how it was, he looked down at the soup spoon trembling in his fist and said, in a voice heavy with sorrow, "Not so hot." He had come to the city to see me, but also to gain an audience with the literary agent to whom he had sent his latest opus, a manuscript titled "Beyond Pragmatism" by which he hoped to advance William James's psychological theories into the twenty-first century—a hope against hope for this obdurate eccentric inventor who rarely read books published after the Hague Convention and whose manifestos were riddled with hyphenated to-days and plastered with Ko-Rec-Type. The agent had not returned his calls. Having paid for our disappointing lunch, my father repaired to a telephone booth across the street, where, for the tenth time that day, he tried to reach her, only to lose a quarter to the out-of-service apparatus. With uncharacteristic fury he slammed the receiver down. A few blocks uptown we found another phone booth, this one occupied by an African American man, prompting my father, until then the least bigoted person I had ever known, to combine a garden-variety epithet with a racial slur. "Papa, take it easy," I said—or something to that effect. "What's the matter?" But I knew perfectly well. It was no longer my father's city, the one he'd invented for me, his son. It had become an unfamiliar, hostile place. As I led us away from that phone booth, in my father's murky pupils I read an accusation of betrayal, as if I, not the city or his agent, had let him down.

Now here I was, a few years later, my father dead and me, his son, suffering from his ailments, his insomnia and his indigestion, his infelicities and failures and disappointments, not to mention a hefty slice of his egocentricity, feeling no less betrayed than he by the city that had been our mistress. By then Paulette and I had completed our migration to the Bronx. Though our window faced the northern tip of Manhattan, and though Grand Central Terminal was but a twenty-two-minute train ride away, we'd turned our backs on the real city. In the shallows across the turbid waters we watched a snowy egret—a feathered white vase—do its slow-motion dance for fish. We kept a pair of binoculars handy. Like having one foot in the country, we told ourselves and the friends we had ditched downtown.

They assumed that the move had been voluntary, but I knew better: I knew the city had already forsaken me, that I had failed to live up to its promises. Not that we never enjoyed ourselves, my wife and I. We took regular trips to Europe, ate good meals, threw parties packed with Manhattanites who risked nosebleeds and blown eardrums to venture north of 14th Street. But an undercurrent of distress ran through my contentment. It was this undercurrent that often woke me in the middle of the night. I felt bloated with regrets, thinking we should never have left Manhattan, that we might as well have buried ourselves alive. I tried to reassure myself. I told myself I had wanted light, air, sunshine, fewer car alarms and idling, poisonous-fume-spewing buses. If I never lived to see Upper Broadway—that ragtag tunnel of produce stands and baby strollers—again, it would have been too soon. Besides, the city wasn't the city anymore. It had been co-opted by the sitcom crowd.

The popularity of TV shows like *Seinfeld* was commensurate with its cultural decline. How I missed seedy Times Square! How I longed for the days before the peep shows succumbed to Walt Disney! Such had been my logic, my excuse, for abandoning the city and the dreams of my youth, a move that would prompt me, on those sleepless nights, to stumble into the bathroom and demand of my no-longer-quite-so-young reflection in the medicine cabinet mirror, *What have you done to my dreams, fucker?*

From the bedroom my wife asks, "Peter, what are you doing?"

I'm a poor underdog / But to-night I will bark / With the great Overdog / that romps through the dark.

"Brooding," I respond.

"For god's sake, come back to bed!"

Then I say to myself: Wait, it's not over. There's still time. You're still young, you can still do it. You know the meaning and worthiness of art, that it makes life bearable by translating experience, letting us see universals and particularities in a kind of flickering way, that every artist holds the potential to delight and heal others by touching them with something genuine, something of deliberate beauty. New York hasn't forsaken you, chum, I assure my reflection in the mirror. That's your sense of gloom talking. Nor have you forsaken it. You just wanted some peace and quiet in which to create.

Here was hope springing eternal; here was my childhood innocence shining its bright dim-witted light again—the same innocence that forty-four years prior had turned an ad slogan on the side of a gas storage tank into a divine revelation. Despite my grown-up sense of gloom, I was still a child, still besotted, still as prone to bad judgment in hope as ever, still as wide-eyed with curiosity, expectation, and optimism as a six-year-old. Still as eager and willing as ever to march headlong into the arms of the enemy, of Berenice, of my father's ex-mistress, as if by conquering her I might make up for his sins.

VII. ASHES & ECHOES

I'd meant to spend that September at a writer's retreat but came home early to attend a gala at Lincoln Center (and to pick up some warmer clothes; I hadn't realized how cold it gets in the Adirondacks). That morning I tried on my tuxedo to discover that it no longer fit. I was about to head downtown to rent one, when the telephone rang: the woman who'd invited me to the gala, calling to tell me that it had been called off. I asked her why.

"Have you got a TV?" she said.

Like half of the country, I spent the next five hours sitting with my hand to my lips in front of the TV. The city that I'd loved, resented, felt challenged and betrayed by, whose slushy sidewalks and oven-like summer subways I'd cursed—this place where I had been loved, mugged, produced, embarrassed, paid, exhibited, that had made me proud and angry and excited and bitter and exhausted and joyous and hungry and regretful, that had been the setting of so many youthful enthusiasms, where I'd walked arm-in-arm with and courted and made love with women, where I had suffered, celebrated, laughed and cried ... whose myriad streets I could navigate blindfolded or by smell, whose subway turnstiles I'd jumped, whose taxi drivers and waiters and shoeblacks I'd tipped, whose cafés and galleries and atriums I'd haunted, whose streets I'd jay-walked, whose muffins and bagels I'd ingested by the score, whose store windows had sampled my evolving reflection, whose landlords had charged me rent, whose employers had paid my wages, whose supermarkets and delis had supplied me with milk and pickled herring, whose water supply had kept me hydrated and hygienic, whose sewage system had eliminated four-and-a-half decades' worth of my excretions, whose thrift stores and flea markets had provided me with furniture and clothing, whose populace had endowed me with friends, lovers, acquaintances, clients, and occasional enemies—that this setting that had graced a hundred charming *New*

Yorker covers could be changed so suddenly into a tragic place, a grim place, a war memorial, a Pearl Harbor, a Waterloo, the Alamo, a place to feel reflective and sad, made me wonder: What would future six-year-olds make of that blazing skyline? Would they look upon it with wonder and joy as I once did? Would they see a city of dreams? Or would they see only the memory of a single disastrous day, twin columns of air where a pair of skyscrapers once stood?

Was I feeling sorry for the city, or for myself? Was there a difference? Sometimes it takes a disaster to put us in touch with our innocence, to remind us of just how romantic our delusions have been. Seeing her ravaged made me fall in love with New York all over again, made me embrace her with fierce protective pride. Even the city's past calamities—the Black Tom explosion, the Triangle Shirtwaist Factory fire, the Fraunces Tavern bombing, the Kew Gardens train crash, tragedies quaint by comparison, were caught in my embrace, as were the rumble of the El, tuberculosis windows, horse walks, Horn & Hardart, those stately clocks along 5th Avenue, the sunken treasures under the swirling waters of Hell's Gate. In a fervor of indignation, I reclaimed my city, the one that I'd inherited from my father. Nothing—not even an army of terrorists—could take her from me again.

VIII. SEPARATION, DIVORCE & RECONCILIATION

In the end it wasn't terrorists or my own sense of failure that separated me from New York, but a tenure-track job at a decent university. It's been four years since I left the city. And though New York has never entirely left my thoughts, this is the first occasion I've really had to look back. I live in an A-frame on a lake in central Georgia. Two paintings hang on the wall behind the desk where I sit writing this. The top painting is an interior of a subway car rendered in mute grays and browns, with passengers asleep or reading books or gripping subway straps, as Chris Rowland and I did when we were fifteen. The painting underneath it is of the Empire State Building at night, its teeming windows represented by daubs of yellow paint, a full moon burning alongside its glowing blimp tower. From that painting I have only to turn my head a few degrees to see, through the slats of the venetian blinds on the doors that open onto my deck, the lake and the weather-beaten dock from which I swim jutting into it. As places go, none could seem farther away from New York.

From my dock, swimming, I count two hundred strokes to the other side of the inlet and as many coming back. These days, that and a three-three teaching load is all the ambition I need, and thanks to the lake I have plenty of water to supply it. Between stretches of work I swim sometimes two or three times a day. With every stroke I push more of the past away, along with my memories of New York.

Who am I kidding? I'll carry that city with me forever. It's in my bones, my flesh, my DNA, my genes. It's the egg that my father fertilized and that gave birth to me. With every stroke I swim deeper and deeper into the teeming metropolis of my dreams.

❖ *How the Vest Was Won*

> "The king hath yesterday declared his revolution of setting a fashion for clothes which he will never alter. It will be a vest. I know not well how, but it is to teach nobility thrift and it will do good."
> —Samuel Pepys in his diary

THE KING WAS CHARLES II, THE YEAR 1662. Thus what began life as a cassock in the mid 1400's and evolved into a doublet by the first half of the 16th century underwent its final transformation, becoming a small, sleeveless jacket shorter in length and open in the front, providing ample opportunity for men of the period to show off their frilly shirts. The vest was born.

Others were less enthusiastic than Mr. Pepys. In his own diary of 1666 John Evelyn records how when the King "put himself solemnly into the Eastern fashion of the vest ... divers courtiers and gentlemen gave his Majesty gold to wager that he would not persist in this revolution."

They should have kept their purses shut. For though the history of men's fashion is replete with styles that have come and gone (stove-pipe hats, spats, leisure suits), vests endure, and have for over four-hundred years, longer than neckties and shirt collars.

A waistcoat, a "coat of the waist." Who needs a coat for the waist? No arms, no legs, no collar. A square yard of fabric—hardly enough to keep oneself warm in. You can't tuck your pants or shirt into a vest. As for those silly little pockets, they're good only for pocket watches and snuff boxes and other things no one uses anymore.

What good is a vest? You may as well ask what good are a peacock's feathers. Vests are made for showing off. Poor hairless and featherless man, his rubbery flesh available in but a few dull shades, his choice of suits equally dull. And the necktie—that skinny, skimpy concession to male individuality. A man needs more. Like the peacock, he needs to strut his stuff, to show his true colors. Hence the vest!

It was another king, King George IV, who initiated the fashion of leaving the bottom button of his vest undone. He did so by accident, having forgotten to button it before attending a party in his honor. His friend and fashion arbiter Beau Brummel was quick (so to speak) to follow suit. The habit persisted.

As did vests, growing more functional in the 1800's, made of lush fabrics depicting everything from hunting scenes to naval engagements, their mysterious myriad pockets hiding everything from love letters to pearl-handled derringers.

Perhaps not entirely by coincidence there followed the age of the fop, whose extraordinarily expensive vests featured buttons of perfumed wood and mother-of-pearl, and floral fabrics that, according to Marc Constantin and his Almanach des Belles Manieres, could "be seen from one end of the street to the other." Admired or loathed, the wearers of such vests were impossible to ignore.

Over time those brilliant expensive fabrics were replaced by plainer stuff, velvets and silks of rich but solid color, cypress greens, rich burgundies, and heady violets. In the late 1800's, the fabrics came in paisleys, plaids, pinstripes, and checks. These in turn were followed by still more sober fabrics, until vests grew as plain as the clothes worn over them, paving the way for the three-piece suit.

Today vests once again trumpet rich fabrics, and so they should. For unlike a suit, the vest is no starched-down disciplinarian, no buttoned-down banker or solicitous clerk, no stiff-collared preacher, but a colorful orator whose locutions are as inspiring as they are connivingly manipulative. The vest is the Elmer Gantry of garments.

But a vest is more than a manipulator. It is a seducer, a set of signs and signals both as subtle as a whisper in the dark and as obvious as a fire engine's flashing lights and puling siren.

Note the geometry of the vest: a series of V-shapes or chevrons aimed downward, indicating a man's belly as the way, not only to his heart, but to his other desires, his masculine center of gravity, the focal point of his libidinal urges. Sexual attraction may begin with the eyes, but from there it makes a beeline south. Indeed, it may be argued that the "humble" vest with its array of buttons and arrow-shapes pointing groinward serves a more vital function than any other garment in a man's closet, in a word: procreation.

As a boy I instinctively felt the power of vests, out of fashion when I came of age in the early 1970's, available only in musty thrift shop racks or as a dull component of even duller men's suits. Inspired by a popular TV series called *The Wild, Wild West*, a James Bond-western hybrid whose hero wore tight fitting ones of dazzling brocades, I had my mother make one for me. With my tight brocade vest, I reasoned that like James West, the show's hero, I, too, could beat up a dozen bad-guys at once, including pimply-faced Bobby Mullins, who went to St. Mary's and tormented me constantly at the bus stop we shared.

So off we went, my mother and I, to the local fabric store where, like prospectors digging for gold, we sifted through the bins and racks of elaborate brocades, to emerge with a yard and a half of the most expensive fabric in the place, along with six filigreed gold buttons no less ornate and costly. An hour later I stood and watched from behind as my mother stooped over her brown Singer sewing machine, making sure she got the curves on the lapels just right, and that the V-opening below the neck was of just the right scale.

A few days later, at the bus stop, wearing my dazzling vest, when—predictably—Bobby Mullins shoved me, this time I shoved him right back. Was it my new vest, or had I grown pugilistic overnight? Anyway we traded blows. My second jab found Bobby's nose, which, broken, spattered blood across my golden vest. I left the stains there: a testament. Blood and gold, silk and snot, brocade and gore.

Years later, when I was making my living as a caricature artist doing private and corporate functions and needed to keep my drawing arm free, unencumbered by a sleeve, I wore fancy vests that I designed myself. But the sleeve thing was really just an excuse. It was the peacock in me, not the artist, who needed his vest. I had a tailor sew me half a dozen, each more elaborate than the one before. Two years later I outgrew them all, my chest having broadened from swimming pool laps.

These days I rarely wear vests, mainly because I never see ones that I like. The referees of fashion can't seem to get it right. Vests shouldn't be loose-fitting or boxy. They should slim the wearer by emphasizing the V-shape of his torso. By no means should they come down to the thigh, lest they resemble the doublets of yore. And the buttons should be of modest size, lest they resemble coals on a snowman. A vest should have lapels; without them they look flimsy.

As for the fabric, if it calls no attention to itself, what's the point? Perhaps not as extravagant as a peacock's plumage, but more than a wink or a whisper, somewhere along the continuum from mild charm to brazen flirtation. The same fabric should be used on both the front and the back, plain satin backs being an economic compromise, since backs tend to wear out faster than fronts. But as they are worn nowadays often without jackets, vests should look good from all sides.

Finally, a vest should never be made of recycled neckties, washable paper, denim, or canceled American Express cards.

Oh, and remember: leave the bottom button undone.

Who are we to argue with kings?

❖ *Swimming to The End*

ON LABOR DAY WEEKEND A FEW YEARS AGO, some friends and I decided to swim across the Hudson River. That may not sound like a great idea. And in fact unless you're a skilled swimmer with an escort, and depending on bacteria levels, tide tables, and boat traffic, it probably isn't a good idea at all.

We had an escort. Paul claimed to know the river by heart. He was a tidal expert and kept tabs on the river's bacteria levels. From a dock at the Riverdale Yacht Club in his rubber Zodiac, he piloted us across the river to our starting point. He and a team of three kayakers would be guiding us back across the river as we swam, the yacht club dock our final destination. We had timed our swim with the slack tide: the short period when there is no tidal motion or current in a body of water. In the Hudson, slack tide occurs when the river's current is counterbalanced by the incoming estuary tide. According to Paul, slack tide would start at 3:30 PM and last a half hour. Once it began, we had only that long to complete our swim. Otherwise we'd be dragged downstream.

Once we got to our starting point, there was some confusion getting underway. One of the swimmers forgot his goggles; another suddenly confessed to having next to no experience in open water, let alone water with currents, tides, barges, and freighters. Two of the three kayakers that were supposed to escort us failed to show up. Since the exhaust fumes from its outboard were sure to asphyxiate anyone swimming less than a dozen feet behind it, Paul's Zodiac proved quickly useless as a guide boat.

By the time we got in the water it was a quarter to four: slack tide had already peaked. The crossing would take at least thirty minutes. By then the current would be flowing rapidly again, or the tide would be coming in. I wasn't sure. We decided to swim anyway.

The river was gray-green and murky, too murky to see my hand break the water in front of me. Bits of gel-like matter passed between my spread fingers. The river tasted of mud, salt, and something I tried not to think about. I aimed for the yacht club: a tiny white triangle on the now distant shore. Every time I looked up, the triangle was further to my left. I was drifting. We all were. The Zodiac spluttered by.

"Oh-point-two-five!" Paul shouted, meaning we had three-quarters of the distance yet to cover. I felt like I'd been swimming forever.

I kept going.

A few days earlier, the students in my writing workshop had challenged me to give them some recipe or formula for plot. Like most writing teachers, I approach the subject with dread and loathing. Having invoked Philip Larkin's recipe ("a beginning, a muddle, and an end"), I drew two points on the whiteboard, about three feet apart, and connected them with a straight line. Then, using a dotted line, I showed how, about two thirds of the way through a typical story, the trajectory symbolized by the straight line is thwarted: something unanticipated occurs, throwing the plot off its predictable course, sending it in a whole new direction, toward a surprising, yet inevitable, end.

As I kept swimming, seeing my target veer further and further to the left in spite of my efforts to compensate for the current, I thought of the illustration I'd used in class: how the author begins with an inciting event, Point A, which then leads into the heart of the story—the middle (muddle) of the river, with its somewhat anticipated complications (barges and freighters churning up wakes); how the plot widens and deepens as it progresses toward the distant Point B, the likely or obvious outcome, the distant white triangle. But then, about halfway across, something unexpected happens: The current builds, the tide comes in; a cramp grips the calf of one's leg. The plot has shifted; the path twisted. The element of surprise comes into play. And there are bound to be many more surprises in store.

I was some two hundred yards downstream of my target. The current was growing stronger and stronger. I tried to fight it, swimming at a sharp angle to it. That's when my left leg gave out; I couldn't move it. The cramp seized my calf first before corkscrewing its way up into the rest of my leg and thigh. I stopped swimming and treaded water, and told myself to keep calm. When the cramp subsided, I started swimming again, aware that I was now at least three hundred feet downstream. The Zodiac was nowhere to be seen.

The image of the plot curve kept recurring to me as I swam on, that simple line on a whiteboard delineating drama: incident, event, surprise, the unexpected. Could that simple line with its unanticipated twist at the end represent the tragedy of this day? Had I inadvertently followed the rules of plot to a "T"—as in Tragedy? Who was it that said tragedy was all very well when it occurred on a stage, but that in real life it seemed closer to absurdity? If one of us died on this day, on this glorious, cool, sunny day with not a cloud in the sky, would it be tragic, or absurd? Or both?

And how fitting that, viewed on a map or from the sky, the course of each of our journeys would correspond exactly to that classic plot curve, bending like a bow from Point A (best laid plans, hopes and aspirations, innocence) to the wholly new and unanticipated Point C (comedy, tragedy, irony—the shedding of innocence, but in any case, The End). Would people trace the last moments of our lives on that graph and say, "They died dramatically, in perfect form, with strict adhesion to the rules of good storytelling?" Would they think silently to themselves, "Like all good endings, a surprise—but in retrospect, inevitable"? Or would they think, "Unbelievable; highly improbable, if not altogether impossible, and hence, unsatisfactory.

Another draft, please!"

For me that day, swimming onward, with the shore refusing to arrive any closer no matter how hard or fast I stroked, the plot had begun to seem all too inevitable. The pedant was about to be hoisted by his own petard. Would the other swimmers likewise drown, victims of my my pedagogy? Would we all be the victims of the perfect plot?

It took me another fifteen minutes to reach the rocks. By then I'd suffered a second bad cramp, this one in the other leg. I was barely able to beach myself.

Twenty minutes later, we'd all made it to dry land. The current carried one swimmer a few thousand yards downstream, almost as far as the Spuyten Duyvil; another swimmer was swept all the way to the shores of Inwood Hill. A third nearly made it to the George Washington Bridge. Had we set off a few minutes later, she might have been swept to the Verrazano Narrows or beyond.

In the end, the plot had twisted itself back into a more-or-less straight line, with comedy tempered by the potential for tragedy, rather than tragedy itself. We had survived our dramatic journey, full of tides and turns treacherous currents and other hazards unpredictable and unknown. The air was crisp and sunny and dry, and so was the champagne we drank to celebrate our crossing and toast the tale that we'd lived to tell.

❖ *Swimming with Oliver*

1.
After a swim, that's when I miss him most. In November, when the water temperature is in the sixties, when I've toweled off and put on my bathrobe and started up the leaf-strewn lawn from the dock to my house, that's when I say to myself: I have to phone Oliver and tell him what a glorious swim I've just had. I'd often call him on weekday mornings after a swim.

Then I remember: I can't phone Oliver. Oliver's dead.

2.
We met in the winter of 1986, at Simon & Schuster, his publisher, soon after *The Man Who Mistook His Wife for a Hat* came out. I was still living in New York then, and had been assigned to interview him for a magazine. The office was at Rockefeller Center. On the street corner a vendor was selling hot chocolate from a cart. Having somehow intuited my subject's love for hot chocolate, I bought two Styrofoam cups worth and rode the elevator with them in a paper bag.

They'd set us up in a conference room. I found him there, a big shy Santa Claus in a white physician's coat with a lush salt-and pepper beard. He sat there with his knees spread apart, gripping them with his big hands, leaning forward into my questions.

"Would you say all people exist on a continuum of pathologies?"

"Ahm ... yes, I suppose you could say that."

"When you talk to people, are you constantly aware of their tics?"

"If you're wondering if you're being diagnosed, the answer is no."

Having drained the liquid part of his hot chocolate, twirling a finger over the sediment at the bottom of his cup, with his characteristic stutter, he said, "I'm—I'm—I'm ... tempted to—to—to ..."

"Go for it!" I urged.

In tandem we licked hot chocolate sediment from our fingers.

3.

Ten years later, I read "Water Babies," his essay in the *New Yorker* about his passion for swimming. Myself a swimmer, I thought: how fun it would be to swim with Dr. Sacks. I dashed off a letter—third item down on my bucket list of things to do before I died: "Swim with Oliver Sacks."

His reply came a few days later, handwritten in green Flair on cream stationery with a cephalopod logo. The writing was barely legible.

He'd be delighted to swim with me.

4.

In the gloom of morning he calls from his car phone. "Olivah heah. Meet me on the Kappock Street ramp in five minutes?" With my black gym bag holding my Speedo, goggles, cap, and towel, I hurry out of my Bronx apartment building, up the steep hill, and under the highway overpass slathered with graffiti. The sun has just broken over building tops.

He stands smiling next to his pulled-over Lexus. "I'm pathologically early," he says.

5.

Mozart on the car stereo. Oliver sipping from a water bottle, discussing his book-in-progress, a chapter about his childhood embrace of metals, chemicals, and minerals. We take the Saw Mill River Parkway north toward Connecticut.

Does this man know, has he any idea, what it means for me to sit with him in his car like this, guiding him toward my favorite lake for a swim? I remember those daydreams I used to have when I was a kid of the Beatles coming to my house for dinner.

6.

The lake is on the former summer estate of a robber baron, now a state park. At its center: a small island with the remains of a decorative stone lighthouse. Swimming is prohibited. We have to scramble up some rocks and bushwhack our way to the swimming hole, where, if the ranger comes by in his truck, we'll be hidden from view.

We undress and put on our Speedos. Since our first meeting Oliver's trimmed down. A swimmer's body: top-heavy, barrel-chested, and covered with gray fur, like a bear.

We swim twice to the stone lighthouse and back. Afterward we lie on a smooth rock, sunning ourselves. Bird songs. The wind whispering through tree branches.

"A beautiful day," I remark.

"We live on a very beautiful planet," says Oliver. "It will be a pity if we destroy it."

7.

We drove to my parents' house. By then my father had suffered the first of a series of strokes that left him unable to recognize people and things, including me. He'd been an inventor. While he sat in his chair in the living room, I took Oliver to see his laboratory at the base of our driveway. Papa's last project had been a revolutionary transformer using spools of flat, lasagna-like copper in place of regular round wire for the windings. Oliver, lover of metals, was drawn instantly to a heap of copper scraps. He asked if he could take one. "Yeah, by all means. My father would be pleased."

As we left the laboratory I explained how, walking up the driveway as a boy, I'd pass by the window and see my father at work inside, always with a big grin on his face.

"An inwardly directed man," said Oliver.

8.
For the next fifteen years, Oliver and I swam together. In pools, lakes, rivers, ponds, creeks, bays, estuaries, oceans. Twice we swam across the Hudson River, jellyfish and other matter oozing between our fingers. Though we timed our swims to fit the twenty-minute slack tide window, the second time we still got caught and swept downstream by the current. In torn Speedos we scrambled laughing up the rocks.

9.
Like my father, Oliver had a British accent, though his was the real thing, while my father's was something of an invention. Though both men intimidated me with their genius, Oliver was much more forgiving of my intellectual laziness and ignorance.

After swimming, we would go for a stroll in the Bronx Botanical Garden. These strolls functioned as a scratchpad on which Oliver worked out topics relevant to his latest work-in-progress. My role was primarily that of an ideal listener. Every so often I'd throw a question his way, or supply a useful analogy. But mostly I listened.

Usually our walks took the same path, beginning with a tour of the Members Only garden, with its medley of wildflowers, then through the fern section, then into the woods, until we found ourselves walking along the Bronx River toward the Snuff Mill, stopping at a waterfalls to watch the water cascade in a white, curtain-like sheet.

10.
One day we discuss memory. Oliver distinguishes between two types of memory: procedural and episodic. Procedural memory applies to things

we do without having to "remember" or even to think about them.

"The test for procedural memory is if you can do something else at the same time," says Oliver. "Procedural memory is what we use when humming a symphony or reciting Shakespeare."

"Or swimming," I say.

"Yes," says Oliver. "Or swimming."

Episodic memory is more complicated. "With episodic memories," Oliver explains, "the individual parts are connected or flow into each other like the links of a chain—though 'flow' and 'chain' don't fit very well together." As we keep walking, Oliver arrives at a better analogy: a series of bridges below which, in a person with no episodic memory, there is a bottomless chasm.

"This is what happened to Clive," Oliver tells me, referring to the English musician who, owing to a traumatic injury, lost his episodic memory and couldn't remember what had happened a moment ago, or the moment before that. "Clive's life consists of an endless series of discrete moments existing completely independent of each other except when they're united in some pattern by some procedure or design—like the notes in a symphony."

We discuss other cases involving amnesia, including Jimmie, the Lost Mariner in the book that Oliver refers to simply as "Hat" or "The Hat Book," and another man who, to compensate for his lost memory, never ceased talking, as though the only way he could pass safely from moment to moment—bridge to bridge—was on a river his own words.

"That was his way of avoiding the abyss," Oliver says.

11.

In the fern garden we study the names in Latin. Vulgaris: common. Salvaris: wild. Praecox: precocious. Spicata: spiked. The droll absurdity of plant names. "Snake root." "Strawberry bush." Back at the magnolia trees, I cup a fat white blossom in my hands.

Oliver: "Look at it calling forth—all of nature signaling, putting up banners, saying, 'Reproduce! Reproduce!'" His expression turns suddenly wistful. "Maybe that's why I feel the way I do today."

"What way is that?"

"Ahm ... nauseated."

"I doubt that's what nature intended," I say.

Oliver laughs his snorty laugh.

12.

At an outdoor café table we trade different substances that we'd like to swim in. Oliver would like to swim in a sea of gallium, the metal with a melting point of 85.6 degrees, the same as chocolate.

"Why not just swim in a lake of chocolate?" I ask.

"I love chocolate," he replies, "but I love metals."

"A sea of mercury?" I suggest.

"That would be very unhealthy."

"What about Dutch gin?" (Oliver loved Dutch gin; a phalanx of the empty brown ceramic bottles lined the counter of the kitchen in his Greenwich Village apartment.) "You could get drunk while swimming."

"True, but since alcohol's density is lower than water's you'd have to be an extremely strong swimmer, and even then you would probably sink like a stone."

13.

A kiwi, a pomegranate, a persimmon, other exotic fruits: that's what my wife and I serve him the first time he comes over for breakfast. Our guest is delighted. Nothing he won't try once. He doesn't care if it satisfies his appetite as long as it satiates his curiosity. The fruits could be poisonous; he would still try them. Oliver loves novelty, variety, eccentricity, excess. No wonder the elements amuse him. He approaches the periodic table like a child in a *gelateria*.

At our kitchen table, Oliver reads the Revised Standard Version of the Bible, the only one we have ("You really must get the King James"), quoting the "nasty God of Ezekiel," the "carrot and stick" God: *He whose testicles are crushed or whose male member is cut off shall not enter the assembly of the Lord.*

14.
When it's too cold for lake swimming or when we don't have time for a day trip, we swim at Riverbank State Park on the Upper West Side. The park was built over a sewage treatment facility. When it first opened people avoided it because of the smell. The problem has since been remedied, sort of.

Arranging items in his trunk, transferring them from an array of pockets and bags, Oliver indulges in some OCD counting:

1. Goggles in plastic bag
2. Plastic bag in coat pocket
3. Shoehorn out of gym bag
4. White sneakers in bag
5. Remove orange sneaker #1
6. Remove orange sneaker #2
7. Put on white sneaker #1
8. Put on white sneaker #2
9. Shoehorn back in gym bag
10. Seat cushion in plastic bag …

I'm reminded of Beckett's Molloy sucking his stones.

15.
We've changed and showered and stepped from the locker room onto the pool platform to find a group of lifeguards gathered around the shallow end, keeping us at bay as one of their number emerges from the water with a very small brown object caught in a fish net.

"Fecal matter," the lifeguard pronounces grimly. A toddler has shat in the pool, which is subsequently closed. As we re-dress back in the locker room, I can't resist saying,

"What does a little fecal matter, anyway?"

Oliver: "One little turd and civilization grinds to a halt."

16.

We'd start lake swimming as early as April, with a ceremonial frigid plunge. We'd drive to one of several lakes up in the Catskills. Oliver's driving was a blend of skill and aggression, augmented by Tourettic outbursts. "Shit! Bugger! Fuck!" He hated being stuck behind another vehicle, especially one that obstructed his vision ("Swinish SUVs!"). He'd slap the steering wheel, bang his fist on the dashboard, kick the floor. If I happened to be driving, he'd snarl, "Overtake! Overtake!"

17.

Breakfast at a greasy spoon. With Oliver you had to be careful what you ordered, since he would invariably order the same thing, then get mad at himself—and you—if he didn't like it. I order a corn muffin: a mistake. Though good in other respects, the muffin is very crumbly.

"Ach," Oliver says, picking crumbs from his lap with thick greasy fingers as if they're inch worms or ants. "I despise crumbs. Why did we order these damned muffins? I never eat muffins. Now I know why. They're much too crumby. I've never seen so many crumbs. Ach! Ugh! Remind me never to eat a corn muffin again!"

18.

We stay at a lakeside hotel, in one of six small cabins dotting the shore. With wetsuits on we swim twice around the lake, then take turns sitting on a rock, helping each other off with the skin-tight wetsuits. The resultant tableaux is half vaudeville skit, half comic book, Laurel and Hardy meet Plastic Man.

The hotel is under new management. We're the first customers of the season. They haven't turned the heat on in the cottages. They give us extra blankets. It's too cold to sleep. We spend the night shivering and talking. Oliver shares his sexual proclivities with me, a secret I'll keep for the next twenty years.

Oliver: "I don't initiate, but I don't refuse."

His sex life in a nutshell.

19.

"When you hear a piece of music in your head," Oliver asks later that day as we explore the lake's perimeter by foot, "what is it that you hear, exactly?"

"I hear the music," I answer.

"Note for note, fully orchestrated, or a simplified version?"

"Note for note," I say.

"As though you're listening to a recording?"

"Yeah. That's right."

"Interesting ..."

"Why? What do you hear?"

"The raw melody line — as if a child were playing it on a toy piano or a xylophone."

20.

I asked him once if he'd ever encountered an old enemy, someone he once detested, but then, seeing this person years later, felt the urge to hug them. He had. I asked: "Do you think that response is the product of nostalgia? Masochism? Narcissism? Or a healthy outlook?"

"Maybe a bad memory," he answered. "I know that I've run into people from my past whom I've disliked or even despised, but who sparked wild enthusiasm when seen again twenty years later. I think the mere fact of having one's survival thrust in one's face by the survival of another may explain it. They're still alive and so are we. A continuum is established and upheld for which we can only feel grateful, even if the other person happens to be some whoreson whose guts we hated, who beat us up or made fun of us or gave us a stiff caning.

"Having said that," Oliver continued after a pause, "were he still living and were I to see my old headmaster at Braefield, my impulse wouldn't be to hug him but to give him a swift solid kick in the rump."

"How often did they cane you in that place, anyway?" I asked.

"I don't know. Daily, twice a day, once every twenty minutes."

"No wonder you carry that seat cushion around with you."

Snorty laugh. "Very good!"

21.

In low moods, Oliver puts himself down, lamenting his lack of significant accomplishments as a "real scientist"—like Darwin, like Luria, like Mendeleev, his heroes. Oliver: "Ah, yes, Sacks. He had such promise, such potential. Pity he never amounted to much ..."

I cheer him up or try to. "You're something as good or better than a scientist," I tell him. "You're an artist. You make beautiful things with words. You entertain and move and educate millions of people. Your books are works of art."

"Yes ... ahm ... I've had that thought from time to time."

All the time I'm thinking to myself: If he hasn't amounted to very much, what have I amounted to?

22.

Oliver had an absolute horror of dog feces. One day, as we get out of his car near Riverbank, he steps in a pile.

"Damn it, Peter! Why didn't you warn me? You're a young man with a young man's vision. Didn't you see it? These people with their shitty dogs. No other city in the civilized world is so full of dog shit! It's everywhere! Remind me never to park along Riverside Drive again. A brand-new pair of sneakers—ruined. I'll have to throw them out or boil them. I'll have to boil my car. I'll have to boil this stretch of sidewalk. The entire Upper West Side—all of New York City—the entire world, must now be sterilized through boiling."

23.
Discussion (while walking through the botanic garden) inspired by glorious yellow and red tulips, their burning mouths open to the sky. Subject: Cryptogamic plants. "Cryptogam": a plant (fern, moss, algae, or fungus) reproducing by spores but that doesn't produce flowers or seeds. Cryptogamic: plants in which the reproductive organs are concealed (unlike tulips and most other flowers that flaunt them in order to attract insects). Phanerogamic: the opposite meaning. Plants are phanerogamic when their reproductive organs aren't merely visible, but gaudily displayed.

I ask Oliver, "Is man cryptogamic or phanerogamic?"

"Both," he says. "On the one hand, our genitalia are located up front and forward, designed to attract attention or at least to be seen. Baboons come to mind. With humans the whole issue of hairlessness and the invention of clothes complicates things, though a few tribes today still go around completely naked. As for the design of the human body itself, its erect posture, that raises the question why—assuming he wants our genitals to be hidden—God didn't provide for their concealment as he does with the elephant, for instance, and other mammals, and not just by a dab of pubic hair, either."

"Other mammals don't walk on two feet," I observe.

"That's right," Oliver says. "As we must in order to use our opposable thumbs. If our pricks are exposed in the process, so be it."

We sit by the waterfall observing a lone Canada goose as he stands there, motionless, admiring the view, apparently.

"Another argument for man's essential cryptogamia," Oliver continues, "is the fact that despite being clothed and having his genitals otherwise hidden for millennia, man still reproduces himself very successfully. Clothes don't seem to have been an impediment."

"If anything they're an enhancement," I remark.

"Right, which raises another question: were we to shed our clothes and be more 'at ease' with our nakedness—with the visibility of each other's exposed genitals—would the sexual urge 'relax' and become diminished? In itself that might not be such a bad thing, but it tears a hole in the argument that nakedness is man's natural state. Whatever else nature wants of us, it wants us to reproduce as much as possible."

Oliver scrutinizes me. "Now you," he decides, "with your macho leather jacket, you're definitely phanerogamic."

"What about you?" I say.

"Me, I'm strictly cryptogamic."

The Canada goose stands there. We wonder what's going through its mind. A moment of pure contemplation? A moment of aesthetic appreciation? A state of mental and physical suspension? A form of meditation? A hypnotic trance induced by the steady white noise and endlessly repetitive visual of the waterfall?

"All of the above," Oliver decides.

24.

We discussed the varieties of weeds growing along the shore of a pond, the bull rushes and horsetails and skunk weeds. Oliver knew the names of almost every plant. I wondered why, with nature so prolific and intent on experimenting, it hadn't produced a masterpiece.

"What makes you so sure it hasn't?" Oliver said.

Me: Are human being nature's masterpiece?

Oliver: That's highly debatable, considering we may be the first species to destroy the planet.

Me: So what species is, then?

Oliver: Maybe nature's masterpiece is a cockroach, or a fungus, or a bacterium.

Me: A bacterium?

Olive: Nature doesn't hold to our value judgments.

Me: What's the point, then?

Oliver: Of what?

Me: Of evolution, if the best thing it can come up with is a lousy bacterium?

Oliver: Evolution doesn't have a point; evolution *is* the point. Nature exists to adapt and experiment.

Me: But evolve why? What for?

Oliver: If you're talking about an agenda, I don't think nature has one.

Me: What about survival? Isn't survival an agenda?

Oliver: I suppose, but then you run into the problem of an involuntary agenda, one that can exist without free will. I'm not sure that a tree or a plant or a bacterium can be said to possess a will, not the way humans do. On the other hand, plants demonstrate a remarkable degree of persistence and determination, as when a bud shoots up through a crack in the pavement, or when plants flourish in the least hospitable environments. The point, as you say, if there is one, is that all things long to persist in their being. Spinoza said as much two hundred years before Darwin. A stone wants to be a stone. A flower—if it dreams at all—dreams of being a flower. A bird longs to be a bird. And presumably, hopefully, you want to be you.

25.

Of mentor-disciple relationships, Russell Baker once remarked that no matter how much more successful an older writer may be, it's a mistake for a younger writer to ever expect much in ther way of sympathy from him. The older writer has relatively little time left; as far as he's concerned, the younger writer has his entire life ahead of him. Therefor older writer envies younger writer despite how little accomplishment or renown younger writer has achieved.

When I looked at Oliver, I saw someone whose talent and accomplishments I would never begin to approach, let alone match, a man who, though nearly a quarter century older than me, had as much or more vitality and curiosity, and was far more industrious, intelligent, intuitive, and knowledgeable.

And when he looked at me, what did my friend see? Youth, time, infinite possibilities, inexhaustible potential: a (comparatively) limitless future. A flesh-and-blood bundle of luxuries.

26.

Another trip to Huntington State Park. The last stretch takes us down narrow, twisty roads.

Oliver: "How much longer? I don't like all these curves. Isn't there a less curvy way to get there?"

A few miles from the lake, a tree-surgery truck blocks our lane. Despite a small pickup headed our way in the opposite lane, in a bold move Oliver pulls around the tree truck. But the pickup truck's driver refuses to give way. Soon we're face to face with him. Finally, Oliver is forced to give in. Reverse: his least favorite direction. As the small truck passes and I cringe, Oliver rolls down his window.

"What's the problem?" he asks the pickup truck driver.

Pickup driver (stern-faced, lock-jawed, steely-eyed): "Obstructed lane stops."

Then he drives off.

"Was that psychotic behavior?" asks Oliver as we head on. "Would you say the driver of that truck was psychotic? I mean what sort of person behaves that way, do you know? I've never seen anyone act so absurdly. What did he mean by what he said, anyway? It sounded like some phrase out of some sort of strategic military manual. Obstruction lane *what?* What on earth was he going on about? Is this science fiction? And his face—did you see that face? The face of of of of—of a cretin, a fascistic face! Those dull, deep-set eyes, that snarling, vicious, half-twisted mouth. I can't do it justice. I doubt Poe could do it justice. Tell me: what sort of person has a face like that? I don't think I'll ever forget it. I'll have nightmares about it. A patently psychotic face. Only I've met psychotics, and none of them were that disturbing. I mean, there really was something sadistic in that man's look, in the furrow of his brow, in those hard, cold, cruel, Satanic eyes. And just what point was he trying to make, anyway? What do you call such behavior? You're a writer—how would you describe it? Aggressive—is that the word? Confrontational? Assertive? Was this a demonstration of what is meant by the phrase 'to assert oneself'? 'Self-assertion?' Is that what he was up to, what he was demonstrating? That's the problem with this country, with all its confrontational, aggressive, righteously defensive, self-assertive, don't-tread-on-me, Wild West aggressiveness. A showdown—isn't that what we've just experienced? One needs to carry a six-shooter with that sort of mentality. But no, really, I ask you in all sincerity: might that person have been insane? Is it possible? ..."

Oliver's tirade lasts all the rest of the way to the lake.

27.

As we're walking toward our swim hole, an old man fishing along an embankment sees us and jokes, "If we catch you, we keep you." I joke back that I prefer to be fried in olive oil, with a dash of pepper and salt.

"You're very sociable," Oliver says as we walk on.

"That's me doing my imitation of a normal person," I say.

"Well, you're very good at it."

28.
Oliver's loves (a non-exhaustive list in no particular order): cycads, cephalopods (especially cuttlefish), orange Jell-O, swimming (especially the backstroke), ferns, copper, the heavy metals (the heavier the better), Mozart, Mendeleev (the periodic table), Darwin, schmaltz herring (and herring of any persuasion), Swiss Miss (diet), Alexander Luria, spicy Thai chicken/coconut soup, big bathtubs, Dutch gin, motorcycles, minerals, his patients, his friends, yellow pads and colored Flair pens (green, purple, red), his standing desk, his Montblanc fountain pen, his Selectric, smoked salmon, radishes, Proustian sentences, Gibbon's footnotes (and footnotes generally, including, perhaps especially, his own), hard cider, hot coffee (especially on the road), punctuality, his neckworn pocket spectroscope ...

29.
We took a few road trips together. In Woods Hole Bay, Oliver swam while his friend Paul Theroux and I paddled kayaks. In Vermont, we visited Saul Bellow and his family at their farmhouse. In group situations Oliver tended to listen rather than speak. He did so as Mr. Bellow shared with me his idea for a children's book he had been wanting to write for a long time. Having delivered himself of his children's book concept, Bellow leaned close and, sotto voce, gesturing toward Oliver, remarked to me, "He's a rare bird."

30.
At the Shakespeare Festival in Stratford, Ontario, we sit through a dress rehearsal of his friend Jonathan Miller's production of *King Lear*, with Christopher Plummer doing a marvelous palsied Lear.

On the way back from Canada, we discuss possible titles for Oliver's nearly completed memoir. He likes "The Garden of Mendeleev," but worries that not enough people know who Mendeleev was. We come up with some alternatives, including two inspired by Flaubert's "The mind, too, has its erections": "Sacks' Mental Erections" or "My Chemical Hard-Ons," by Oliver Sacks.

Other topics for the drive: Kaleidoscopic patterns under eyelids. Mental symphonies: imagination or hallucination? On fitting in, being or wanting to be "one of the gang."

We take turns behind the wheel of Oliver's Lexus, seeing who can obtain the best gas mileage. I win.

31.

Christmas holidays. Riding the Amtrak from Washington, D.C. to New York. We board the "Quiet Car": no cellphones or radios of any kind permitted, hushed voices: "A library-like atmosphere encouraged."

Eureka! we think.

No sooner are we seated in the Quiet Car than we consider the possibilities. Why not quiet gyms and quiet restaurants, quiet cafés, bars, and beaches? How about a Quiet Brothel or a Quiet Construction Site? Our minds race with possibilities. Quiet Buildings. Quiet Streets. Quiet Neighborhoods. Quiet Counties. Quiet States. State motto on license plate: "Shhhh!" Imagine Quiet Radio Stations (instead of listening to talk or music, you tune in to silence). Quiet Books. Quiet Websites. "Quiet for Dummies." Is it our imaginations, or do all of the passengers in the Quiet Car seem more sophisticated, better dressed, better looking, healthier, wealthier, wiser, and wittier?

Oliver and I (quietly) read our books. Oliver: *Proust Was a Neuroscientist*. Me: *Out Stealing Horses*. When we get bored we wander to the café car, Oliver bracing himself, his legs unsteady as he navigates the swaying aisles. We snack on hummus, olives, tea.

Back in the Quiet Car, Oliver is in a chatty mood. He whispers, discussing the distinction between romantic and clinical descriptions. I'm not sure how long we've been talking, whispering—five minutes, ten?—when a tall passenger wearing expensive tortoise-shell bifocals materializes, crouching in the aisle so that his face is level with ours, a middle-aged face with thick gray hair brushed back and parted in the middle. His complexion is red; his eyes bulge.

"Excuse me," the man seethes, "but you are talking"—his lips spell the words for us—"very loudly. This is the quiet car. If you want to talk loudly, move to some other car. This is the quiet car." His jowls tremble. He looks as if he is headed for apoplexy.

I say, "I didn't think we'd been talking that loudly."

"Yes, yes—you were talking very loudly and this is the *quiet* car." The man returns to his seat.

Oliver and I exchange looks, then bury our chastened heads in our respective books. After a few moments Oliver opens the little vellum notebook he keeps with him always and writes, using one of the three colored Flairs he likewise keeps on hand at all times: *Was that a bit exaggerated?* He hands pen and pad to me.

I write: *I think we've just encountered a Quiet Car Fanatic.*

Oliver (writing): *A Quiet Asshole.*

Me: *A Quiet Hole.*

And so on. We giggle like school kids—silently.

This is, after all, the Quiet Car.

32.

In some ways he was like an older brother or an uncle to me; in others more like a father. Like a father he could be critical. On learning that, at fifty-three, I'd become—not on purpose—a father myself, his response: "That's kid stuff, Peter. At your age you should know better." He disapproved of my saying "different than" (as opposed to "different from"). We disagreed over the proper use of "that" vs. "which."

He could get angry, too. Once, at a swimming camp in Curaçao, while pulling ahead of him in a race I accidentally kicked Oliver in the face with my foot. I had no idea that I'd kicked him. Later, in his room, I found him seated at the desk strewn with papers, with more sheets of paper scattered on the floor, all with strange diagrams drawn on them with his red and green Flair pens, the sort of diagrams football coaches draw for their players, filled with circles, arrows, and Xs. They were Oliver's schematics of "the event," proving, beyond any doubt, that I and no other swimmer in the pack had kicked him in the face, as if he were preparing for a tribunal. I pleaded guilty. It took him a day or two, but eventually he forgave me.

33.
I was still living in New York when Oliver learned about the melanoma in his right eye. He'd picked me up for a swim. As soon as I got in the car I noticed the strained look on his face. I thought his sciatica might have kept him up. It had been acting up lately.

As we pulled away he said, "I'm afraid I've had some rather distressing news." He explained to me how he'd gone to the movies two days before to see the latest Star Trek film. At some point while watching the movie he became aware of a strange, burning shape, like a glowing coal, in the upper corner of his vision. As the dark screen brightened the glowing coal disappeared, but soon it reappeared, along with flashes like camera bulbs going off.

"At first I thought I was having a visual migraine," Oliver explained, "only it affected just one eye, making it an unusual one, since migraine auras originate in the brain and typically effect vision symmetrically."

The visual distortions persisted throughout the movie and afterward, when he got home. Oliver phoned his ophthalmologist, who, it turned out, was away on vacation. Another doctor was covering for him. The doctor, who saw him the next day, found a growth close to the retina. It might be a tumor, the doctor said, or a blood clot from a hemorrhage, though the color was more indicative of a tumor. If a tumor, it might be a melanoma. If a melanoma, then—worst case—it might have already metastasized to the liver, as eye melanomas are known to do once they've grown to a certain size.

"And if it has metastasized?" I asked. "What then?"

"That would be a death sentence, I'm afraid."

He said it matter-of-factly. I remembered the story he once told me of Bishops Latimer and Ridley being burned as heretics at the stake. *Play the man, Master Ridley.*

34.

We had our swim. Afterward, as we walked back to the car (he with a cane now; since breaking his leg in the mountain fall recounted in *A Leg to Stand On*, he'd not been all that steady on his feet), he spoke of how the news had changed his perspective on things, how it had forced him to consider his achievements, to ask himself whether, were he to die in a few weeks or months, his would have been a worthy, a satisfying life. His friend Stephen Jay Gould came up in the ensuing discussion, so did Susan Sontag, Hume, Gibbons, Freud, and others who had lived life to the fullest and faced death bravely, and even (in Hume's case) with great good cheer. Then there were less positive examples, like the polymath physicist John von Neumann, who had been an atheist until he learned that he had eighteen months to live, whereupon to the dismay of his fellow atheists he became a Catholic and lived out his remaining months in fear of hellfire and damnation.

"I don't see that happening to you," I said.

"Nor do I," said Oliver.

35.

In his office he reads to me from a slim vellum notebook: the diary that he's kept since learning of his eye tumor, recounting that moment in the movie theater. The notes sound like notes from one of his case studies, only now the patient is himself. He describes blind spots drifting like clouds over the newsprint in the *Sunday Times,* and how the day will soon come when he'll have to say goodbye to bright colors and stereoscopic vision *(Goodbye to All That,* the title of Robert Graves's autobiography, keeps occurring to him). He smiles while reading, amused as ever by his own words and observations, despite their being occasioned by a life-threatening illness, his own. He approaches his own mortality with the same spirit—sympathetic, curious, with wry, deadpan humor—as he approaches his patients' symptoms: with empathy and interest rather than detachment; sympathy, but not pity; concern, but not alarm; clarity without coldness. Like good poetry, his notebook is the record of emotions recollected in tranquility.

36.
The growth is malignant. Worse, it's right next to the optic nerve. Radiation treatment will be risky. The good news: the tumor is small enough so that it probably hasn't metastasized yet. He orders his priorities: life, sight, eye. He's already decided against enucleation—a gruesomely scientific term for having one's eyeball removed. Radiation offers the best prognosis.

"Either way, I'll probably lose all sight in that eye and with it my beloved stereoscopic vision. Still," Oliver says, "if it saves my life, the loss will be worth it."

I ask him what he plans to do for the holidays. He says he's not sure. Usually he goes to D.C. to visit a friend and the friend's family. On one hand, the distraction may do him good, he says. On the other, he doesn't want to have to be merry around strangers.

37.
Every now and then, however, the clinical detachment dissolves. When it does, Oliver's beleaguered eyes lose their focus. Gravity draws down

the edges of his lips. Under his gray beard his jaw tenses. He steps out of his clinical observer's role and into the body of a man diagnosed with cancer. The poet/scientist vanishes; the helpless patient takes his place. He needs the detachment offered by language, by analysis, by thoughts and words sweeping across the pages of a notebook, the alchemist turning despair and terror into language.

38.
"Let's have a walk, shall we?"

Bundled up, we leave his Greenwich Village apartment in search of lunch. The Japanese restaurant is closed. We go to the Bus Stop Café. It's afternoon. Oliver orders a buttered bagel and coffee. I ask for a glass of wine. Tomorrow Oliver goes for his liver test (one reason he abstains from alcohol himself, though he doesn't much care for wine anyway: too sour; at home he even puts sugar in it, or mixes it with Jell-O). If the test results are negative, it will mean that the cancer hasn't metastasized; if not, there will have to be other tests to determine for certain if the cancer has spread or not. One way or the other, he'll know the worst.

39.
At noon the next day Oliver phones. No metastases.

40.
In 2009, having accepted the first of several visiting positions in pursuit of a new academic career, I left New York City. That pursuit led me here, to Georgia, to my lakeside house.

Whenever possible, on my visits north, Oliver and I swam together. Otherwise, at least every other weekend, typically after my morning swims, I'd phone him, my Speedo still dripping, to rub in his face the fact that I lived on a lake (as he had once), in an attempt to entice him to visit. During one such call, after we'd spoken of other things, he shared with me his bad news: after a long remission the melanoma had metastasized to his liver. Some treatments might extend his life for a few months, but there was no cure.

"This is it," he said.

Apart from his assistant Kate and other people in his inner circle, he hadn't yet told anyone. He would make the news public in writing, probably in a *New York Times* essay. He didn't seem all that scared or sad or even concerned. His words carried more resolve than anything.

He shared with me his determination to use well whatever time he had left. "I'll spend it with my friends, swim and take walks, read and play the piano, laugh and have fun." But the thing he wanted to do most of all was to write.

"You sound resolved," I said.

"My cancer is resolved. Why shouldn't I be?"

"Well, Oliver," I said, "it's probably no comfort, but dying is just about the only thing that you haven't done yet in your life."

Snort. "Very good."

I'd carried my cellphone out onto the deck, where I could look out at the lake as we spoke. Afterward I stood there, holding it, crying.

41.

I remember my last visit with him. We and his partner, Billy, were swimming together in the back yard pool of his Rhinebeck home. The pool was just big enough for the three of us to swim back and forth abreast of each other. Afterwards Billy and I had a push-up contest on the pool deck. Then we sat there, the three of us, lounging under a pergola in our wet bathing suits.

It would be our last swim together.

Two weeks later, back in Georgia, I awoke to an e-mail from Kate saying that Oliver had died that morning at two o'clock. He died peacefully in his sleep within days of putting the finishing touches on what would be his final essay.

42.

December. My last lake swim of the season. The water temperature has dipped below 60 degrees. At first the lake is painfully cold, but then, after a few dozen strokes, it feels as comfortable as if would were the water a dozen degrees warmer. I do my usual swim to dock four houses away and back, two hundred strokes each way, thinking, as always, while stroking and breathing, of Oliver.

Whenever I swim now, for as long as I keep swimming, I'll think of him. I'll swim for us both.

❖ *The Strange Case of Arthur Silz*

IN THE LOFT BATHROOM OF MY LAKESIDE HOME in Georgia hangs a painting my father did many years ago. It's a small painting done in a narrow range of earth tones—sepia, umber, terra cotta, sienna (raw and burnt), bistre, brown madder, and caput mortuum. The subject is a group of heads sculpted from clay, arrayed on the shelf of a battered cabinet. With their set lips and vacant eyes the heads remind me of the Easter Island statues and of the fate of all who looked directly into the eyes of Medusa, the winged Gorgon with venomous snakes for hair, whose gaze turned them instantly into stone. Dead center on the painting, just below the jaw of the second head to the left, there is a small triangular black hole where the canvas has been pierced. It is through this hole that we broach the story of Arthur Silz.

The painting once hung in my father's laboratory, or the Building, as we called it—the rotting snake and mouse infested stucco shack at the bottom of our driveway where my father conceived and built the prototypes for his inventions, his Mercury Switch, his Color Coder, his Induced Quadrature Field Motor, his Neutralized Cathode-Ray Deflection Tube, his Null Type Comparison Reflectometer... When not inventing things, Papa wrote books, philosophical and etymological tracts and science fiction novels. He was also a more-than-competent painter. His paintings filled the Building, mostly scenes from his travels—markets, piazzas, and landscapes—painted postcards.

When I asked my father about the clay-head painting, I was twelve or thirteen years old. He explained that it was one of the first paintings he'd ever done, in the late nineteen-forties, when he lived in New York City, in a Brooklyn Heights apartment where the Promenade is today. In fact his apartment building was demolished to make way for that pedestrian walkway, with its splendid view of Manhattan, and the new expressway that would run underneath it.

He did the painting in the studio of a Greenwich Village artist from whom he took lessons on Sundays, a German artist named Siltz. Tall, red-headed, with a thick accent, piercingly pale blue eyes, and a fiery temper to match his flaming hair, Siltz had a pet saying, a mantra that guided him through his existence: "It is something I must do." He was married to a quietly devout woman. They had an infant daughter. Occasionally Siltz hired models to pose in the nude for him and for his students. One model was a young "fraülein" named Helga. Pretty, with tight blond curls and a cherubic face, she couldn't have been much older than eighteen. Siltz was in his thirties. One Sunday afternoon, after a painting sesson, with Helga dressed and gone, Siltz asked my father who was cleaning his brushes, "Tell me, what do you think of Helga?" To which my father replied, "She's a nice girl," or something to that effect, prompting Siltz to declare, "I intend to run off with her!" Questioned by my father as to the wisdom of this proposal, Siltz replied, in his strong accent, "It is something I must do."

That was the story behind the painting that currently hangs in my bathroom, except for a footnote my father threw in as an afterthought, speaking to me from behind the spinning lathe or while typing with two fingers on his black Royal portable: how, years later, while hiking alone in the mountains of Mexico, his former painting teacher met with a sensationally violent end. He was stoned to death by indigenous locals who mistook him for the devil. My father read about it in a newspaper.

Needless to say this footnote stuck with me. It's not the sort of thing you forget, after all. Still, over time I did forget about it, until after my father died. Of his many paintings I'd inherited only a handful, the others having been given away or lost when the Building burned down a dozen years before my father died. I remembered the painting of the clay heads and wondered if it had been among the casualties.

I phoned my mother, who swore she had seen it hanging in Eve Bigelow's house. Eve and her husband had been friends of our family's for years, regular guests at my flamboyant mother's lavish dinner parties. I phoned Eve, who by then was a widow.

Indeed, Eve had the painting. "Would you consider trading it for one of mine?" I asked (I, too, am a painter).

"Of course," Eve said. "If I can find it. Why don't you come over and help me to look for it?"

It took a while, but we found the painting. It was in the Bigelow garage, poking out from behind a stack of storm windows. The edge of a window had pierced the canvas.

"I'm so sorry," Eve said.

I didn't care about the hole. I was thrilled to have the painting.

At the time I was still living in Manhattan. I hung the painting in the vestibule of the Upper West Side apartment I'd bought with my wife. I meant to patch the hole, but never got around to it. Every so often, seeing it, I would recall the tale of the German painter and his supposed violent death on a Mexican mountaintop. Such an incredible story! Had my father not told it to me, I wouldn't have believed it.

One day I tried to verify it. The Internet had come of age. Something that sensational had to have left a footprint in cyberspace. I googled Siltz, artist, murdered, Mexico, mountain. Nothing. I tried other search terms. Still nothing. Hours later, convinced that my papa had either dreamed the whole thing up or been pulling my leg, I gave up.

Ten years went by. In those ten years I'd been divorced, fathered a child, left New York, and moved to Georgia, to an A-frame on a lake.

Since I happened to be looking at it while on the phone, I mentioned the painting of the clay heads and the story my father told me about Siltz to Clare, one of my two half-sisters (my father married thrice).

"You wouldn't happen to know anything about that, would you?" I asked Clare.

"The crazy German?" said Clare. Yes, she'd heard the story. She went on to tell me how her mother, who had been friends with Siltz's widow, took her and her sister to the widow's apartment one day for lunch. "There were paintings on all the walls," Clare said. "This was in the spring of 1956. I know, since we'd just learned that your mom [the woman our father left Clare's mother for] was pregnant with you." The German artist's name, Clare told me, was Arthur *Silz*. She spelled it for me. S-i-l-z. No 't.'

Armed with the correct spelling, I did another online search and found the newspaper article, which appeared in the September 15, 1956 issue of the *Village Voice*. Headlined "Village Painter Is Murdered in Mexico," it begins:

> September 8, San Cristobal, Mexico. Six Indians of the Chamula tribe are in jail in this isolated Mexican town, implicated in the murder of a Greenwich Village artist. The cause of the murder could simply be stated as the ignorance and superstition which is still deep-seated among the remote villages of this mountainous state of Chiapas.

The *Voice* article goes on to explain how Silz, who had rented the same house in San Cristóbal de las Casas every summer for several years, having declared his intention to spend all his time painting and not leave town even for the local fiesta, took leave of his studio one day to hike Uitepéc, the highest mountain in the valley. From its summit he noticed the peak of an even higher mountain, Cerro Tzontehuitz—the highest in Chiapas—and, the reporter infers, made up his mind then and there to climb it. According to the article, Silz, who neither spoke nor understood a word of Spanish or the local Indian dialect, was unaware that Tzontehuitz was one of the most dangerous mountains in Chiapas. Apart from the desolate, steep paths threading through areas of dense jungle and skirting abysmal canyons, it was inhabited by superstitious tribespeople untouched, the article states, by Western civilization.

Silz was forty years old when he died. He left behind his wife and their nine-year-old daughter. He hadn't run off with Helga after all.

My obsession with Arthur Silz's story coincided with a period in my life when I had wandered into a wilderness of my own. Divorced, having quit New York City after thirty-six years for the boondocks of central Georgia, my own young daughter living far from me with her mother — whom I'd met and gotten pregnant soon after my divorce and from whom I had since become estranged — I felt lonesome, isolated, at odds with my radically new life, despite having, consciously or not, chosen that life for myself.

My sense of isolation was dramatically heightened by my having recently been put on paid administrative leave by the university where I taught while it investigated charges of misconduct brought against me by a student. The investigation took an agonizing sixty-four days during which I was not allowed to teach nor set foot on campus, nor could I concentrate enough to write, or even to read. That left me with exercise. And though I swam several miles a day in my lake, at night, night after night, I'd waken at one or two in the morning, unable to go back to sleep, infused with a blend of insomnia, anxiety, anger, fear, regret, and sadness — mostly sadness — until one morning, around three o'clock, I found myself sitting in the bathroom of my loft, gazing at the painting of the clay heads from my vantage point on the commode, staring deep into the little triangular hole in its center. On the sink counter nearby, a quartet of prescription vials stood arrayed: Ambien, diazepam, Xanax, trazodone, and some other prescription, a sedative or an antianxiety drug with sedative effects: more than fifty pills altogether, enough, I thought, to do the trick if swallowed with a sufficient quantity of gin (preferred by me to vodka).

But at that moment the little black hole at the center of my father's painting commanded my attention. I felt myself falling into it, tumbling through the rabbit hole in that canvas and into the lurid story behind it. Suddenly, I was Arthur Silz trekking a sun-dazzled, jungle-strewn trail up that mountain, negotiating treacherously steep, narrow paths, bushwhacking through rainforest, broaching isolated, primitive populations, in search of—what? What drove Arthur Silz to his terrible fate? What had he been looking for? Who was he? I had to know.

"It is," I told myself, "something I must do."

When my father studied with him in the late forties, Silz was a painter of repute, with work in the collections of the Metropolitan and the Brooklyn Museum of Art. He taught classes at the Art Students League —where he himself had studied—and workshops in Provincetown. He was something of a reactionary; when abstract expressionism was taking the art world by storm, Silz continued to do figurative work, portraits and landscapes of quaint stone cottages and anachronistic fishing boats in harbors, paintings distinguished by their earthy palettes and heavy brushstrokes (not unlike the brushstrokes in my father's painting of the clay heads, which clearly displays Silz's influence).

Among images of Silz's work available online, I found a portrait of the artist standing before his easel, necktie raffishly loose and askew under his painter's smock. He stands against a dull ochre background, eyes squinting, strong bony jaw and flaring nostrils turned upward, eyebrows raised, brow furrowed, lips pursed, his red hair—which looks more brown than red in the painting—shooting up from a sloped forehead. The head in Silz's self-portrait bears an uncanny resemblance to the second clay head from the left in my father's painting, the one with the triangular hole below its jaw. With its jaundiced pallor and  mask-like squinted eyes, there's something both admonitory and cadaverous about Silz' expression, as though he were assessing his talents from beyond the grave. I can imagine Silz applying the same judgmental squint to the products of his avant-garde contemporaries, to a Rothko or a Kline or a Pollock. How their vast, splattered, streaked, and stained canvases must have vexed Silz, who still believed in the painter as observer and a painting as a kind of glass case wherein the artist's goods are displayed like cakes in a bakeshop window.

Like van Gogh—whom he surely admired—in his portrait before the easel, Arthur Silz wears his tunic loosely buttoned. Like van Gogh, Silz set himself against the tide of current artistic fashion. Like van Gogh, he went south for inspiration, seeking his equivalent of Vincent's "high yellow note"—not in fields of rippling wheat or poppies or sunflowers under the blinding Provencal sun, but in the jungle-clad mountains of southernmost Mexico.

The *Village Voice* article goes on to piece together the story of Silz's murder. However thorough, the article merely whetted my curiosity about Silz and his circumstances.

Effectively under house arrest in my lakeside lockup, I spent the next several weeks researching, determined to fill in that hole in my father's painting by uncovering more pieces of Silz's story, and the stories of other men connected with it, stories that in their sensationalism rival the most convoluted jungle fiction, *Savage Mutiny* meets *Raiders of the Lost Ark*.

In the days preceding Silz's imprudent excursion, two fellow German expatriates tried to talk him out of going. One of those German expats was a man named Wolfgang Cordan.

Born Heinrich Wolfgang Horn in Berlin in 1909, Cordan was an author, translator, anthropologist, and ethnologist. He was also a homosexual, which may be one reason why he left Germany in 1933, the year of Hitler's appointment as chancellor. He fled first to Paris, where, under his penname, he wrote and published L'Alemagne Sans Masque (Germany Unmasked), a booklet condemning the Nazis for which André Gide wrote the preface. From Paris he moved to Amsterdam, where he edited a leftist journal. He also wrote and published an essay on surrealism that earned him a place in the Dutch avant-garde.

During the Nazi occupation of the Netherlands, Cordan joined the resistance. Having learned that a group of Jewish children living in an orphanage had been marked for transport to a concentration camp, he and another resistance member kidnapped and secreted them to a hiding place. (For his part in that deed a commemorative grove of apple trees in Israel bares Wolfgang Cordan's name.) Another time, Cordan and a friend were riding their bicycles together. As they rounded a corner, Cordan recognized a Gestapo informant. With a pistol he was carrying, Cordan shot the *spitzel* dead in front of an apartment house. Though he and his friend evaded capture, that night Cordan watched as Gestapo officers rounded up a dozen of the apartment house's occupants. They were lined up against a wall and shot.

After the war, Cordan journeyed through Central and Southern Europe and Northern Africa, taking photographs, settling briefly in Italy, then in southwest Germany, where he served as a newspaper editor before relocating to Havana. Following a trip to Madrid—during which the landing gear of his airplane failed, forcing it to crash-land on its belly—he left Cuba for Mexico.

It was while hiking the jungles of Mexico that Cordan became immersed in the study of Mayan ruins, especially their hieroglyphs, for which he developed a unique controversial system of interpretation that formed the basis of his doctoral dissertation *Systema di Mérida* (The Merida System). Among Cordan's many interpretations was what his contemporaries characterized as an "extremely loose" translation of the *Popol Vuh*, the sacred book of mytho-historical narratives of the K'iche' kingdom in Guatemala's western highlands.

The same year he published his translation of the *Popol Vuh*, Wolfgang Cordan took a professorship at the University of Merida in the Yucatan. Meanwhile he continued to explore the jungles of Mexico and Guatemala, uncovering archeological treasures. Among Cordan's findings was an Olmec carving dating between 1,150 and 900 BC. The size of a bank vault door, the carving depicts a man of characteristic Olmec features—thick legs, no neck, small feet, wearing a tall headdress with banded decorations, a round earplug with a curved tassel, sharp claws or talons on his feet, and a breechcloth tied with a square knot. Except for his arms and legs, he is portrayed in profile, carrying a knife or a baton in one hand, and a bundle of what is probably maize in the other. Though it was first discovered in the 1920s, because of its remote location only a handful people knew where the Olmec sculpture was, and even fewer had seen it—among them another German expatriate, "B. Traven," the elusive author of *The Treasure of the Sierra Madre*. Without disclosing its location, in 1964, to great fanfare, Cordan published his photograph of the Olmec relief.

Two years later—ten years after Arthur Silz was murdered—Wolfgang Cordan would himself die mysteriously in the jungle. He was fifty-seven years old.

The following words from *Secret of the Forest: On the Track of Maya Temples,* his memoir published two years before his death — words that might have served as his epitaph — suggest that Cordan may have died a contented man:

> The world-weary European who, heartsick and weary of civilization, escapes to and dies in the jungle, whose corpse is sheathed by the jungle's twilight shadows, dies intoxicated with freedom.

In the opening pages of *Heart of Darkness*, Marlow reflects on the primitive urges that drive men to confront the darkness at their innermost depths by way of "the mysterious life of the wilderness that stirs in the forest, in the jungle, in the hearts of wild men." Having bewitched him with its primeval depths, before driving him mad, the jungle inflames Kurtz with a sense of omnipotence, anointing him supreme ruler of his own abominable empire, a Dominion of Darkness. In abandoning civilization, Kurtz morphs into a primeval god. Through Marlow, Conrad warns us of the "the longing to escape, the powerless disgust, the surrender, the hate" experienced by those who, like Kurtz, succumb to their inner darkness.

My confrontation with my own inner darkness wasn't my first. I'd been there before, many times, as a matter of fact, starting in my mid-twenties, when, in despair over an injury that had cost me the use of my left hand (I'm left-handed) and a coincidental broken leg, I hobbled on crutches to the end of a rotting New York City pier, where I stood overlooking the dark East River, luminescent ice floes drifting by, the Brooklyn skyline blazing across the frigid waters.

No, I didn't kill myself, but I thought about it — as I would think about it, off and on, now and then, with increasing regularity, for the next thirty years, until the dark thoughts became so much a part of me I hardly noticed them. When, in my forties, a therapist I had been seeing asked me, "Do you ever think of suicide?" the question took me by surprise, since by that time a more appropriate question would have been, "Do you ever *not* think about it?" I realized then that there was something very wrong with me, that the darkness I'd been taking for granted was a dangerous condition—no less dangerous than any potentially fatal disease, or an incursion up an unknown mountain inhabited by suspicious, primitive people.

My therapist referred me to a psychiatrist, who put me on drugs. Prozac, Zoloft, Paxil, nortriptyline, trazodone—we tried them all with various degrees of success and failure. But something more than chemical was going on. I was drawn to my darkness, unable to resist the tidal tug of those suicidal thoughts, drawn to them like matter to a black hole—like that black hole in my papa's painting of those clay heads that drew me so deeply into Arthur Silz's suicidal excursion.

Exploring jungles is a risky business. As well as the psychological hazards dramatized in *Heart of Darkness*, one has to fear the many physical dangers and diseases presented by the environment. When the jungle is in Central America in the first half of the twentieth century, to the list of dangers one must add suspicious and often hostile indigenous locals, marauding bandits, hard-hearted revolutionaries, and the competing interests of other explorers, some of whom would stoop to anything, including murder, to protect their findings or claim others'.

It was doubtlessly with these things in mind that Wolfgang Cordan tried to dissuade Arthur Silz from hiking alone up into the mountains of Chiapas. How the two men met isn't known, nor is the precise nature of their friendship entirely clear, though clearly they were friends. Apart from their Germanic roots and a shared love of the Mexican wilderness, both men were strong-willed, brave, fiercely independent, bound to their adventurousness by a sense of duty and destiny. Though Cordan was homosexual, and Silz remained married to his wife in New York, in all likelihood both men were more wedded to their sense of adventure than to other people. Like most explorers, they were most likely loners. And like most explorers—like Kurtz and his pursuer Marlow—within the ruin-encrusted jungles, among other things they explored themselves, their own inscrutable, dark depths.

I imagine them hiking the mountain trails together, or sitting on the verandah of one of their lodgings, sharing a bottle of tequila or schnapps while trading stories, the artist and the anthropologist. I see Cordan spreading out his latest photographs, and Silz his latest sketches, each of them offering their appraisals, comparing notes, nodding, affirming each other's talents, brothers in arms—one armed with a camera, the other with a sketchbook. In their own way they may have loved each other. As Cordan wrote to another friend, "When deep contact [is made] between men of about the same age and of equal spiritual development, a lightning flash occurs that breaks down all barriers and fuses their natures."

That Silz and Cordan had hiked the nearby mountains together is without question. Evidence suggests that on one of their hikes they may have made an important archeological discovery. What they discovered isn't known. What is known is that on or around August 17—ten days before Silz was murdered—he wrote to several of his friends, including Professor José Weber, a schoolteacher in San Cristóbal, about the discovery, saying that he and Cordan had been warned by "a rival explorer" working in the same area not to exploit it, to stay away from the site, that in venturing anywhere near it, they would put themselves in grave danger. All this was recounted by Dr. Weber in a letter he wrote to Silz's sister, Mrs. Hilda Silz Royce then of Hillsdale, California. Weber sent a copy of the letter to the United States Embassy in Mexico City.

Who was this "rival explorer?" No one living knows. Weber died in 1982. Neither Silz's letter nor the one Weber wrote to his sister survive. Assuming that the U.S. Embassy in Mexico still has a copy, it is buried deep within its archives.

Nor is it entirely clear that Silz viewed the "warning" as a threat. What is certain is that Silz understood that in undertaking what—in the same letter to Weber—he referred to as his "mission" into the mountains, he would be putting himself in jeopardy, that on top of the risks that he had already been warned about, he faced this other danger as well.

Wolfgang Cordan knew it too. Which is why, a day or two before Silz set off on his journey, having failed to talk him out of it, he arrived at Silz's lodgings with a pistol.

"Take this with you at least," I imagine Cordan saying, yanking a Luger or a Mauser from the waistband of his jungle-hiking shorts. Having lowered the pistol onto the veranda table, next to the bottle of tequila or schnapps, Cordan stands there, looking down with a mixture of derision and admiration at his artist friend, who remains seated, his arms folded stubbornly across his chest, eyeing the weapon with distaste, as if it were something dead dug up from the ground.

"Take it," Cordan insists.

Silz shakes his head.

"Why not?"

"Because—I am a peaceful man!"

"Take the pistol, or you'll be a dead peaceful man."

As Cordan must have realized by then, there was no arguing with his fellow German, from whose lips he had no doubt heard the words "It is something I must do" many times. And so, early on the morning of Friday, August 17, carrying a map, a knapsack, water, some food, and his sketching equipment, Arthur Silz left San Cristóbal de Las Casas for a three-day hiking trip.

❖

Wolfgang Cordan had more than sufficient cause to fear for his friend, the hazards of jungle forays having been brought home to him seven years earlier, in 1949, when fellow explorer Carlos Frey, whose son Cordan would adopt, met with his own mysterious death in the jungles of southern Mexico. In his memoir Cordan tells the story.

Born Charles Frey, "Carlos" was an American who, in 1942, at age eighteen, fled his country for Mexico to avoid the draft, only to find himself no less eligible for military service there. What began as an escape turned into an adventure, one that took Frey through the country's most remote areas mainly by foot and boat. In the Usumacinta River valley by the Guatemalan border, Frey met and married a native Indian girl and established himself as a pig farmer, albeit not a very successful one. While pig farming he learned that occasionally the local Maya visited a secret city supposedly hidden deep within the forest. Frey had heard rumors that within that city was a temple, and within the temple a golden statue that the Maya worshipped. Frey yearned to see that golden statue.

Frey cut a most unusual figure. A Caucasian gringo, a combination of suntan and filth rendered him as dark as the natives. He seldom bathed and rarely cut his hair or shaved. Apparently he stank. As one of his Lacandón friends told him—Lacandóns being notorious for either speaking the truth directly or saying nothing at all—"The river is handy, Don Carlos. Why don't you see to yourself a bit? We are not savages."

It took some doing, but eventually Frey convinced an Indian friend to take him to the secret city. Indeed, the city existed, in the mountains about a hundred miles south of Palenque at what is now the archeological site of Bonampak. And there *was* a statue: about a foot and a half tall, though that it was made of gold is highly doubtful—jade is more likely. In any case, soon after Frey laid eyes on it, the statue disappeared. On his own Frey returned to steal it. Hard-up for cash, he took it to Mexico City, where it quickly found a buyer.

By then, though Frey's native friends couldn't have doubted that he had stolen their statue, they seemed willing to forgive him. Nor did they seem to mind him bringing photographers to their place of worship, or the occasional scholar. But when, early in 1949, Frey returned once more to the ruins, this time leading an army of Mexican archeologists and officials—along with doctors, journalists, scholars, photographers, engineers, draftsmen, engravers, and a detachment of soldiers to protect them all—he may have gone too far.

By then news of the newly discovered temple had spread around the world, causing a sensation. Overnight, the name Bonampak—a corrupt Mayan translation of "Painted Walls"—had attached itself to hastily constructed hotels, souvenir items, even a popular rum drink. With expeditions arriving weekly from everywhere, the peace and spirituality of the jungle were soon obliterated.

As jungles will, this one took its revenge. When he met his end, Frey had been leading three members of an expedition—a photographer named Morales, a draughtsman named Gomez, and a mestizo guide—to a supply camp to fetch a generator. Instead of hiking through the swamps to the camp, Frey opted to take a shortcut via the river in a dugout canoe. Morales alone retuned to the site. According to him, they'd been paddling and portaging for some time, going against the current, arguing as to whether or not they should turn back. They were paddling up a small waterfall when suddenly the canoe turned crossways in the current and capsized. The upturned canoe was discovered days later by several Lacandón. Soon afterward, Frey's body was found lodged under a tree that had fallen into the river. Gomez's body was located nearby. Two days later, the mestizo guide's drowned body was found.

A capsized canoe seemed a likely explanation for one death, perhaps two, but not all three deaths. One possible conclusion: the same Lacandón who found the three men had murdered one or more of them. Another explanation: in his fear of the river voyage and his anger over their refusal to turn back, Morales either killed the others, or let them drown.

Ten years after Frey died, in 1959, Cordan would have even more reason to be wary of "rivals." Carrying through on threats, a gang of pistoleros broke into his San Cristóbal house. As he tells it in *Secrets of the Forest*:

> Carlitos [Frey's adopted son] and I escaped, miraculously. Professor Weber hid us in his school, in the same city, for twenty-four hours, and then prepared our flight. My collections were broken, my archives destroyed, and my hunting weapons stolen. And this was no consequence of a political feud, but the envy of a local archeologist using methods to do away with competition.

Confronting a midlife crisis, a middle-aged artist abandons the jungles of New York City, along with his wife and young daughter, for the jungles of southernmost Mexico. A hunter armed with a knapsack, a canteen, some food items, and a sketchbook, driven by forces he scarcely comprehends, he sets out in pursuit of that most elusive and inscrutable object: himself.

The student who brought the charges against me was a male student named Jack. Why he brought the charges I'm not sure, though he'd made it clear that he was angry with me. I know he struggled with criticism, and that he felt ostracized by others in our program. Since he was my advisee—and since I liked him and admired his gifts—for a time I took him under my wing, putting extra energy into his papers, even having him over to my place several times, to boat, swim, and even for supper. But over time my solicitousness cooled. I grew weary of Jack's sudden, mercurial mood-swings from egotism to brooding self-doubt. More and more I found his presence intimidating, menacing even. I increased the distance between us. I stopped having him over. I did my job, but nothing more. It never occurred to me that he might view my distancing myself as an act of betrayal. Indeed, I had betrayed him—worse, I'd done so not aggressively or with malicious intent, but apathetically, heedlessly. Was that what made him go after me? I'll never know for sure.

The charges that Jack brought were as follows: over the summer break, in July, at a private party at which several students were present, I engaged in "inappropriate behavior" by skinny-dipping in a swimming pool. The pool party was to celebrate the new yoga studio that the pool's owner had recently opened in town.[1] It was a very hot afternoon, 104 degrees at four o'clock. Having chatted among some guests indoors, a New Age crowd by and large, mostly adults with a sprinkling of graduated seniors and one graduate student, I ventured out to the pool. There, three guests sunned themselves at a table while

---

[1]. Three years later the same pool would be the site of a bizarre murder. Summoned at one a.m. by a 911 call, police arrived to find two men—Marcus Lillard, a car salesman who'd recently lost his job, and Clark Heindel, the Yoga studio owner whose pool it was, and a woman, Dr. Marianne Clopton Shockley, a professor of entymology at the University of Georgia in nearby Athens. All three of them were naked. The woman lay dead in the hot tub. There were blood stains on the pool deck. According to both men, the woman had accidentally drowned. Sensing foul play, the police separated the two men for questioning, taking Lillard into their vehicle and asking Heindel to wait on his front porch. When one of the officers went to get him, Heindel wasn't there. The officer stepped into the house, called Heindel's name, and heard a gunshot. Heindel shot himself in his bedroom. Lillard was charged with the murder. It was later determined that Heindel was not a suspect. Before opening the yoga studio, Heindel had been a clinical psychologist. I was one of his clients. It was Clark who helped get me through my investigation.

three others tossed a red inflatable ball around in the pool. I went to fetch my bathing suit from the back of my car to find it wasn't there; I'd left it at home, a twenty-minute drive.

I asked if anyone had a spare swimsuit I might borrow.

"What do you need a bathing suit for?" one of the sunbather's said. "Skinny-dip!"

The suggestion was reiterated by several of the other sunbathers. I remember saying to myself, "Yeah, why the hell not?" Another part of me—the part that grasped that with respect to public nudity the protocols of Central Georgia differ markedly from those of St. Tropez or Paradise Beach—hesitated. A mental tug of war ensued: at one end, my sense of modesty, at the other, an equally opposite fear of being considered a prude. Meanwhile the sun scorched, the water beckoned.

I asked if anyone would mind. Shrugs and assurances.

So I skinny-dipped. I went to the far end of the pool and, as discretely as possible, undressed under a towel and stepped into the shallow end, where I stayed just long enough to cool myself off. Then I got out and, just as discretely, dressed.

Jack hadn't been at the party. He heard about my skinny-dipping from the female grad student who had been there, who told him about it in passing, having found it amusing. She had no idea that in doing so she would cause me so much grief. Nor did it cross my mind as I climbed naked out of that pool that I had just done something incredibly foolish that would jeopardize my job and result in a sixty-day misconduct investigation—a torment that would deliver me to the brink of suicide in the loft bathroom of my lakeside A-frame.

Why did I do it? It wasn't just the heat or that I'd forgotten my bathing suit. Maybe I wanted to be young and carefree and innocent again, to show-off my aging yet well-preserved swimmer's body, to prove to myself that, though no longer young, I was not yet old. Maybe I wanted to tempt fate, to do something risky, to loosen—if not free myself entirely from—the shackles of a tenured faculty position, to challenge the secure life I had opted into, with its monotonous benefits and tedious meetings. Maybe I wasn't thinking at all.

In *The Unbearable Lightness of Being,* Milan Kundera writes: "Anyone whose goal is 'something higher' must expect someday to suffer vertigo. What is vertigo? Fear of falling? No, vertigo is something other than fear of falling. It is the voice of the emptiness below us that tempts and lures us, it is the desire to fall, against which, terrified, we defend ourselves."

Was it my own vertigo that lured me naked into that swimming pool, my own "desire to fall," the urge to plunge from stifling safety and security into the cool depths of the unknown? That naked dip in the Yoga studio owner's pool: was it my climb up Tzontehuitz?

The more I delved into Arthur Silz's story, the more convinced I grew that something beyond sightseeing or secret archeological discoveries had sent him hiking alone up into those mountains, that he had been driven there by more than curiosity or a sense of adventure.

Though my father's testimony suggested a fiery, stubborn, impulsive nature, according to the *Village Voice* reporter, Silz had been a man of pacific disposition. Perhaps he was all of those things—or, to use today's terms, bipolar, or a borderline personality, a classification not uncommon with artists. Or am I again conflating my story with Silz'?

At any rate, the more I learned about him, the more I identified with Silz, convinced that his fateful hike had been every bit as much a confrontation with himself, with his own quirky nature, as with that mountain. Some sail off to find themselves, others climb mountains, still others venture off into the darkest, deepest jungles. To find ourselves, first we need to get lost. We must leave everything we know—or think we know—behind.

As for me, did I really want to die on a commode in Georgia? Was I really willing to abandon my five-year-old daughter—as Silz abandoned his? Oh (I hear you say to yourself as did I), "Silz didn't intend to die." That's debatable. At the very least he meant to confront his demons, to ambush them on that Mexican mountain.

Instead the natives did it for him.

The *Voice* article continues:

> While still within the valley he took the wrong trail and started in the direction of a town called Chenalo, rather than on the correct path leading straight to Pantelo. The Thursday evening before, however, while talking to his friend, he had said that if he did not appear for six days after leaving, search parties were to be sent out for him.
>
> By the following Friday, Silz had still not returned, and this same friend—Cordan or Dr. Weber; the article doesn't specify—arranged for a search party of eighty Indians to comb the region where Silz had disappeared. Later that day, the party returned a message saying that a murder had been committed in Mukén, a little-visited settlement on the slopes of Tzontehuitz. The article continues:

> That evening a posse of 80 arrived at Mukén at midnight and arrested five of the six men named as implicated. The sixth, who had left the day before on business, was arrested some hours later. The men, brought to jail in San Cristobal early Sunday morning, confessed their guilt and told where the body had been buried. Another posse, returning to Mukén, recovered Silz's body from where it had been buried, wrapped in his poncho, on the edge of a deep canyon.

From the confessions of the arrested men, the *Voice* reporter pieced together the story of Silz's murder. Though Silz was a strong, experienced hiker, apparently he hadn't been prepared for the steep, narrow, rocky, at times ambiguous trail—if it could be called one—that climbed Tzontehuitz. The map he'd brought proved worthless. When not filtered through a canopy of vegetation, the sun's rays broiled him. He realized he hadn't brought enough water.

Lost, disoriented, and fatigued, in the middle of the afternoon, Silz found himself at the end of a trail facing the edge of a sheer canyon. To one side he noticed the thatched huts of a small village. Stumbling with exhaustion, he made his way toward them. As he did, a group of female villagers who'd been working outdoors, cooking and washing clothes and tending sheep, ran off screaming. Exhausted, at a loss for what else to do, Silz found a nearby tree and sat there, on a stone in its shade.

It wasn't long before the village men arrived back to discover—to their amazement—this tall, pale-eyed, red-haired man sitting on that stone, his face ruddy and glowing from a mixture of sweat and sunburn, his lips and tongue parched, his eyes wide with bewilderment and fright. In their native language they questioned him. Who are you? Where did you come from? What are you doing here? Not understanding a word, his mouth too dry in any case to speak, Silz could respond only by shrugging his shoulders and shaking his head.

One of the men sent for a man who spoke Spanish. In Spanish this man repeated the same questions. Who are you? Where do you come from? Again Arthur Silz smiled, shook his head, gestured, but could not answer. It must have been at this point that the women, who had gathered to watch from a remove, became truly frightened, their fears fortified by an ancient Mayan legend wherein death emerged in the form of a white devil from the underworld, sometimes disguised as a goat, to cast a spell over the countryside, killing crops and cattle.

"He is the devil!" one of the women offered. "See how bent over he was coming up over the hill? Just like a goat!"

"No," said another. "He's not the devil. He's an angel. Look how light his skin is!"

"I tell you he's the devil, the white devil! Look at his red hair—and those pale eyes!"

On one thing the villagers could all agree: whoever this strange man was, he had to have come from another world. And since—as the *Village Voice* article goes on to explain—according to their beliefs, only spirits, good or bad, were incapable of speech, he must be either an angel or the devil.

To make sense of what happened next, it helps to know something about these villagers. At the time of Silz's unplanned visit, the Chamulas were a tribe of about sixteen thousand living in rural settlements throughout the highlands of San Cristóbal. They spoke the Tzotzil language. They were subsistence farmers, living mostly on corn, beans, and other vegetables. Though they used fertilizer, irrigation was unknown to them. Their main agricultural tool was a long, pointy stick. The fieldwork was organized by family, with men and women taking equal part, and each person's share dependent upon his or her relationship to the family. Despite these primitive conditions, they formed active relations with Indian and non-Indian centers outside of their communities, bringing produce and other products of their labors to the markets there. When not harvesting their own fields, they were in constant demand as laborers at nearby coffee farms. They lived pliably under two systems: the Indian system, with its pre-Conquistadorian organization, and the national, capitalistic system of their European conquerors.

All this is set forth in *Juan the Chamula*, a memoir by Mexican anthropologist Ricardo Poza, who proceeds to itemize the characteristics of a typical Chamulan. They include:

—a strong constitution, enabling him to work in the fields
—a sense of collective unity limited to the ethnic group

—an active distrust of anyone who is not Indian
—a love of cane liquor, consumed to honor the living, the dead, and the gods
—a readiness to fight when drunk
—a fear of reprisals by the living and the spirits of the dead
—a strong ethical sense
—deep religious convictions

With these qualities in mind, let's return to the *Voice* story:

> In the end the frightened women prevailed. With a combination of sticks, stones, and machetes, the tribesmen, acting as one, attacked him. Silz tried to run, tripped, fell, and was probably killed instantly. After burying Silz's mutilated corpse in a nearby shallow grave, the men burned his knapsack and belongings.

Misconduct investigations—especially those conducted by Human Resources departments at universities—are cryptic affairs. To protect accusers and accused alike, all parties are sworn to silence. As a further protective measure, often the suspect is isolated, subjected to what is euphemistically referred to as "paid administrative leave," told to do no work, and in some cases barred from the place of employment. Though protective in theory, in practice these measures have a punitive effect on the suspect, who—far from being presumed innocent—is made to feel like a pariah and a menace. Making things worse is the fact that the accused is advised to speak with no one about the investigation lest it be "contaminated." Apart from hiring a lawyer—who will cost lots of money and who will likewise be kept in the dark—the suspect has no one to turn to other than the investigators, who exist—or seem to—for no greater purpose than to establish guilt, a process that may take days, weeks, or months: no one can say for sure. Meanwhile the accused molders away in their exile, growing increasingly despondent as each day slashes a black mark across what had been a perfectly good reputation.

By week six I had begun to lose my mind. Though I'm sure the good people at my Human Resources department had no malicious intent, and that the investigation they carried out was ultimately both thorough and fair, the process itself was a form of torture. One night I found myself quite literally writhing on my carpeted bedroom floor, wondering whether and how I could endure more.

What kept me going were visits to my psychologist (coincidentally the owner of that pool), along with constant phone calls from friends and family, some lasting hours. When not in therapy, or talking on the phone, or swimming, or sleeping or trying to sleep, I was at my computer, learning more about Arthur Silz, determined to learn exactly what happened to him. What had driven his executioners to their pointy sticks and stones? What, ultimately, made them murder him?

When it comes to grasping—or trying to grasp—Arthur Silz's story, the saying "the devil is in the details" has never been truer. As for me, I could only speculate. Or let someone else—a skilled Mexican poet who lived much of her life in Chiapas—do so for me.

Born in 1925 in Mexico City to wealthy, well-educated parents of European stock, Rosario Castellanos was still in her twenties when her parents died. By then she and her family, stripped of its wealth by the revolution, had relocated to a ranch in Chiapas. Left to her own devices, Castellanos went on not only to become one of Mexico's leading poets, but a diplomat serving as Mexico's ambassador to Israel, a professor, and a fiction writer, with her memories of Chiapas supplying the background for many of her stories. Much of Castellanos's writing is imbued with an intense, ironic melancholy, and when she died freakishly at forty-nine by electrocuting herself with a hair dryer, many suspected her death was not an accident.

Among the stories that make up her 1960 collection *Cuidad Real* (City of Kings) is a powerful allegorical tale titled "La Tregua" (translated by Robert Rudder as "The Truce"). It describes a gruesome encounter between a lost tourist and the inhabitants of a rural Mayan hamlet in Chiapas. Written within a few years of Arthur Silz's murder, the story is clearly based on that event, which occurred while the author was living in San Cristóbal de las Casas, and about which she no doubt heard many accounts and rumors.

Narrated in the third person from the viewpoint of one of the village women, "The Truce" opens:

> Rominko Pérez Taquibequet, of the village of Mukenjá, carried two pails of fresh water. A woman like all the others of her tribe, an ageless stone, she walked rigidly, silently, balancing the weight of her load. As she climbed the arroyo with each swing of her legs her fingers ached; the blood pounded at her temples. Fatigue and delirium shaded her eyes. It was two in the afternoon.
>
> At a bend in the road, without a sound to announce his presence, a man appeared. His boots were splattered with mud, his shirt dirty, torn to shreds; his beard showed several weeks' growth.
>
> Rominko stopped in front of him, stunned by surprise.

Convinced that the stranger, who cannot communicate, is a *pukuj* or "evil spirit," and aware that those who set eyes upon a *pukuj* are known to go mad, the terrified woman prostrates herself at the stranger's feet, weeping and wailing, confessing her frailties and begging forgiveness. Equally terrified, not understanding a word she says, in what may be interpreted as a symbolic gesture denoting the violence loosed upon indigenous peoples by Europeans when faced with radical cultural incomprehension, the stranger pushes Rominko away. Rominko screams, alerting the village men, who have been off somewhere distilling cane liquor—an illegal act that in the past has brought terrible punishment by the Ladino authorities, who've been known to burn perpetrators alive in their huts for lesser crimes. Given this and the stranger's violent gesture, it's not surprising that he is viewed as a threat.

In the story's ultimate scene, the villagers unleash their collective fury on the stranger, murdering him in a scapegoating ritual in the hope that it might relieve, temporarily, their bad luck. In destroying the devil, they hope to appease the gods and save their community.

> The men looked around for what they could find readily at hand for the attack: cudgels, stones, machetes. One woman, with a smoking incensory, made several turns around the fallen man, tracing out a magic circle from which he could no longer escape.
>
> Then they unleashed their fury. Cudgel that pounds, stone that crushes skull, machete that severs limbs. The women shouted from behind the walls of the huts, inciting the men to finish off their criminal work.
>
> When it was all over, dogs came to lick the gore. Later the vultures arrived. The frenzy was prolonged artificially by drunkenness. All night dismal screams echoed through the hills.

Ironically, in relaying the story through her narrator, Castellanos, a wealthy Ladina of mixed European ancestry, refers to the stranger as a "caxlán," the Mayan word for a light-skinned foreigner derived from the Spanish word for "Castilian" (which, it so happens, is "castellanos"). At least one critic takes issue with the narrator's—and by extension Castellanos'—reducing Rominko to a generalized archetype, the timeless indio, "an ageless stone," while alternating freely between the Maya words for "foreigner" *(caxlán)* and "devil" *(pukuj)* to permit—if not enforce—the impression that, while the narrator can distinguish between the devil and a tourist, the story's Maya protagonists cannot.

Though it brings us as close to the historical event as we're likely to get, Castellanos' fictional rendering still leaves much room for speculation. For instance: how probable was it that a hiker of Silz's experience, familiar as he was with the terrain, was so unprepared for this three-day hike to not have enough water with him to last at least that long? Accepting that he'd run out of water, how likely is it that his mouth was so dry he couldn't speak at all — enough, at least, to assure the suspicious locals that he wasn't "incapable of speech"? How probable is it that, confronted with this unarmed, seated, and obviously weakened specimen of human or devil, the village men would see fit to murder him then and there, in front of their women, in cold blood? Had Silz been the aggressor? Did he "push" them to murder? If so, it doesn't jibe with the "peaceful" man who refused Wolfgang Cordan's pistol. Had his killers been furtively distilling *pozol* (cane-sugar liquor), as implied by Castellanos' story? Were they afraid that he would tell on them?

And just how likely is it that, as the *Village Voice* reporter claims, Silz's decision to hike Tzontehuitz had been a last-minute change of plan? Isn't the more likely explanation that he had planned to go there all along? And why would he have said otherwise, except to keep his true destination a secret?

To account for their motives, the *Village Voice* reporter had only the testimonies of the arrested men—men who, though the report doesn't say (and no subsequent articles exist to tell us) were probably either acquitted of their crime, or received relatively light sentences: the latter a distinct possibility, given the cultural factors involved and the wish to maintain the delicate balance that existed—then as now—between the need for so-called "civilized" society to protect its citizens and to respect, or tolerate, the autonomy of isolated indigenous groups with their own distinct codes and cultures. Given those conditions, it would have been a simple matter for that mysterious "rival explorer" to bribe a group of indigent locals into carrying out a murder on his behalf, especially the murder of someone as foolhardy as Silz, who not only made it possible, but may have invited it.

As for the "significant" archeological discovery that he and Wolfgang Cordan supposedly made in the jungle, it remains a mystery. Cordan doesn't seem to have spoken of it ever again, nor does he allude to it in any of his several books. His own suspicious death ten years later while on an archeological expedition in Guatemala, followed by the death of his Locandón guide and best friend six months later, all but guarantee that the mystery will never be solved.

Puzzling and tragic though it was, according to the *Village Voice*, Arthur Silz's death could be seen as, if not necessary, logical. As for the *Voice* article, it ends on this conciliatory note:

> Putting oneself in the place of both Mr. Silz, who knew little about the region, and of the terrified Indians, one can understand the tragedy.

Along with the artist himself and his paintings, Arthur Silz's murder has since been almost entirely forgotten. Sensational though it was, it's probably unreasonable to expect the memory of a single murder in Chiapas to have survived, given that place's bloody history, one that dates back to the annihilation of the Aztecs—who weren't exactly averse to violence themselves—by the conquistadors, and beyond. Even if Silz hadn't been pelted to death on that mountain, the years between then and now would in all likelihood have erased his memory. Those men who murdered him merely started the job that time would finish.

Or rather Arthur Silz had been lost to time, until I found him, hidden in a painting of some clay heads my father did long ago, the one that hangs in the bathroom of my A-frame on a lake in Georgia—a painting that, like Pandora's jar, when opened released its flood of evil. Along with the evil, though, as Hesiod tells us, the last thing that comes out of Pandora's jar is always hope.

For me things have improved. I survived my university's zealous HR inquest, which turned up no findings against me. It seems that skinny-dipping, though hardly sanctioned by them, falls somewhere outside of my university's code of conduct, hence I broke no rule. My administrative leave has ended. I've gone back to teaching. I'm working, sleeping, and eating better. Though not entirely eradicated, my sense of isolation is much less strong than before. Nor do I feel at all suicidal. For the time being, anyway, I've escaped my dark jungle.

Today the municipality of Chamula, the place nearest the village into which one day in September of 1956 a parched, sunburned, disoriented, and frightened Greenwich Village artist stumbled, is a bustling tourist destination. The locals wear bright costumes. There's a thriving market for vegetables, rugs, baskets, and other items from the weavers' cooperative next to the church. The village boasts an ethnographic museum and a handicraft shop. It is best visited with a guide who can advise on local customs and the propriety of taking photographs.

From Chamula, I'm given to understand, tour buses depart regularly to within two miles of the ancient ruins and murals of Bonampak.

"Take water and insect repellant," a tourist website advises. "Wear non-skid shoes; hydrate constantly."

Works Cited

"The Kuhreihen Melody"

Boym, Svetlana. *The Future of Nostalgia.* New York: Basic, 2001. Print.

Cook, James. *The Voyages of Captain James Cook... With an Appendix, Giving an Account of the Present Condition of the South Sea Islands, &c.* [S.l.]: [Nabu], 2010. Print.

Frauchiger, Fritz. "The Swiss Kuhreihen." *The Journal of American Folklore* 54 (1941): 213-14. Print.

Harper, Ralph. *Nostalgia: an Existential Exploration of Longing and Fulfillment.* Cleveland: Press of Case Western Reserve University, 1966. Print.

Hofer, Johann, Johann Jacob. Harder, and Johannes Hofer. *Dissertatio Medica De Nostalgia Oder Heimwehe.* Basileae: [s.n.], 1688. Print.

Kaufmann, Walter Arnold. *Nietzsche, Philosopher, Psychologist, Antichrist.* Princeton, NJ: Princeton UP, 1974. Print.

Nietzsche, Friedrich Wilhelm, and Friedrich Wilhelm Nietzsche. *The Gay Science.* Mineola, NY: Dover Publications, 2006. Print.

Ruskin, John; David Barrie. *Modern Painters.* New York: Knopf, 1987. Print.

Sedikides, Constantine, and Jochen Gebauer. "Yearning for Yesterday: Should It Really Be Avoided?" *Scientific American* (2010). Print.

Stead, Naomi. "The Value of Ruins: Allegories of Destruction in Benjamin and Speer." *Form/Work: An Interdisciplinary Journal of the Built Environment* No. 6 (2003): 51-64. Print.

Thoreau, Henry David, and H. G. O. Blake. *Summer: from the Journal of Henry D. Thoreau.* Charleston, SC: BiblioBazaar, 2008. Print.

Voznesenskii, Andrei, Vera Sandomirsky Dunham, and Max Hayward. *Nostalgia for the Present.* Garden City, NY: Doubleday 1978. Print.

Wilson, Janelle L. Nostalgia: *Sanctuary of Meaning.* Lewisburg: Bucknell UP, 2005. Print.

Yoshida, Kenko. *Essays in Idleness; the Tsurezuregusa of Kenko*. New York: Columbia UP, 1967. Print.

"The Opening Credits to *Rebel Without a Cause"*

Alexander, Paul. *Boulevard of Broken Dreams: The Life, Times, and Legend of James Dean*. New York: Viking, 1994. Print.

Aristotle, and Gerald Frank Else. *Aristotle: Poetics*. Ann Arbor: University of Michigan, 1967. Print.

Beath, Warren Newton. *The Death of James Dean*. New York: Grove, 1986. Print.

"Cymbal-banging Monkey Toy." Wikipedia. Wikimedia Foundation, 2 Dec. 2012. Web. 20 Mar. 2013.

Flaxman, George A. "A Brief History of CINEMASCOPE." *A Brief History of Cinemascope*. Movie Collector, 2000. Web. 20 Mar. 2013.

Frascella, Larry, and Al Weisel. *Live Fast, Die Young: The Wild Ride of Making Rebel Without a Cause*. New York: Simon & Schuster, 2005. Print.

Hart, Martin. "Technicolor History 1." *Technicolor History 1*. American Widescreen Museum, 1999. Web. 20 Mar. 2013.

"James Dean Jacket from Rebel Without a Cause.": Lot 1014. Liveauctioneers.com, 2004. Web. 20 Mar. 2013.

"James Dean vs Charles Darwin: Rebel Without a Cause." *The Fine Art Diner*. Blogspot, n.d. Web. 20 Mar. 2013.

Mitchell, Rick. "Everything You Wanted To Know About American Film Company Logos But Were Afraid To Ask." *Hollywood Lost and Found - Studio Logos - Warner Bros*. N.p., n.d. Web. 20 Mar. 2013.

"Manet's The Dead Toreador and The Bullfight: Fragments of a Lost Salon Painting Reunited." NGA: *Manet's The Dead Toreador and The Bullfight*. National Gallery of Art, Washington D.C., 2013. Web. 20 Mar. 2013.

Plato. "The Internet Classics Archive | The Republic by Plato." *The Internet Classics Archive / The Republic by Plato*. N.p., n.d. Web. 20 Mar. 2013.

"Rebel Without a Cause (Nicholas Ray, 1955)." *Simons Film-Related Rants and Musings*. Wordpress, 18 Dec. 2008. Web. 20 Mar. 2013.

Sperling, Cass Warner, Cork Millner, and Jack Warner. *Hollywood Be Thy Name: The Warner Brothers Story*. Rocklin, CA: Prima Pub., 1994. Print.

Stern, Stewart. "Rebel Without A Cause." *Rebel Without a Cause*. The Daily Script, n.d. Web. 20 Mar. 2013.

Van Ostrand, Maggie. "The Ten Most Gross and Disgusting Celebrity Deaths / Film School Rejects." *Film School Rejects*. N.p., 24 Mar. 2008. Web. 20 Mar. 2013.

"The Strange Case of Arthur Silz"

Castellano, Rosario, *City of Kings*. Trans. Robert S. Rudder, Gloria Chacón de Arjona, Latin American Literary Review Press, 1993. Print.

Cordan, Wolfgang. *Secret of the Forest; on the Track of Maya Temples*. Garden City, NY: Doubleday, 1964. Print.

Danien, Elin C., and Robert J. Sharer. *New Theories on the Ancient Maya*. Philadelphia: U Museum, U of Pennsylvania, 1992. Print.

"Details of the Death in Mexico of Arthur Silz, 55, U. S. Artist, Revealed by American Embassy." *Kansas City Times* [Kansas City, Missouri] 12 Sept. 1956: 10. Print.

Kennedy, Hubert C. *The Ideal Gay Man: The Story of Der Kreis*. New York: Haworth, 1999. Print.

Lamb, Dana, and Ginger Lamb. *Quest for the Lost City*. United States: Long Riders' Guild, 2004. Print.

Morley, Robert. *Telling and Being Told: Storytelling and Cultural Control in Contemporary Yukatec Maya Literature*s. The University of Arizona Press, 2013. Print

O'Connell, Janna. *Prospero's Daughter: The Prose of Rosario Castellanos*. University of Texas Press, 2010. Print.

"Olmec Relief Looted 45 Years Ago Found in France." The History Blog RSS. N.p., 24 Sept. 2015. Web. 14 Feb. 2016.

Pateman, Roy. *The Man Nobody Knows: The Life and Legacy of B. Traven*. Lanham, MD: U of America, 2005. Print.

Pozas, Ricardo, Alberto Beltrán, and Lysander Kemp. *Juan the Chamula: An*

Ethnological Recreation of the Life of a Mexican Indian. Berkeley ;Los Angeles: U of California, 1962. Print.

Rath, Heather. "Chamula, Mexico: A Step Back in Time with the Tzotzil Indigenous People - The Travel Word." *The Travel Word RSS*. N.p., 28 July 2011. Web. 14 Feb. 2016.

Ross, John. "Zapatista Villages Become Hot Tourist Destinations." www.counterpunch.org. N.p., 16 Feb. 2009. Web. 14 Feb. 2016.

Shreve, Dwayne. "Introduction to Finding the Lost City." *Finding the Lost City: The Story of "Carlos" Frey in Mexico*. MostlyMaya.com, 1997. Web. 14 Feb. 2016.

Silz, Arthur. *Arthur Silz: Oil Paintings*. New York: Hudson D. Walker, 1938. Print.

Sykes, Barbara Anne. "Village Painter Is Murdered in Mexico." *Village Voice* [New York, New York] 19 Sept. 1956: 1+. Print.

Acknowledgments:

"The Kuhreihen Melody," *Missouri Review*, April 2012. Winner, Dana Award for the Essay, 2012; Winner, Missouri Review Editor's Prize, 2012, Dana Award for Best Essay, 2012, Best Notable Essay, 2013 (Cheryl Strayed: Guest Editor), Pushcart Nomination (by Wally Lamb), 2013

"The Muffin Man," *Alimentum,* Winter 2011

"Eagle Electric," *Florida Review*, Fall 2006. Pushcart Prize Nomination, 2007 (published in modified form in *Life Goes to the Movies*, a novel, Dzanc Books, 2009)

"The Opening Credits to Rebel Without a Cause," *Gettysburg Review,* May 2017

"Some Field Notes on Setting," *The Writer Magazine*, Winter 2008

"The Bones of Love," *Ploughshares*, December 2008

"Barber," *Madcap Review,* April 2016

"Noise," *Bellevue Literary Review*, Fall 2016

"In Praise of Stripes," *Catapult*, April 2017

"My New York: A Romance in Eight Parts," *Missouri Review*, Fall 2013. Best American Travel Writing 2014, Selected by Guest Editor Paul Theroux, January 2014, Best Notable Essay, 2014

"Swimming to The End," *Poets & Writers*, January 2016

"Swimming with Oliver," *Colorado Review*, Vol. 43, Spring 2016

"The Strange Case of Arthur Silz," *Gettysburg Review*, Oct. 2016

Parts of some of the essays in this collection appear in slightly different form in *Confessions of a Left-Handed Man* and *The Inventors.*

Peter Selgin is the author of *Drowning Lessons,* winner of the 2007 Flannery O'Connor Award for Short Fiction. He has written a novel, three books on the craft of writing, and several plays and children's books. *Confessions of a Left-Handed Man,* his memoir-in-essays, was a finalist for the William Saroyan International Prize. His memoir, *The Inventors,* won the 2017 Housatonic Book Award. His essays have appeared in the *Colorado Review, Missouri Review, Gettysburg Review, The Sun,* and elsewhere, and in *Best American Essays* and *Best American Travel Writing.* A graphic artist and illustrator as well as a writer, Selgin's visual art has been featured in *The New Yorker, Forbes, Gourmet, The Wall Street Journal,* and elsewhere. He is Associate Professor of Creative Writing at Georgia College and State University in Milledgeville, Georgia.

THANKS

In random order: Patrick Dillon, Susan Forrest Castle, Peter Nichols, Charlie Thomas, John Domini, Michael Nethercott, Christopher Rowland, Audrey Selgin, Nevzat Murtishi, Walter Cummins, Allen Gee, Billy Collins, Vincent Stanley, Fred Eberstadt, Vivian Gornick, Megha Majumdar, Jessica Papin, and—in memorium—Clark Heindel.

www.ingramcontent.com/pod-product-compliance
Lightning Source LLC
Chambersburg PA
CBHW030107100526
44591CB00009B/315